The Triple Design Matrix

Other titles by Eleanor Haspel-Portner

Beyond Human Design
Cosmic Guidance for Mastering You Life
Cosmic Secrets
Astrology Essentials
First Degree Reiki Manual
Second Degree Reiki Manual & Workbook
Marriage in Trouble: A Time of Decision

The Triple Design Matrix

THE DREAMRAVE DESIGN SYSTEM

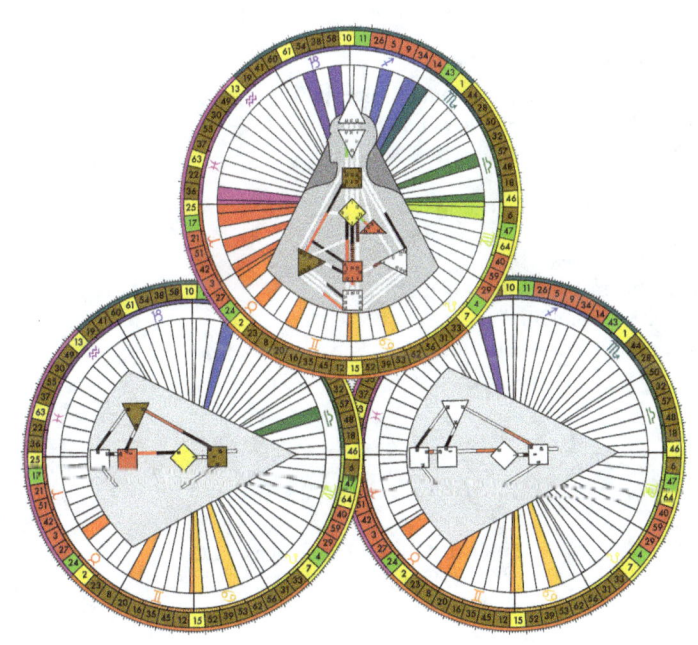

Ra Uru Hu
Eleanor Haspel-Portner, PhD
Marvin Portner MD

The Triple Design Matrix: The DreamRave Design System

Copyright © 2025 NOBLE SCIENCES, LLC.

All rights reserved.
No part of this publication may be reproduced, transmitted, transcribed, stored in a retrieval system, or translated into any other language or computer language in whole or in part, in any form or by any means, whether electronic, mechanical, magnetic, optical, manual, or otherwise, without the prior consent of the publisher except for the use of brief quotations in a book review.

Library of Congress Control Number: 2025901063

ISBNs:
978-1-931053-18-1 (Paperback)
978-1-931053-19-8 (Ebook)

BODY, MIND & SPIRIT / Human Design
PSYCHOLOGY / Personality
HEALTH & FITNESS / Alternative Therapies
BODY, MIND & SPIRIT / New Thought
SELF-HELP / Personal Growth / Success

Book Design by Michelle M. White

Author's websites
www.nobleenergywellness.com
www.DrEleanor.com
www.moptu.com/DrEleanor

Published by Noble Sciences, LLC
Mount Pleasant SC

Our primary goal at Rave Life Sciences is to make Human Design & Health information available as quickly as possible to the public and professionals. This module is not a perfectly constructed text; it is a preliminary text for practical use.

Publisher's note: This book is not intended to replace a one-on-one relationship with a qualified healthcare professional and is not intended as medical advice. It is a sharing of knowledge and information from the research and experience of the authors. You are advised and encouraged to consult with your health care professional with regard to matters relating to your health, and in particular regarding symptoms that may require diagnosis or immediate attention.

*To Ra Uru Hu (Alan (Robert) Krakower),
who entrusted me with documenting
the science of Human Design and introducing
the DreamRave. I am ever grateful
for this multidimensional data that validates
the Four Worlds of Consciousness and Noble Energy
Maps®, which have the potential to change
how we understand consciousness and communication.*

*To my dear husband and soulmate,
Marvin M. Portner, M.D.,
you inspire and encourage me to always be my best Self.
Your recognition and understanding of our
creative process and the importance of our work
have allowed us both to flourish.
I am deeply humbled and blessed to always
have you by my side.*

Table of Contents

Statement of Purpose … 1
Triple Design Matrix: Explication & Amplification … 9

BOOK ONE
The DreamRave Design System
15

Foreword … 17
Preface … 19
Introduction to The DreamRave … 23
The Dream Keys: Introduction … 27
The Dream Keys: Basic Concepts … 33
Three Realms: The Light Field, The Earth Plane, The Demon Realm … 41
The Earth Plane: The Tao … 47
The Light Field … 59
The Demon Realm … 79
The Lines … 95
Clinical Applications Introduction: Overview … 105
Transits to the DreamRave … 119
Archetypes in the DreamRave … 121
The Senoi … 125

Reversals in the DreamRave Designs	127
Case Studies	129
Conclusion	147
Book One References	148

BOOK TWO
DreamRave Keynotes & Clinical Applications
149

Foreword	151
Preface: Triple Design Matrix	153
The Dynamics of the Triple Design Matrix	161
The Dream Keys Keynotes	171
The Lines in the Hexagram	229
Clinical Application	245
Book Two References	259

BOOK THREE
DreamRave Basics & Keynotes
261

Introduction	263
The Light Field	285
The Demon Realm	293
The Earth Plane	299
Conclusion	305
Book Three References	309
About the Author	311

Table of Figures

Figure 0.1: The Mandala of Synthesis® 13
Figure 0.2: The Lunar Dream Matrix 14
Figure 1.1: DreamRave Keys 34
Figure 1.2: Ra Uru Hu's Human Design Chart 44
Figure 1.3: Ra Ura Hu's Solar and Lunar Dream Design Charts 45
Figure 1.4: DH's Human Design Chart 130
Figure 1.5: DH's Solar and Lunar Dream Design Charts 131
Figure 1.6: Example Reflector Human Design Chart 140
Figure 1.7: Reflector's Solar and Lunar Dream Design Charts 141
Figure 1.8: Example NM's Human Design Chart 143
Figure 1.9: NM's Solar and Lunar Dream Design Charts 144
Figure 2.1: The Design of Forms 158
Figure 2.2: Example Reflector Human Design Chart 167
Figure 2.3: Reflector's Solar and Lunar Dream Design Charts 168
Figure 2.4: DreamRave Keys 172
Figure 2.5: Ra Uru Hu's Human Design Chart 182
Figure 2.6: Ra Uru Hu's Solar and Lunar Dream Design Charts 183
Figure 2.7: Freud's Human Design Chart 216
Figure 2.8: Freud's Solar and Lunar Dream Design Charts 217
Figure 2.9: D.C's Human Design Chart 246
Figure 2.10: D.C.'s Solar and Lunar Dream Design Chart 247
Figure 3.1: The Design of Forms 266
Figure 3.2: DreamRave Keys 273

Statement of Purpose

When Ra and I presented this material in Sedona on January 29-30, 2000, our work with the DreamRave and its Clinical Applications was in its infancy. The "voice" had only told Ra that his dog Barley was in a Mammalian Matrix, a Matrix active in humans when they slept. This 15-Gate Matrix that Ra called the DreamRave receives its incoming energy imprint horizontally rather than vertically. When Ra shared "everything the voice told him," all he knew about the DreamRave was that it operated during the sleep cycle.

Because of my background, trained as a Jungian Analyst and psychologist, with extensive experience analyzing and working with the dreams of thousands of patients, Ra relied on my expertise to help him understand DreamRaves. I first noticed that it made a difference in how a person functioned if they had a defined Sacral Center and lost it during sleep compared to another person who had an undefined Sacral Center and gained it during sleep. Noting this clinical difference in my patients and clients was critical to recognizing the multidimensional nature of consciousness and the potential of the Human Design System to expand to include how we function in all Matrices.

As I read this book that Ra and I wrote more than twenty years ago, I was gratified to note that we talked about integrating the Matrices. Ra stated several times that we can only understand our complete design when considering how we are impacted by the cosmic energies coming in through various Matrices and transits.

Learning about how your Matrices shift with your consciousness opens the door to understanding the depth of your unconscious and how it functions over time. This book shows you the underpinnings of Human Design analysis and the importance of looking at all layers of consciousness before making assumptions about how someone functions in daily life.

Over the past several years, I began integrating the information from Noble Energy Maps®, my proprietary expansion of the Human Design System that includes critical developmental stages in a baby's first three months of life, with the Kabbalistic Tree of Life. Ra always said that the Human Design System was a synthesis of the Tree of Life, Chakras, Astrology, and the I-Ching. Since I am versed in all these systems, I am decoding the information in Noble Energy Maps® and how it is informed by understanding the Paths of Intelligence in the Kabbalistic Tree of Life. The knowledge of the Four Worlds, or Matrices we function in, expands Noble Energy Maps® depth of interpretations and further scientifically validates the Body Graph and its structure. This work is extremely groundbreaking and exciting.

Since this book is source material, I did not edit any original language when updating this book. Maintaining the integrity of source material is a substantial value of mine, and in that vein, I kept Ra's work intact. Based on clinical and statistical observations, I have noted where I evolved my thinking. While editing and reviewing this material, I felt great gratitude and respect for the work Ra and I jointly did. I am especially indebted to Ra for bringing my awareness of the Four Worlds to consciousness and providing a system I could use to verify and document how the Four Worlds function.

The black text in this book is the original unedited text transcribed from a Seminar. The blue text is my current commentary.

STATEMENT OF PURPOSE

With the Human and Mammalian Design Information and other ancillary knowledge given to him in his trust, Ra Uru Hu is responsible for ensuring that this knowledge is disseminated and validated with integrity and professionalism. This knowledge is a true synthesis of science and spirit and, as such, needs verification. It is not a belief system but a testable logic system that is being documented (Haspel E. et al., 2000). Ra Uru Hu oversees the integrity of Design, which was transmitted to him in 1987. He brings forth the information as appropriate and teaches its application in its form and structure. This work's essence and purpose is disseminating this information in its proper Form.

> I completed several statistical studies in 2000 and additional statistical and case studies between 2000 and 2002. The statistical studies documented Type as a valid construct based on the Human Design 64-Gate Matrix and the 15-Gate Spiritual/Dream/Sleep Matrices. In addition, I verified the structure of the Human Design Sacred Geometry Body Graph as sound. I could verify the structure of the body graph through several rotational factors common to the Centers and the mathematical distribution of constructs such as Profiles. However, we cannot base interpretations relating to behavior or personality characteristics on the structural integrity of the Body Graph. Using the structural integrity of the Body Graph to make such interpretations would be a misuse of statistical analysis.
>
> The statistical analyses of the Human Design Body Graph and the Dream Design Body Graphs that Ra shared only provided a partial picture of Consciousness in humans and mammals. More calculations were needed to complete the Matrices of the layers of Consciousness, the Four Worlds hypothesized in the Kabbalistic Tree of Life, and the proven physiology of sleep, dreams, and emotional release. As a trained social scientist, astrologer, and developmental psychologist, I used twin

kittens as subjects to document additional calculations that expand the Human Design model to include the Four Worlds of Human Consciousness.

Over the 20 years since my original statistical research, I have continued to do clinical case analyses. I can verify the reliability of Integrated Noble Energy Maps® in their capacity to operate as a reliable tool for guiding and empowering individuals to manifest their full potential. I had hypothesized that 99% of the general population would be Manifesting Generators, based on my clinical readings of over 15,000 Integrated Four World Body Maps or Noble Energy Maps®. Based on a recent sample of one hundred forty-four people at a Human Design Conference, Nameh Marsin validated statistically that 99% of the population function as Manifesting Generators in their Integrated Noble Energy Maps®. This means that 99% of the population is here to manifest their full potential at three months of age and can make choices based on their core Self beginning at that age. This knowledge is empowering and scientifically sound, and, in my view, is essential for you to know and live.

Rave Life Sciences is dedicated to disseminating information to healthcare professionals and those whose professional responsibilities concern the health and well-being of their "patients" and "clients." The focus and purpose of Rave Life Sciences is integrating Design and its information with day-to-day client concerns, leading to an ever deeper and broader recognition of its personal and professional value. The experiential aspect of living with the information is under the guidance of Marvin M. Portner, M.D. He integrates Design into his holistic medical practice by using the Body Graphs of his patients to help determine areas of vulnerability and appropriate treatments. He is involved in validating and documenting case material and embryological development following Design information. Marvin M. Portner, M.D. is available for clinical consultations, integrating this information with his solid base in medicine.

How living one's Design affects health and psyche is clinically documented and impacted through experiences, understanding, and knowledge. Rave Life Sciences' task is to make this information available to professionals for their use and the use of their patient/client base. Eleanor Haspel-Portner, Ph.D., teaches the application of Design in people's lives. She does individual readings and works with couples, groups, and parents. She works with families and businesses in the application and documentation of the value of Design in successful healthy living. She is responsible for the publication of social scientific studies. Statistical analysis of Design is well underway, and scientific verification has been established.

Because it is necessary at this point to document all the work with scientifically valid studies and research, we are working with many groups to educate them on the possibilities open to them and allow participation in pilot studies by those interested in working with us. Eleanor Haspel-Portner, Ph.D., is designing and developing these programs. She is available to help design programs that utilize Design applications and to consult with individuals about their life paths.

Another area of exploration in Rave Life Sciences involves the presentation, teaching, and development of the DreamRave and DreamRave Design System knowledge. The DreamRave, the Design of our Sleeping Life, differs from the Design of our Waking Life. Rave Life Sciences is also working on the Mammalian Design System; the knowledge and its application are being readied for presentation to the public.

In addition, Rave Life Sciences is working to create a foundation of design-aware professionals by documenting research and design applications in various settings. Only through the verification of applications and their validity can we state clearly and scientifically that this is a logical, testable system that proves capable of supporting and enhancing health, Consciousness, and the well-being of humans and mammals, in fact, of all Life Forms. As part of this research and application, training Ra Uru Hu, Marvin M. Portner, M.D., and Eleanor Haspel-Portner, Ph.D., are developing teaching programs so other professionals can carry the work into the marketplace and all areas of life and health.

Rave Life Sciences educates professionals interested in utilizing Design in their life process and in the care and health of their clients/patients. As part of this endeavor, Rave Life Sciences has developed a publishing program in which Modules, Transcripts, and Primers are available, which disseminate information of a didactic nature about the design process in health and health-related areas. We make all materials available as quickly as possible, even when they are being documented and proven.

Areas under development by Rave Life Sciences, LP include Rave Biology, including Rave Medicine, Anatomy, Physiology, and Embryology; Rave Psychology, including DreamRave Analysis and Design; Family Analysis; Organizational Analysis; Business Applications, Communication Applications, the Mammalian Design System and its applications for Humans, Veterinarians, and Breeders. The fundamental purpose of Rave Life Sciences is to understand how Design can and will be applied to facilitate the communication of consciousness and health at the foundational level of human and mammalian life. Research monographs outlining studies and the statistical methodology and findings will also be published. The data is currently being gathered and is being analyzed.

As part of the training program and the dissemination of this material to interested individuals and groups, audio/visual learning tools are available. Tapes and indexed CDs from seminars are available.

Ra Uru Hu
Marvin Portner, M.D.
Eleanor Haspel-Portner, Ph.D.

STATEMENT OF PURPOSE

Ra and I stopped working together in 2002 when we ended our legal partnership. Ra continued his mission of getting Human Design out to the general public. I continued my mission of scientifically exploring the Human Design Synthesis encompassing the Tree of Life, Astrology, Chakras, the I-Ching Hexagrams, and Developmental Psychology. Over the past twenty years, I have done thousands of readings and studied thousands of charts clinically. The material in this book is essential and can change how you think about consciousness and yourself.

In reviewing and adding commentaries to this book, I remembered that when Ra and I presented this material at a seminar, I presented the Sleep Architecture first, Ra presented the DreamRave structure and Keynotes next, and we both presented thoughts on how the DreamRave interfaces with waking life. I presented the Case material.

Triple Design Matrix: Explication & Amplification

When Ra and I presented the DreamRave material at the first Rave Life Sciences Seminar (November 1999), we had only its basic matrix and some preliminary clinical data. Material presented at that seminar was based on a study of 3500 Solar and Lunar DreamRaves (SDR and LDR); some interesting patterns emerged in terms of how to work with and use the DreamRave Matrices. Since that time, we have been able to flesh out the keynotes as well as the Matrix in a practical way both scientifically and clinically.

As the primary researcher working with the Triple Design Matrix (TDM), i.e., the Waking Rave Design Matrix (WRD), the Solar DreamRave Matrix, and the Lunar DreamRave Matrix as an integrated whole, it has become clear to me that the use of this vehicle provides a holographic life design image placing an individual's consciousness into the holographic collective universe in a multidimensional manner. The TDM makes this information easily accessible to the individual. The TDM allows an individual without a great deal of study or effort to comprehend their life purpose and to get a beginning picture of how transits affect their consciousness on multiple levels of their being.

When we sleep, we move through all the phases of brain wave consciousness that have varying activations of the different parts of the brain. Current research on the brain and its activity levels during sleep makes it clear that understanding our awareness during this important process in our daily life is essential to understanding ourselves and our Type (as the term is used in basic Waking Rave Design (WRD) charts).

In my statistical analysis of over 30,000 cases including clinical data on Heart Attack deaths, Fibromyalgia patients, Aids patients, addicts, and matched general populations, it is proven that Type holds up despite clinical differentiations, and it is not affected by experience in life. This research holds up in both the Basic WRD and in the SDR and LDR. My research has proven that there are Five rather than Four Types that hold across all Matrices (cf. "Revised Research Verifies 5 Types in the Human Design System," Eleanor Haspel-Portner, PhD. Rave Life Sciences. August 2001 & "The Triple Design Matrix: Type Statistically Verified Across the Matrix," Eleanor Haspel-Portner, Ph.D., Rave Life Sciences, August 2001).

My most recent work has proven to me that other calculations are necessary to further elucidate the DreamRave Matrices. These confirm both the timing of the sleep cycle in the course of a night and pinpointing individual content filters from the collective archetypal level of consciousness. I do not, however, currently have access to such material easily. As a result, I am releasing what I do have and trust that you all will take it as preliminary. Please pay attention to when the material was recorded as the dates of the presentations are quite relevant to their accuracy and represent the reliability of the material in terms of its veracity. Not all the material is fully accurate as presented early on although I have attempted to edit and add notes where relevant to update the materials to date. As William James said, "Science is mutable."

As always, I will do my best to keep you abreast of the parts of the material that stand up to scientific scrutiny as well as those that do not. What I am presenting currently is clearly stated as either theory or documented research: clinically, statistically, or both. The research is documented and scientifically proven in the most rigorous statistical manner currently available. All data has been analyzed using the SPSS program (Statistical Package for the

Social Sciences) with the assistance of a trained statistician who is independent of Rave Life Sciences and the design community at large but who is well respected in his field. The clinical observations are based on our clinical casework and involved looking at over 6000 cases using the TDM; in all these cases we know both the medical and psychological background of the individuals.

We find our work in using the TDM very exciting. We hope you find it useful for your process and self-awareness.

Eleanor Haspel-Portner, Ph.D.
Pacific Palisades, California, September 2001

> Since this book was written, my work and research with Dream Designs has continued. In 2002, I did an additional calculation to determine the Sleep Design of a Mammal. Ra was not knowledgeable in either Sleep Architecture, i.e., the stages of sleep and dreaming, or in the extensive literature and research done on Dreams and their meaning and significance in health.
>
> As a Social Scientist, Clinical Psychologist, and extensively trained Astrologer, I knew intuitively that documenting the Sleep Design of a Mammal would be significant in expanding our understanding of the Matrices. I calculated both the Solar Minute Design and the Lunar Minute Design and found that they delineated critical times in a baby's early development. As I worked with the eight Charts forming Noble Energy Maps®, they validated the integrity of the Sacred Geometry Body Graph, the connections between the Kabbalistic Tree of Life and Noble Energy Maps®, and detail a roadmap to self-actualization as hypothesized by Carl Jung.
>
> Much of what Ra taught has held up from a structural perspective, i.e., the Sacred Body Graph is valid. From a content perspective, Type, Definition of Type, The Patterns of Orientation, The Three Matrices that Ra was given, and the one I was given are valid and have direct connections

with the Paths of Intelligence of the Tree of Life. Ra's Interpretations of the Dream Designs have many important insights and hypotheses, but much of what he said remains to be documented in clinical explorations.

It has been my honor to research Noble Energy Maps® because I can say with complete confidence that the Integrated Noble Energy Maps® is a highly sophisticated psychological instrument that is proving to be highly useful clinically. It is a valid and reliable tool that can help individuals identify where they are gifted and what pathways are optimal in manifesting their full potential. I have proven that 99% of the general population are Manifesting Generators and are here to manifest divinity.

I am currently integrating the Noble Energy Maps® into my teaching of the Four Worlds as described in the Kabbalistic Tree of Life. To my delight, working with the Four Worlds and Noble Energy Maps® confirms that Ra was indeed given a system that is a synthesis. I am eternally grateful to be doing this important and groundbreaking work. May you recognize your multidimensional nature and live your potential fully.

      Dr. Eleanor
      Mount Pleasant, SC, October 2024

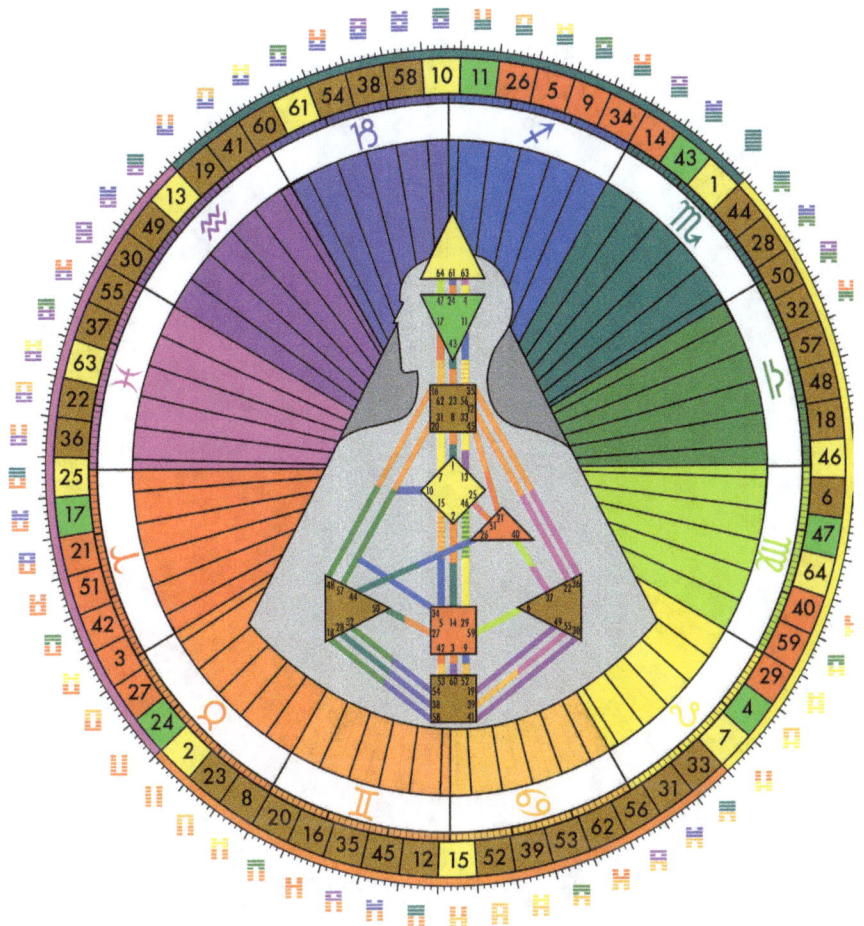

Figure 0.1: The Mandala of Synthesis®
(The Human Design Mandala)

THE TRIPLE DESIGN MATRIX

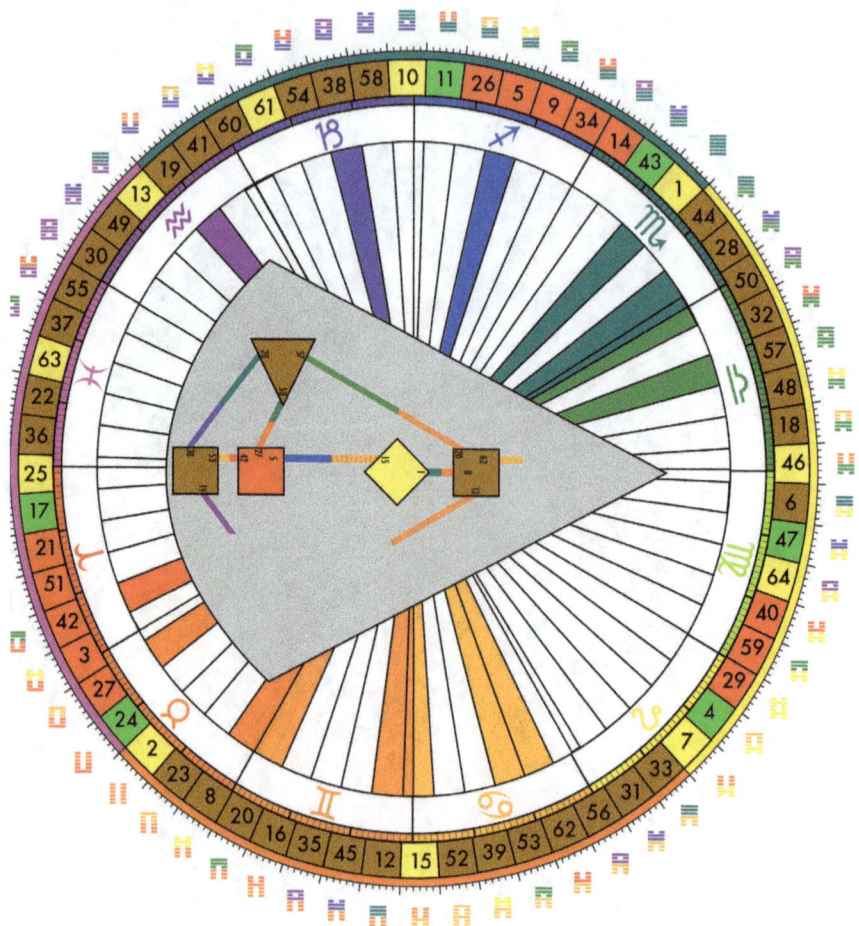

Figure 0.2: The Lunar Dream Matrix

BOOK ONE

The DreamRave Design System

Seminar Transcript & Updates
Recorded January 29-30, 2000
Sedona, Arizona

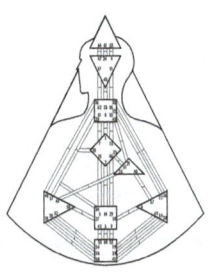

Foreword

While Rave Life Sciences primarily focuses on educating professionals who affect their patients' and clients' lives and health, we are acutely aware of this information's practical value/application. Until now, the information has been available to those who had private readings or consultations and those who wanted to study Design in more depth. With the founding of Rave Life Sciences, a new chapter in disseminating this information and knowledge has begun. Enough documentation based on this information and knowledge exists to make it essential for the information to reach many people as quickly as possible for the benefit of everyone. Rave Life Sciences is putting together modules (monographs) for professionals. At the same time, Rave Life Sciences is releasing companion information for practical use and application in the lives of the people with whom those professionals work.

This information is simple, straightforward, and understandable to everyone. It is based on your own Human Design Body Graph and is something you can take in, try out, and live with. You are already living in your body with your energy mechanics. Now you can have a tool that can tell you how that body is Designed and how it is meant to run.

Your Body Graph is the map. Once you have the map and spend a little time learning the terminology, you can begin to know, understand, and experience how it works. You learn to know and be who you are. The journey into the knowledge of oneself is ancient. However, that journey now happens with some simple tools that can change your life, your health, and your family's health forever. It occurs without therapy, drugs, or pain. It happens by knowing your Design and by living who you are. Enjoy the journey and Love Yourself.

> Since Ra and I presented this material, I have gathered data on thousands of cases clinically and have found consistent patterns in the Four Worlds approach to working with the Human Design Matrices. The Human Design Body Graph only documents the cosmic influences on development from three months before birth and at the moment of birth. I documented energy maps of Consciousness, including Body Maps for the Spiritual/Dream, Emotional, and Physical Worlds and the Human Design Mental/Waking World. When I considered the Birth Date and the Postnatal dates to generate Body Maps, the timing documented developmental critical times in early human development. Since all eight Human Design Body Maps, as they represent the Four Worlds, exactly correlate with critical times in Early Human Development, as a social scientist, I can confidently say that Noble Energy Maps® is a reliable and valid description of an individual's energy flow and Consciousness. In addition, it shows predisposing patterns of energy flow that influence behavior in specific ways. I am currently designing studies to document these patterns.

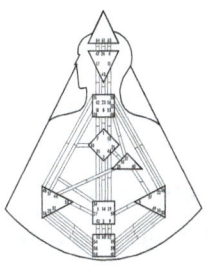

Preface

This book is an edited transcription of portions of a DreamRave Seminar presented by Ra Uru Hu, Eleanor Haspel-Portner, Ph.D., and Marvin Portner, MD, in Sedona, Arizona, in January 2000. It has been edited by Eleanor Haspel-Portner, Ph.D., to remain as accurate to the actual transcript as possible to retain the flavor and nuances of the Seminar. Some but not all grammatical corrections for readability have been made. In addition, some clarifications were added to make the reading material initially presented orally and with Illustrations and gestures understandable. We have taken the editorial liberty of Capitalizing some Keywords for emphasis. In a few places, we reorganized the information for logical sequencing.

One of our purposes at Rave Life Sciences is to preserve the foundational source materials presented as close to their original form as readably possible. We aim to make this material available to as large an audience as possible without intervention from other "voices" who are not in touch with the Source.

We do not intend to make this a perfect finished piece that provides a logical or interpretive text. The time for that kind of modality will come later when this information is preserved and available as the primary source material. These transcription series workbooks all have companion tapes and indexed CDs from which they were made. The tapes and CDs are available through Rave Life Sciences [Now available through www.nobleenergywellness.com]. Because the material is minimally edited, it is generally possible for you to read it while you listen to the tapes or CDs. This technique will be valuable for some people.

As we know from Design work, people learn in different ways. Thus, we intend to provide everyone with materials to understand and assimilate the information quickly. No one way works for everyone. Also, since not everyone can travel to seminars, we hope to provide material in a form that is as "real life" as possible.

The workbooks have pages for notes [these re-edited books do not have pages for notes]. The books are designed to present the material close to the source form. Interacting with the material allows you to internalize it. Work with the knowledge you gain and use it. As you experiment with it, keep notes for your process.

Change within our being takes seven years as our body cells entirely change during that time. We are in the beginning learning phase of our process with Design material until all our cells have been touched by the internalized knowledge. Those of us who have been experimenting with living our Design for a number of years have consistently been profoundly affected and changed. The experience of being oneself carries a deep sense of integrity and validation for our Human experience. The relief and the surrender to being oneself allow us to enter correctly into all things in our life and begin to allow the unfolding of all that is rightly ours. We are, in fact, designed just as we are, and as we live that Design, we truly experience life.

Be yourself. It is your right.

> When Ra and I presented this Seminar in Sedona in 2000, our work with the DreamRave was in its infancy. When Ra spent time telling Marvin and me "everything the Voice told him,"

he had no information about the Sleep design other than that when humans slept, they moved into a mammalian matrix and slept horizontally. The Mammalian Matrix has 15 rather than 64 Gates or activated hexagrams. Ra did not know what to make of the sleep design he had labeled the DreamRave.

Within a few days of looking at the DreamRave, I noticed that how my clients' Dream Design affected them had clinical ramifications in their decision-making and, thus, in their lives. Ra was skeptical about my observations because he needed to profoundly understand sleep architecture or physiology and have the psychological background to understand unconscious nuances related to the DreamRave.

I taught the first DreamRave Class in November 1999, and after that class, Ra began to flesh out keywords and ideas about how the Mammalian Design might function. Ra was only open to input when it resonated with his beliefs. Thus, this transcript is an early attempt on Ra's part and mine to understand and expand the importance of our discovery of the depth to which the Human Design Matrix could take us. As I work with the Four Worlds and the Integrated Noble Energy Maps®, I recognize the profound depth of what Ra and I recognized as significant. I am deeply grateful to Ra for entrusting me with this sacred work. It is to honor Ra and my commitment to him to document this work that I am releasing these original books we wrote together with my updated commentaries.

Please recognize that this book is source material showing the development of our thinking and the pieces we were working with in the beginning to flesh out our understanding of a very complex area of human consciousness.

I am committed to continuing, expanding, and documenting this work. The Four Worlds and using Noble Energy Maps® can change our understanding of Consciousness and Sleep.

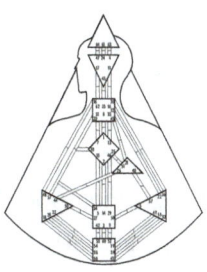

Introduction to The DreamRave

Throughout the ages, man has been fascinated by Sleep, especially Dreaming. The DreamRave allows us to understand the Mechanics of this process in a whole new way. It provides a very deep understanding of the nature of Consciousness and its integration between our different States of Being in terms of our functioning and our Programming by the Neutrino Field.

Humans spend a third of their lives Sleeping. During this time, their general alert, wakeful posture of Vertical alignment changes and becomes Horizontal. As Horizontal Beings, Humans experience their nature as Mammals. Programming of the Neutrino Field shifts accordingly.

> In 2001, I asked Ra if the Neutrino Field impacts us differently when we sleep than when we are in a vertical position. I wondered this because of the structure of the hexagrams of the I-Ching and the yin/yang structure. If the hexagrams turn on their side when we sleep, how the energy stream impacts us could be significant. Ra did not know the answer to this question; it remains an area open to investigation.

Calculating The DreamRave

Because we are Designed and function as Humans and as Mammals, our nature is understood best when we consider the Human Design Rave Chart with its 64 Gate Matrix and the Mammalian Design DreamRave with its 15 Gate Matrix. The Human Design Rave Chart involves two calculations: the Personality Gates corresponding to the Zodiac positions and their corresponding Hexagrams of the I Ching at the time and place of birth, and the Design Gates corresponding to the Zodiac positions and their corresponding Hexagrams at 88 *Solar* Degrees before birth. The DreamRave Chart also involves two calculations: the Personality Gates corresponding to the Zodiac positions and their corresponding Hexagrams of the I Ching at the time and place of birth, and the Design Gates corresponding to the Zodiac positions and their corresponding Hexagrams at eighty-eight Lunar Degrees before birth. A third Chart is calculated, which places the Human Design Rave Chart into its 15-gate Matrix and looks at it Horizontally. The Solar DreamRave represents a Chart with the Design side calculation done at 88 *Solar* Degrees before birth.

By looking at the integrated nature of the three Rave Designs that make us uniquely Human, we can begin to understand the complex dynamic of our programming as a whole. In our work, we have looked at the integrated Designs of thousands of people. *Using the Solar and Lunar DreamRaves in addition to the Human Design Rave Chart provides an insight into the invisible third of our Sleeping life in much the way that the Design side of the Rave Chart provides a depth of understanding that would be impossible without it.*

In the Rave Design Chart, 36% of the general population are Generators (Haspel-Portner, E. et al., 2000), about 18% of the general population are Generators in their Lunar DreamRave, and 23% are Generators in their Solar DreamRave. Manifesting Generators in their Rave Design Chart comprise 34% of the general population, with .5% in the Lunar DreamRave and .7% in the Solar DreamRave.

Reflectors represent only about 1% of the general population in their Rave Design Chart. In comparison, about 70% of the general population are Reflectors in their Lunar DreamRave, and 60% are Reflectors in their Solar DreamRave. 8% of the general population are Manifestors in their Rave Design Chart, only 0.1% are Manifestors in their Lunar DreamRave, and 0.4% are Manifestors in their Solar DreamRave. Projectors comprise 21% of the general population in their Rave Design Chart, 12% of the general population in their Lunar DreamRave, and 17% in their Solar DreamRave. These frequency statistics show the significance of the different Designs in the same populations, and they hold up well across many separate samples of the general population (Haspel-Portner, E., 2001).

Various preliminary statistical analyses have confirmed that the DreamRave Matrix is valid as a construct, and we have found it clinically helpful.

> Based on the Four Worlds Matrices calculations, the expanded designs show that more than 99% of the general population in their Noble Energy Maps® are Manifesting Generators. Psychologically and developmentally, it makes sense that humans are designed to manifest their full potential when they integrate their consciousness and live in all dimensions.

Working with The DreamRave

Begin working with the three Designs first by observing the differences in the Designs and their Gate activations for yourself and those close to you, much like you did your basic Rave Design Chart. As you go through the Dream Keys, look at them in your three Designs and begin to note how Transits impact you and your triple-integrated Designs.

The Dream Keys presented in Part II can serve as a guide for understanding the depth and scope of the DreamRave and its implications for understanding human beings in their relationship with other species and the whole.

The Clinical Applications in Part III provide a physiological and psychological framework for working and guide you through some DreamRave Analyses.

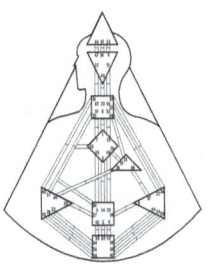

The Dream Keys: Introduction

Let's start today with vanity. Vanity has no place in what I'm talking about today. We're humanity. The way we're designed and our level of awareness generally perceive everything about the nature of life at a deeply personal level. Everything about life is taken at a personal level. We wonder, "What did I do," or "What did I not do." We see things in terms of blame and fault; there is an assumption of meaning in why things happen or don't happen to us. The moment you're involved in the Personality is the moment that you don't get to see the real movie. It is the moment you identify with the Maya that you don't get to see what really goes on, and, more than that, you can't surrender to the Maya.

> Ra describes functioning in the Mental Waking World and advises students to consider the Dream and Sleep Designs when examining their consciousness. When we worked with this material in 2000, we were in uncharted territory both in Design and Astrology. It was only after I did the statistics and worked with the multiple designs that the importance of the multidimensional charts became clear. Ra recognized

> the importance of working with multiple charts but did not have the psychological background to understand how to fully integrate the information. Ra was not an astrologer, nor did he have a background in the Kabbalistic Tree of Life. Based on his background and the focus "The Voice" put on the Body Graph, Ra's focus on the Mental World as a starting point in analysis made sense.

The Program: How it works

We live in a program. We live in a vast program. It extends far beyond our little realm here. It moves throughout this entire cosmos. The Consciousness field that exists on this planet and the experiment, the evolutionary experiment with Consciousness in Form, does not belong to us exclusively; it doesn't. Not only does it not belong to us exclusively, but we understand that it is only the totality and the Consciousness of the totality that matters anyway. We are a component of that. The program runs the movie. The program operates through everything.

> When Ra uses the term "program," he refers to the cosmic energy that impacts our energy field in specific ways at certain times. Astrology calculates the movements of the planetary bodies and the energy frequencies they carry. It is the imprint of these energies and their influence that Ra describes as the "program."

Think about what the program is like. If you're someone who is relatively unhappy in life and you have a forest in your backyard, when you go out into your forest, you deal with the Design of plants. We forget that every blade of grass has a Design Crystal. Every tree, every flower, every mushroom is alive. Everything is endowed with Consciousness, everything. They germinate at different times. They have periods of germination at different times, historically. When you walk through a forest, you walk through a Defined Splenic Center. You can't miss it. Every footstep that you take, the moss that you walk on, the contact that you make with all that life connects to you. It connects to us always. You see the Consciousness that permeates all other forms of life. They are not aliens; they are in the same program.

It is the program that is fascinating. All of us are just, well, you know, we're diverse. We're the little bits and pieces of what comes out of all of that. But it's essential to understand that we are all deeply, deeply, deeply integrated in a vast Consciousness field.

Death

Think about death. It is a nice thing to start with. Let's think about death. You die. Your Design Crystal and your Magnetic Monopole make a quick retreat and go down into the Earth. And your Personality Crystal? It goes up into the Earth's Upper Environment. There are many, many, many thousands of Personality Crystal Bundles that literally are in various positions in orbit, in that sense, around us within the environment. Try to imagine that you have the ability to see Crystals of Consciousness.

Imagine sitting on Mars with a nice, powerful telescope and looking at Earth. What you would see is a Crystal Shell. You wouldn't see the Earth; the Crystals would be in the way. But they're all dead.

The Personality Crystals that you carry inside are wonderful. Our task is to come to grips with the bullshit of the Personality Crystal that stores all kinds of stuff; it processes Consciousness. And then you die. Imagine you have a floppy disk; that's your Personality Crystal. But the computer is dead. It doesn't matter what you have on that floppy disk. You're not going to get anything out of it: there is no computer; there is no body; there is no bio vehicle that allows everything on the floppy disk to come through. Now, imagine you look up into the sky, and it's full of floppy disks, but they have no computers. Here we are, we're measuring, e.g., Mars is in this Gate, and Venus is in that Gate, etc. But I want you to understand something: Mars and Venus have to go through that Crystal Shell first. You see, we're in a Consciousness Field. When you leave your vehicles and your Personality Crystal goes up there into the Bundle, you'll become part of the Shell. The Neutrino Field that's going through the Shell goes through because it's part of the Consciousness Field. It's not just us here in Form. People who channel, people who talk with the dead, all of that stuff, it's just that they're tuning in to part of those bundles. They happen to be down here in Form, but their Crystals resonate with that field. The Life Force, the Consciousness Force of this planet, is vast.

Think about the cells in your body. They're alive. They each have a Design Crystal and a Magnetic Monopole. Think about that. Think about the number of cells, the number of living cells in this room. They're all being programmed. But they're being programmed through their Matrix. It's about the different Matrices. So, the program that's affecting us that comes out as the psychology and drama of our lives is the same program that is affecting every single cell in our bodies. The plant that we're walking beside, the animal that we touch, the bird that flies by, and the Crystals all around us, we're all constantly in this field, this Matrix.

How the Neutrino Ocean Operates

Think about the Neutrino Ocean and the way it operates. It goes in all directions. It comes from everywhere. The beings on the other side of this planet process Neutrinos that we later get. Neutrinos come through us, and what we experience goes through others; it is a constant movement of the same program. It is the only constant. It is the only whole. It is what we all want at the spiritual level: to be in touch with the One. It's my joke about having a Design with no activations: that being could really experience the One.

When we start dividing up the Matrices, the first thing to do is to get rid of the sense that there is a qualitative or quantitative difference and value in those Matrices. The fact that a Mammal has a 15 Gate Matrix just means that Mammals are different from Humans who have a 64 Gate Matrix. There is no way to compare their importance to what goes on in the total Consciousness Field simply by saying, "Well, we've got 64 over here, and they've got 15 over there." Look at a plant, and you say, "That plant has only 4 Gates." Each Matrix processes the program in its own unique ways to make its own absolutely necessary contribution to the totality. Think about all the ants on this planet; the biomass of ants is 70 percent of life on Earth. Let us not forget that they are in the program, too. If they weren't in the program, what they do physiologically and biologically in this life, what they do as part of their connection to us in this vast ecosystem, wouldn't work. If ants weren't here, we wouldn't be here.

One of the things to understand about the way Consciousness operates is to understand that we live in this vanity in which we think, "Uh-ha. This is all about me. After all, I'm an Ego Manifestor, right? It's all about me." My friend Frank kept on saying, "I'm God. When I die, you're all finished." It is a terrible threat. Go out to dinner with someone who says, "When I die, you're asleep." This is true, ultimate vanity.

The Waking Life, The Sleeping Life

What we're going to talk about is the Dream. It is all a Dream. The program doesn't change when you go to Sleep, only the Matrix changes. The program stays the same. The program does not change. Something does change. A dynamic experience takes place from the moment you leave the Waking Life and you enter into the Sleeping Life. Eleanor has some material on the timing of those processes, i.e., where they take place physiologically. But there is something important to understand: our personalities, the passengers, dominate the Waking Life. We don't want to deal with our Design because, after all, we can't. It's unconscious; it's spooky. We live in our Personality Realm, and our Personality Realm means everything to us. All the Passengers, i.e., the Personalities, want to be the Drivers; they want to be the Vehicle; they want to be everything; they want to eliminate the Design in order to be the only Personality in charge. That part of our experiment in living is certainly a development of our Interactive Consciousness. (I'll explain that in more depth as we move along).

When you step into the realm of Sleep, you stop being a person. Let that sink in a little. You stop being an individual person when you sleep. You are no longer guided by a Waking Personality. You do not exist in any way, shape, or Form. It's like being in the Twilight Zone; you suddenly step through the mirror, and when you step through that mirror, you lose your Identity. One of the most common things you'll see in Mammalian Dream Design is that there's very little Definition, and Defined Selves occur infrequently. It is fairly common for us to see a Defined Self in the Waking Life, but it is not common to see a Defined Self in the Sleeping Life. You lose your Identity as a person when you sleep. The Sleeping Life is the only chance the program has, with the arrogant, vain little machines, to make sure that the general program is implemented. So, when you step into your Dream Life, you essentially step into the ant's life, i.e., you become the ant.

If you were the Waking Personality in the Dreaming Life, you would be looking at something remarkably ugly, and it would scare the hell out of you. Instead of being this illusion of individual and feeling, "It's my life," which is not really true, you would be a drone in the Dream World. You're only a cog in the wheel in the Dream World, and the general program must be implemented for you to be a cog in the wheel.

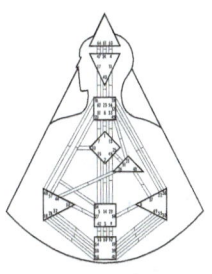

The Dream Keys: Basic Concepts

The DreamRave Keynotes

Look at The Dream Keys. Note that The Dream Keys are divided into three different areas. Basically, the generalized program works on the Dreaming Life, with each of those areas involved in Dreaming representing different areas of Consciousness. One of the reasons why it's been so difficult to bring Personality value understanding to what takes place in the Dream Realm relates to the different states of Consciousness and how the States of Consciousness integrate.

> Note that Ra talks about the importance of the Matrices in integrating Consciousness. He understood the Mental-Waking World but did not have all the mechanics or timing of the integrated field of Consciousness that I documented in the expanded Matrices calculations. Because the timing of the Four World calculations correlates with critical times in early human development physiologically, psychologically, and interpersonally, the value of integrating the layers of Consciousness makes sense. In addition, from a scientific perspective, when

> independent fields document the same timing or data points, we consider that as consensual validation, meaning that the information is considered scientifically valid. The data points in Noble Energy Maps® stand up to this level of scrutiny.

The DreamRave Keys

The Mechanics of the Sleeping Life

Secrets	Possession	Turmoil	Obesssion	Fantasy	Vision
1	2	3	4	5	6

The Light Field
62 Love
20 Sight
57 Attunement
8 Darkness
1 Joy

The Earth Plane
12 Mutation
27 Yearning
50 Sex
8 Time
15 Chaos

The Demon Realm
19 Environments
53 Flight
42 Dying
38 Aggression
28 Fear

Figure 1.1: DreamRave Keys

Consciousness States are similar to what's happened with modern deconstructionism. All kinds of things are, hopefully, established as meanings, but they don't translate because they're really very, very different things. The closest you can get to God is when you go to Sleep.

It's true. The closest you get to the devil is when you're awake. It's just true. When you go to Sleep you become One with everything because your Waking Personality has been stripped from you. We have a Dream Personality that is very different from the Waking Personality. During Sleep, the Waking Personality is not functional. With the Waking Personality deactivated during Sleep, there are no more barriers to allowing the totality to either move through you or to connect to you. This experience is what people call the astral plane or many other names. In the Sleep State, you enter into the Realm of the Whole. You wake up, and you're back in the box.

When you're asleep, there is no box. The Sleeping Life is not confined to the body. It isn't. The body is the illusion of being awake. There is nobody when you Sleep. There's only the Whole.

The Dream Keys provide a structure for entering into understanding about the Dream Life. The Dream Life is not for you to personalize. Once you depersonalize your Dream Life, you can see your life's purpose in another way. Your life purpose is not about what you can actively or not do; it isn't about that. It's about seeing that you make a very important contribution; each and every one of us makes an important contribution to the movement of Consciousness. In Waking Life, you have to do something with Consciousness. That is the illusion of the Maya. That's why we do things with Dreams that don't work. We are not meant to do anything with Dreams. In terms of what you see in your Design, the fact of the matter is that Dream information brings you literally what you process for the Whole. That is what you see in Dreams. You see the aspects necessary for the Consciousness of the Whole, and you actually are participating in that process.

Because things are set up this way, do not dismiss what can be learned from the DreamRave and its importance in understanding the problems translated from the DreamRave into the Waking Life. There is a real Bridge between the two. It's deep. It's very, very difficult to cross those lines. And I will show you as we go through the day that there are only certain places where Bridging is possible.

> Ra began to introduce the concept of Portals here. He alludes to the different Matrices and Gates that act as conduits between the Worlds. My book *Beyond Human Design: Turbocharge Your Practice with Integrated Channels In All Four Worlds* addresses how to read and work with integrated channels.

Programming & The Design of Forms: The Neutrino Field

Imagine that the size of your Consciousness Crystals is about five Neutrinos wide. A Neutrino is incredibly tiny. We're talking about things that are very, very, very small. We're dealing in nanometers. We're dealing in very, very, very tiny spaces. Recognize the nature of the way programming works; we are programmed in a geometry. Human Beings are programmed in a geometry that's literally 88 Solar Degrees. Imagine a Human Being in its Crystal. The Neutrino that feeds goes into that Crystal slightly off 90 degrees. The Neutrino feed into a human being comes in at a slightly off vertical angle. You get one Neutrino at a time, endlessly, in that geometry. That is the Waking program for a human being.

When you look at a Mammal, the triangle graphic describes the body of the Form, and you can see that the Neutrino feed is Horizontal. You can also see, by the way, that in Mammals, the orientation is Horizontal to the right; reptiles are designed Horizontally to the left, but Mammals are Designed Horizontally to the right. What that means is that Mammals receive their Neutrino information Horizontally. That's their way.

As Humans, we walk through our lives, and the Neutrino Field is everywhere; we are permeated by Neutrinos in every direction, but we are not programmed by all of them; at the horizontal level, there is a Neutrino feed that programs the whole Mammalian Environment. We are programmed as Mammals Horizontally when we lie down, and we are programmed as Humans when we are Vertical.

When you are awake and you lie down, you lie down to think, to rest, or to make love. Whatever those things are, in that moment you change your programming. In other words, you take away 49 Gates of possible programming. It does not mean you eliminate those. For example, let's say that you're lying down and musing. Now, when you're lying down and musing like a cat, in that sense, what that means is that those 15 Gates of the Mammalian Matrix become the active program for you. If you have any activation in those 15 Gates, or if the Transits activate any of those 15 Gates, those will be the dominant theme, although you still process it through your whole Design.

There is a change in the nuance of the programming. You can see how that is effective in sexuality. In The Mammalian Design, there is no Solar Plexus Center (Emotional System). Yet when we lie down what we open to is the Mammalian Matrix. Most lovemaking is done horizontally. It means the Mammalian Program comes into us, and it becomes the highlight. It does not take away the other Design that somebody has as a waking being. Remember the Key in this information is that the Waking Personality loses control over being an Active Passenger. As soon as you go to Sleep, you are really in the Mammalian Program.

49 out of 64 Waking Design Gates are asleep when we Sleep. Obviously, we know that when we go to Sleep, we don't stop being alive; in other words, there are basic functions that continue to take place. And if you don't have those basic functions, you're not

asleep, and you're dead. So, one of the things to understand about the sleeping environment is that 49 Gates go to sleep. In other words, 49 Gates shut down for what we call Sleep, but 15 Gates remain active. These are, of course, what we call Mammalian Gates; they are the Gates that then translate into our DreamRave structure.

The Importance of the Dream Keys

Let's translate, first of all, what Freud did. Think about it. It's very funny. Please, think about it. You see, Freud invented an interesting thing. His patients lie down. Do you understand? As soon as his patients lie down, the programming themes that dominated their Waking State became similar to the programming themes that were at work in their Sleeping State. Freud was trying to get to a relationship between those two States of Consciousness and to get the information across through the companionship between those states. Not bad. But, you see, it's very difficult to translate across those States of being because you need the Keys. And if you don't have the Keys, there's no translation.

Only three Gates allow the movement of information across the barrier of that dimension between what is the Sleeping Life and what is the Waking Life. Here, you can see it in terms of the Mammalian Design; you can see it as the three Cross-Species Gates. It is through these Gates that it is possible to move information back and forth; in other words, through the Cross-Species Gates, it is possible to take the Waking experience into the Dreaming Life and to take the Dreaming Life into the Waking experience. These three Gates, because they are the Portals or the Bridging Gates, open up a line of communication; they open up a way to Bridge the different Dimensions.

> Ra describes how consciousness moves between the Worlds and how the portals of the Worlds activate and operate in the

frequency of the World being activated. When he describes the Portals, he describes the Gates that shift frequencies between the Worlds and influence our unconscious functioning components.

Ra was clear that the integration of the Matrices of the Worlds occurs, and each World is state-specific. Ra and I presented this paper two months after I first delineated and taught about the DreamRave and its functions at our first Rave Life Sciences Meeting in November 1999. Neither Ra nor I had all the calculations based on my scientific data when we presented this paper.

When I documented the calculations of the missing Matrices, Ra acknowledged their importance. The expanded consideration of how we function changes what can be delineated in a Chart. As I read this document, I recognize the underpinnings of Noble Energy Maps® and the foundation on which my work is based.

Remember the beauty of the program through Transits. Everybody has access to the Portals/Bridges. One of the most important things for those who have active Dream lives is the Transits that bring the Portals/Bridges; those Transit Mediated times bring the moments that Dreams seem to have an unusual value to them into the Waking State; they may be more than just interesting, a movie, whatever the case.

Recognize that not everyone has Portal/Bridging Gates in their Design, but the program provides them. The program says, "Look, every once in a while, we're going to provide you with access to Portal/Bridging Gates as part of the Cycle to take you and to move this information back and forth." Because we're working in the whole outside of vanity in our Sleep, there are essential ingredients we must be able to translate and bring across into our Waking Life. We must. In the Dream World, we work on three Dimensions of Life. In the waking world, it's all jumbled.

Because Ra did not have all eight charts integrated into Noble Energy Maps®, he relied on transits to learn if a portal or matrix was activated. Using energy maps for each World and their critical timing in early human development, we see that the transits that impacted us early in development activated essential psychological, physical, and spiritual energies in our development. These remain similar to the activations in our birth chart. Moreover, they show our developmental process and how the matrices integrate and serve as predisposing patterns relating to each of the Worlds.

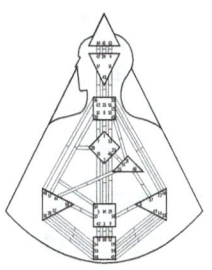

Three Realms: The Light Field, The Earth Plane, The Demon Realm

Three areas need to be brought into the individual Waking Life: The Light Field, The Earth Plane, and The Demon Realm. Through The Light Field, we are brought Love but not schmaltzy love. Through The Demon Realm we are brought our Environments. In The Demon Realm, we deal with heaven and hell, with God and the Devil.

Personality Crystals and Design Crystals stay in Bundles. Personality Crystals the Bundles above the Earth program The Light Field. Design Crystals in the Earth program The Demon Realm. Now, when I say "program," I simply mean that they act as a filter, specifically for the program. Of course, this is the basic dynamic; this is the yin/yang, if you will, of the Dreaming Space. On one side is this potential for Light and the bringing of Light into the Personality. Then, the reality of The Demon Realm says that if the Environment isn't correct, the Light cannot shine. There are both sides of the coin: form on one side and energy on the other, with all of these basic divisions: yin and yang, male and female, and all of that as well. The Mother rules The Demon Realm. The Father rules The Light Field.

For psychological work, particularly with family problems, this knowledge can be extremely helpful. Understand that these themes work in these two different areas. Through The Earth Plane, the most difficult aspect of the Dreaming Life is lived because The Earth Plane deals with all those who are awake while you are asleep. Think about the way in which the Duality of our existence operates. The Sun is up in one location while someone's awake, and it is down in another while someone's asleep in another location. The active, so-called astral plane exists in The Earth Plane because this aspect in the Dreaming Life attunes the Sleeper to those who are awake. Everyone who is asleep in America is attuned to all the Indians running around in Delhi. It's just the way it works.

The Portal (Bridging) Gates

Three Gates are Portal Gates of great importance: the 62nd Gate, the 12th Gate, and the 19th Gate. Understand these as important Gates because these are the "Portal" or "Bridging Gates." The Cross Species or Cross Matrix Gates allow communication between different States of Consciousness as well as between different Species. Everything that belongs to their group is part of that whole ultimate Bridging process. All the Gates in each section carry within them varying aspects of being able readily to have that Bridging experience, of being able to move from one side to the other, to move information, in that sense, from the Sleeping Life into the Waking Life, or vice versa. The Key is not so much what you have in your Design. Remember that. How the program affects what you have in your Design is of most importance. That's what it's all about. It always goes back to the program.

When you come to grips with what you are, that is when you

go through Basic Human Design, and you come to grips with your Type and your Definition. You begin your experiment of living that out. That is when you get to that place that heals your Waking Personality. You heal your Waking Personality, which opens you up to larger spirituality. That larger spirituality addresses how individual behavior impacts everything. "My being myself," how does that work?

The contribution of someone who lives out their nature in their Waking Life begins when they explore their life as a whole, not simply their physical interactive life in the Maya. They experience and learn what's really going on. Read popular writing, like Carlos Castaneda and other people who write this kind of modern shaman mythology stories; they all lead you into the same thing. They all talk about old shamanic stuff, about entering into the Dream Realm, and about the kinds of things that are possible in the Dream Realm. There's always a kernel of truth in everything. There's a kernel of truth in that. That kernel is that you must come to your own nature to tame the beast. The beast is the Waking Personality. Once you've tamed that beast, you really do have an opportunity to enter into a higher dimension of involvement in the life process, not by doing anything, but by being aware that it's there.

For example, I have very little Dream recall; Dreams don't mean anything to me. Yet I understand that regardless of that, while I'm asleep, there is work being done. My Contribution (Gate 8) actively participates in that process (Ra's Charts, pages 44–45). By understanding my DreamRave, I can look at that process, and I can see what it is. Those things that I can learn or be a filter for or transmit in my Sleeping Life may bring a lot of significant understanding and may be of great value to my Waking Personality. Knowledge from my Dream Life may be very important for my Waking Personality and for what my Waking Personality can share with others. So much knowledge comes from the Dream Realm and then gets introduced into the Waking Realm.

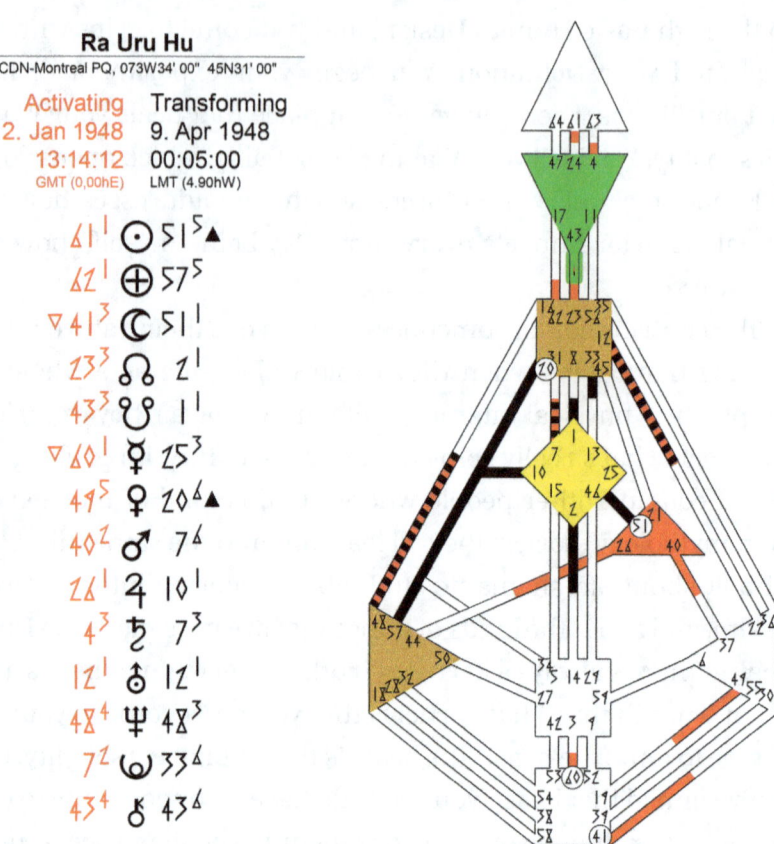

Figure 1.2: Ra Uru Hu's Human Design Chart

THE DREAMRAVE DESIGN SYSTEM

Ra's Human Design Chart

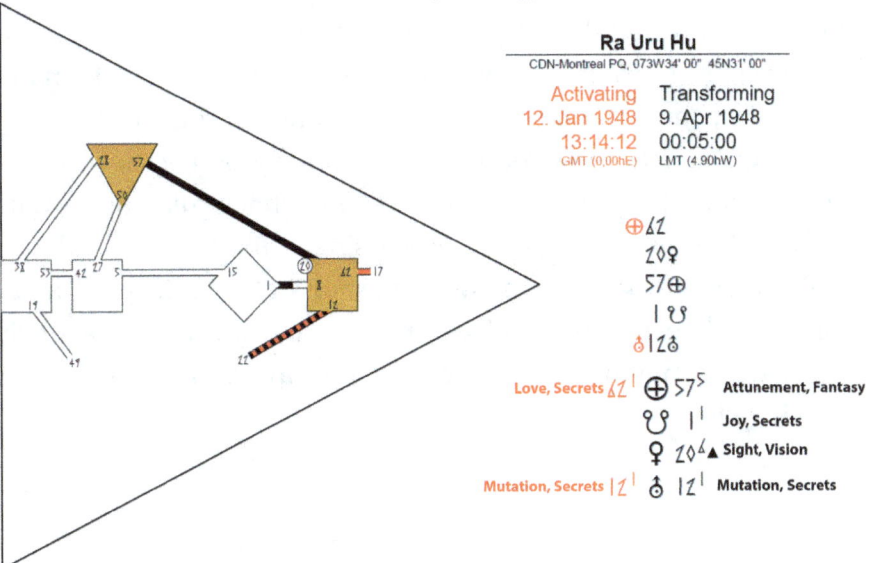

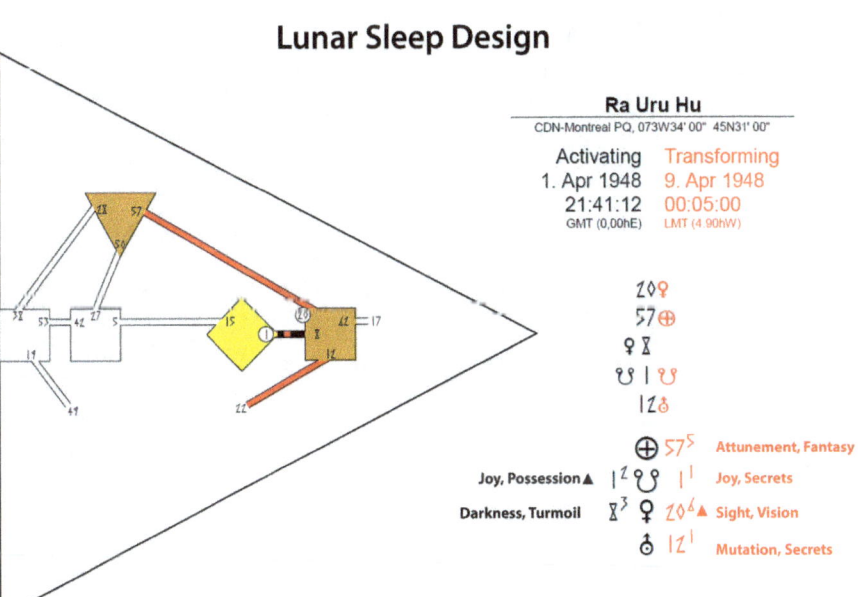

Figure 1.3: Ra Ura Hu's Solar and Lunar Dream Design Charts

This pattern goes back forever. It's very important to see that instead of being haphazard, each of us has the ability to see how it works.

Eleanor had no idea what I would do today because I had no idea what I would do today. What's fascinating about that is that she prepared Transits for you. Once you get through this material today, there's something so important for you to see. You'll see that Transits show you how your contribution comes alive in your Waking Life. When you understand what's going on in your Dream Field and what you're processing in the Dream Field, you will surrender to your own nature in your Waking Life; you'll actually see the Portals, the Bridges, and how they work. You'll actually see the information come across in the way you apply it to your Waking Life.

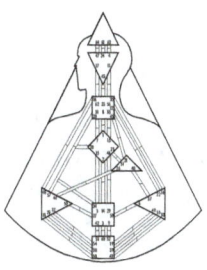

The Earth Plane: The Tao

Let's look, first of all, at the basic divisions and begin talking about them on the surface. The common denominator of the Dreaming Life is The Earth Plane. Mutation rules The Earth Plane. One of the jokes of that is that those who are awake benefit those who are asleep more than they benefit those who are awake. Isn't that great? That's Mutation.

Approximately half of the world is awake, i.e., the Waking Consciousness Field of the Waking Personality feeds the Dreaming Life of those who are tuned in at The Earth Plane. In other words, in your Dream Design, the 12th Gate, the 27th Gate, the 50th Gate, the 5th Gate, or the 15th Gate, any of these five Gates process information for people who are awake when you are asleep. Don't take your Dreams personally. Imagine that you're a woman in America, and you go to sleep. What you're getting is the Waking Life from an oppressed and abused Afghan female. I want you to understand how painful The Earth Plane is as a Field in which we operate.

Any Dreamer and I know many people for whom dealing on the Astral Plane can be a horrible thing. In our language, see Dreams for what they are. The Earth Plane is not astral anything. It's The Earth Plane. It's the Waking Consciousness that Sleeping beings process. That means that we take in the pain of Waking

Consciousness when we sleep. The Astral Plane can be full of violent energies, and all Dreamers experience how scary that can be; look at the Waking World around you and note where people are who are awake when you are asleep. We live in the United States, an isolated continent. Think about people who are awake on the other side of the Planet. You have a billion waking Chinese people who you deal with while you are asleep, and you deal with the dilemmas that exist in their lives.

People who carry Earth Plane Gates have the most disturbing Dream lives. In other words, do not assume that, for example, the so-called nightmare originates from The Demon Realm. The Light and the Darkness have their own equations separate from The Earth Plane. On The Earth Plane, you take in the world of pain. In fact, I'm not overstating the pain of The Earth Plane because, as you know, you're not going to experience a majority of joy from the waking world around you when you sleep because that's not what the world is like. We live on a planet of suffering. Thus, there is tremendous processing at this level.

The Earth Plane Portal/Bridge
The 12th Gate: Mutation

There's always a balance. It's always a fair game in that sense. We process what goes on around us in The Waking Consciousness while we sleep at The Earth Plane, and we take in all of the heaviness. After all, we're taking in the Mammalian quality of all that, so we take in real heaviness. Only this process leads to real mutation and change.

The Earth Plane exists as a Plane of Suffering, which, by the way, is less so now than it's ever been. The Dream Life resists this suffering. After all, the Dream Life is part of the Whole. Thus, it suffers when the Whole suffers. In Dream Life, the five Gates of The Earth Plane bring very, very important Solutions at the Earth Plane level. People with the 12th Gate Portal often wake up suddenly with "The

Solution." Their Solutions are generally mundane. Their information is not about finding God or about getting some mysterious message from somewhere. It is more often, "Oh, yeah, I'd better take the spoon out of the garbage disposal, or it's going to break." The 12th Gate Portal wakes people up with a Mutative Solution that comes out of another Plane of Existence, and it has come across the Portal/Bridge. People who have Earth Plane gates without the 12th Gate Portal/Bridge feel the Energies of the awake world while they sleep without the Mutative Transformation that the 12th Gate Portal/Bridge brings.

One of the first things we are looking for statistically are people who have very uncomfortable Dreams and/or Sleep experiences, be they nightmares or other uncomfortable Dreams and/or Sleep experiences. We'll look at the correlation between Dreaming patterns and the presence of these Earth Plane Gates, but there's more.

Program solutions regularly Cycle, thus providing for all of us. Again, the program rules. So, a Cycle, for example, moves the Moon through the 12th Gate every 28 days. Every time the Moon transits the 12th Gate, you'll think about it differently now. Every time the Moon enters the 12th Gate, think about its importance to a whole world that sleeps at that moment that you're aware of the Transit.

When you're asleep, everybody who is awake programs you. It is Earth Plane stuff. Please, think about it. You're awake now. You program all these Sleepers out there. If you want to be spiritual, you have to have yourself together, and it can't be just one or two or three or four or five or six of us. You can see how difficult it is to transform the Consciousness of this planet. Please understand how difficult it is. By the time we're through with this whole process on this planet in these Forms, we'll be lucky if 50 percent "get it." But hopefully, we'll get there.

In Consciousness, you're awake. Think about all the awake people right now in America who are about to kill, to rape, to beat, to cheat, to steal. Think about all the people in mental institutions, all the people who are suffering. Think about the people on the street, all the people with unhappy lives, all the people who are frustrated. Think about all the stress, all the tension, all of that. All of that goes into the Dreamers on the other side of the planet, and they process that through the five Gates of The Earth Plane.

The vanity of being in the Waking Personality is that you think you're there all by yourself. It doesn't matter what you think, what you feel, what you do. You are in your own movie. "Everybody leave me alone." But, in reality, there's no escape from being in the whole. There's no way out. And there is nothing that the whole understands quicker than hypocrisy because it's so obvious. To the Dreamer, on the other side, who gets your wave and who knows that you've got all this stuff that you're dumping into them, it doesn't matter what your movie looks like on the surface. We're in a Consciousness Field together. *We all endlessly impact each other.* As a concept, I've never met anything more beautiful in my life. But as a practical teacher and as a messenger, if I think about it too much, it's really annoying. After all, I know how difficult it is to get to the point where humanity can wake up. It's not simple. It's not about somebody saying, "Oh, gee, I know my Design." *We are alive on the whole. We are an aspect of the whole. We are never separate.*

The beauty of this work in DreamRave Analysis is that it is a venue for human beings to really be able to understand that they are part of something that is so vast and to see that they make a contribution far beyond what they understand. The very nature of their lives, every aspect of their lives, every breath of their lives, is essential and important for the Whole. The quality of each life and the awareness of that life affects everything all the time. The fact is that you can never be free of the disease and illness and pain and suffering of the whole because every time you go to sleep, you are reminded of it. Every time you go to Sleep, you're brought back into the bosom of the Whole. It says, "Smell this and see if you like it."

The individual can hide behind the veil of the Personality's game and its illusion, but the Dream Life does not allow that to happen. No matter what your illusion is in your Waking Life, you wake up every morning with the heaviness of the world. You do. The speed with which people's Personality covers that heaviness up varies. But everyone wakes up with the heaviness of the world; we all do. Then, we go back into our illusion.

In dealing with The Earth Plane, we begin to understand that slowly, but surely, the weight of the horrors of information from the Waking Realm being processed by the sleepers in the Dream Realm leads through the Portals/Bridges to Mutation, which can change the horrors slowly, very, very, very slowly.

The Gates of The Earth Plane

We begin with the only Tantric Channel in the Human Design Rave Chart in the Mammalian Matrix, Channel 15/5. Remember, in my discussions over the years, I always emphasize the importance of Channel 15/5 as Universal. In other words, Channel 15/5, in one way or another, is part of the Design of every other Form from the single cell upward through evolution. So, The Earth Plane most naturally roots itself in this Tantra of the Universal Life Form.

The Role of Mammals in the Program

I have always had a very deep love for mammals in my life. Because of that, and because of having a Mammal, a dog, Barley, with me in my experience, I was given this additional knowledge about various different Forms and, particularly, about Mammalian Form. One of the things that I shared with my students during the last grey course was the nature of the transition when we leave our current Forms. Basically, that transition involves us moving from being a Consciousness Form operating through two Crystals to a Consciousness Form operating through three Crystals. The third Crystal is not going to come from any place out there; it is going to come from Mammals that are currently here in Form. At some point in the destiny of what it is to live out this Consciousness evolution in Form, we are going to carry within us what was, at one time, Mammalian Life. Thus, our relationship to Mammals is very important. Mammals innocently process in the program all the time. That's what they do; they process that way both in their Waking and in their Dreaming state. In other words, they always busily get the program out.

Gate 5: Time

In looking at Channel 15/5, first of all, look at the 5th Gate: Time. The Dream Realm has no time, i.e., The Earth Plane is a place outside of time. The entrance through The 5th Gate carries the possibility of entering into a timeless void. I don't want to get too dramatic, but it involves the ability to tap into things that are both past and present. Remember that through The Earth Plane, you deal with the Waking Life Consciousness of those who come into you when you sleep.

Waking Life is filled with time as the most dynamic dimension: when you get up when you go to work, when you have to involve yourself in this and that; all that kind of stuff is time related. The whole process of the Waking Life involves a constant movement from the 64th Gate to the 63rd Gate. In other words, that movement from what's gone on in the past to what will go on in the future of those who are awake. In the Waking Life, there is a spectrum. In other words, there is a movement. While you're awake, you can say, "Yesterday I did that. Tomorrow, I will do this." With the 5th Gate, in The Earth Plane, the past, the future, and the present become indecipherable. For example, through the activation of the 5th Gate, your dead father and your future child can be in the same room with you in a Dream, if you know what I mean. Time breaks down.

Explaining time inspired a whole group of physicists and the way they think. And they are all off base. Time has nothing to do with The Waking Personality. Time dissolves and disappears in the

Dream Life; there is no time there. That means that all time can exist at any given moment. But, of course, in the Waking Life, that's not true. In the Waking Life, we're connected to gravity, and our movement through space and time is a reality. Remember, only the Personality Crystal knows anything about time.

The Personality Crystal says, "Hey, it's 5 o'clock. Turn left." It's the Personality Crystal that's caught up in the movement. But the moment you go into the Dream State, what you get through the 5th Gate is Timelessness. That is very important. Remember, the 5th Gate is a potential Mutative Field through which the Dreamer can learn from the Waking Consciousness Field, and out of that can come a new grasp, a new understanding.

The 5th Gate is part of a Logical Channel (15/5). So, by being able to process time blindly, with no boundary, and to bring it together, the 5th Gate in the Dream Life is the Great Synthetic Gate. In other words, things can simply merge together, and a different perspective can be found. By the way, people who have the 5th Gate in their DreamRave think they've had past lives. It's very common, for example, to have a 5th Gate Dream in which you're some historical figure. That happens because many people who are awake may be thinking about that historical figure, or they may make a living out of information about that historical figure. A specific history may have been in the newspaper or the news that day. If information is active in the Waking Wave, the Dreaming person takes it in and says, "I was Joan of Arc." Time gets compressed through the 5th Gate. It doesn't mean that person was or was not Joan of Arc. We're dealing with a Channel of Being in the Flow. This is one of the most important things for the Dream Life.

People who have illnesses associated with Sleep Disturbance feel absolutely turned off by the Waking World. The direct result of wanting to escape the Waking World is that by going to Sleep, these individuals meet the Waking World at the most intense level. After all, through these five Gates of The Earth Plane, they meet the most intense levels of the awake world, and it wakes them up. They can't Sleep. They get to a point of not wanting to go into the Sleep space even if they don't recognize their motivation. The whole flow of life is lived on The Earth Plane. That is where it is. Thus, a deep resistance may emerge about going into that place. And, of course, that can lead to Sleep Disturbance. It's so funny, isn't it, that people resist going to sleep because they don't want to meet Waking Consciousness?

Gate 15: Chaos

The 15th Gate, like the 5th Gate, produces all kinds of interesting and bizarre things which ultimately turn out to be realistic concepts in physics. In other words, time is a momentum, and movement vanishes at the moment of entrance into the Dream World. Time can be a fixed point that can include all times, yet at the 15th Gate, Chaos exists, i.e., as in Chaos Theory. All kinds of things come out of Chaos because with movement into the Dreaming Realm, with no true time, there is no true order.

Remember, the 15th Gate in Human Design is a Gate of Extremes; it looks for its Fixed Pattern so that it can find the Flow that is correct for it. So here, in entering into the Dream Life, time loses its dimensional Quality: Order breaks down. You walk into a room, and it is filled with holes or staircases—in other words, the order breaks down. Things aren't what they should be in the same way that time gets compressed together. The order of how things should happen or should take place breaks down.

In both of those Gates, the Dreaming Life eliminates the vanity of the person. The Dreamer is not interested in the movement of time. The Dreamer is in all time, timeless, oneness, complete, the whole. It's a beautiful space. Who needs differentiation in time when all time is here, in the Dream? But that becomes foolish when it extends to Personality philosophy because the Dream Matrix is a different Matrix than the Personality Matrix. *The DreamRave Matrix works differently than the Human Design Rave Personality*

Matrix of the Waking Life. The same thing is true with the 15th Gate. It can be very disturbing to someone. You see, the Waking Life demands that we honor the Flow, that we honor Time, that we honor the Patterns. It demands all that. It demands that we remain organized in order to be successful as a Species.

Many people who carry this activation into their Dreaming Life on The Earth Plane constantly meet the feeling that there is no time, there is no order. Everything is just Chaos, and that's the flow for them. I've had people talk to me about Dreams in which they are caught in a warp, and all they have is beings flying by them screaming. That's the time Chaos warp. Now, the thing is that you have that in your Design. Understand that in order to be in the Flow there can be no time, no structure. This parallels our seeking of God. You are there. It is the great moment when everything stands still.

Some of the most important mystical experiences had over time involve the experience of time standing still in the Waking State. I had that. I have experienced this myself. There's nothing more frightening, shocking, or unbelievable than the sense that everything has stopped and stood still. That is the magic that always exists in The Earth plane of the Dreaming Life, i.e., everything can stand still. Obviously, that can be very disturbing; it can be very disturbing to the Waking Personality, which desperately needs things to be orderly, structured, and reliable. It's a very different kind of energy for them.

The Three Basic Divisions

One of the things to understand about the Three Basic Divisions and the way they operate is that The Earth Plane is the Tao. The Earth Plane is the Mutative Field, the Merging Field. It is the Merging Field because it is programmed directly by the combination of Personality and Design Consciousness in the waking lives of those who program the Dreamer. The Earth Plane is really the Tao. It is really the place where there is a fusion of what is on both sides, both the Personality Bundle (Light) side and the Design Bundle (Demon) side. But the moment you go to either The Light Field or The Demon Realm, you are in a place outside of the Tao. It relates to perspectives. Neither The Light Field nor The Demon Realm is the essential meeting place. You are going to differentiate programming.

Crystal Bundles and Their Structure

Today, we are providing a description of the out-of-body Mechanics of Crystals of Consciousness, i.e., the Personality Crystals Bundle. Understand this concept of Bundling crystals. Imagine that we have a Bundle and imagine that Bundle is called Christ Consciousness. One of those Bundles is called Christ Consciousness, just like there's one called Buddha Consciousness, and so forth and so on. That's the way we translate the vibration that is processed through those Bundles. Now, think about a Bundle. A Bundle might have two, three, or four million Personality Crystals in it. That seems like a lot of Crystals to us, but it really isn't. There are untold zillions of crystals that make up the bundles and shells that are part of the exterior of our Earth's environment.

If you're dealing with a Bundle that has, let's say, a million Crystals in it, only about two or three percent of those Crystals are designed to incarnate in form. The rest of those Crystals stay in the Bundle.

You belong to a Bundle called the X Bundle, and you incarnate. You come into this life, you go through your experience, your Design Crystal, and so forth and so on, all of that process. You die. When you die, your Personality Crystal goes back to its Bundle. One of the things to understand about the nature of channeling is to understand it as an active relationship between the Crystal and its originating Source Bundle. In other words, our Crystals are specialized. They are specialized for many different kinds of Bundles. They are specialized to come into Form and to go back into their Bundle; by going back into the Bundle, the information of that life, whatever it may be, is shared. It is shared not in a way that we understand it because it doesn't have to do with our kind of hardware. It's not about being a human being.

On the outside, we have a collection of Crystal Consciousness, Personality Crystal Consciousness. Now, every single one of those Personality Crystals, every single one of them is going to process a single stream of neutrinos. Every once in a while, I'll have a Dream. As a matter of fact, one of the few Dreams I remember was a great Dream. In that dream, I was in San Francisco, standing on top of a typical San Francisco hill. I was at the back door of a wooden house with a wooden staircase going down. There was a road going down in front of me, and on the left-hand side was a parked car. At the back of that car, my dead father stood, as well as my dead dog, Barley Baker. Barley hated humans, and he never wagged his tail at people. But there was Barley wagging his tail. And my father was motioning. It was a very funny moment. A part of me said in that moment, "Hey, guys, you're dead."

In that moment, in that Dream, what was really going on? I was not remembering my father. I was getting his vibration in the rotation of the Earth. In the relationship of geometry, there is always the possibility that I can link into that geometry that is going through what once was something that I could call "Father."

The whole business of contacting the dead deals with the connection between Personality Crystals and Personality Bundles. Some people are connected to Bundles. There are people who, through that kind of connection, have a way to anthropomorphize the Bundles as lives and people and all kinds of things. However, understand that this shell of Personality Consciousness acts as a filter of everything that pours through. In other words, it's not just that you're getting the energy of Mars. You're getting the energy of Mars filtered by the Consciousness Field. That Consciousness Field is every Personality Crystal that has ever been in Form, back and forth, back and forth, in forming the shell that is around us.

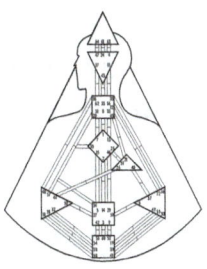

The Light Field

The Personality Crystals program is called The Light Field because of the very fact that they enclose our planet. The Light Field has a specific programming. On the other side, you have The Demon Realm. Within the Earth is a Design Crystal Bundle. It has many names, Shambhala among other names.

Scientists have discovered a compressed iron crystal 2,000 kilometers wide at the center of the Earth in the last five years. That's a nice image. This single Design Bundle is what informs The Demon Realm. In these three divisions of Sleeping Life, we are programmed with a personality accent on one side and a design programming field on the other side. We have the Tao, and the Tao is experienced neither through Personality nor Design but through how it impacts the Waking Life, and the Dreamer takes in that fusion. Out of that, Mutation occurs.

The polarity programming of the Sleeping Life moves through the Yin and the Yang. I'm going to start with The Light Field. Words are so funny. "Light" is a funny word. It is particularly funny when you look at this group. You have the Channel 8/1 and the Channel 20/57. You see, this is the Acoustic Dream Realm. That's why the Light is funny. You have to *hear* the Light. See, people run around thinking you have to see the Light. It's a joke. It's a bad joke. You have to *hear* the Light. *You hear the Light in The Light Field.*

Neutrinos

In their experiments in Japan, the Japanese and the Americans proved that neutrinos had mass. They actually proved that by following a stream of neutrinos through the Earth, seeing that they oscillated, that is, neutrinos turn, and in that oscillation, they actually change. So, the way neutrinos come into the Earth differs from how they go out. This is an important principle to understand about the nature of the neutrino. One of the things to recognize is that oscillation; if I stretch that out, oscillation is music; anything that vibrates is music. One of the magical things about this part of the dreaming process is that, as in the Bible, starting with "In the beginning is the word," this field has the capacity to articulate a process.

The Dream Matrix has three Gates in the Throat Center. These Gates provide an opportunity to articulate the Personality Crystal Bundles. "Gabriel spoke to me," "Jesus spoke to me," "Buddha spoke to me." In the Dream Realm, this is the only place where the Personality Consciousness Field gets a Voice. It gets a Voice. The Angels get to speak to you.

All Dreams can have audio capacity. Only those beings who carry these Gates in the Light Field in their Dream Design are the ones who get tuned in to the station. That is, they do not get the static. They get the exact frequency. In getting that frequency, what really goes on is the ability to bring words to the collective personality field. People who have this Gate hear conversations about their dreams; the things said in their dreams are really things that are special. It has nothing to do with them personally.

These Dreamers are the ones who are most likely to recognize that aspect of Dreams. In other words, if these Dreamers get to

Bridge, they end up giving their Dream frequency some kind of character: "My mother spoke to me," "My father spoke to me," "My dog," "God spoke to me," "The angels spoke to me." Whatever meaning the Dreamer gives it, there is a way here in which the Personality Field gets a Voice

Now, that is something very important. Remember that it is the Personality Plane that carries all our illusions of God and the God Head and Light and Enlightenment, and all of these things. So, it is a way in which the Personality Field as a whole tries to bring in those messages through the Dreamer, through sound.

The Light Field Portal/Bridge Gate 62: Love

Look at the Portal/Bridge. Isn't it cute that Love is in the Detail? Love is in the Detail, and the Detail is in the Music. Now, people who have numerous activations in The Light Field can have very disturbed sleep because of noise. Sounds can be frightening in their Dreams. Or, people may hear music or may sing in their Dreams. All kinds of sound quality stuff goes on throughout this process. The Light Field carries the message of Love being delivered to us constantly by the Personality Structure that is around us. It filters everything with rose-colored glasses. Don't be fooled. Remember what I told you: only The Earth Plane is the Tao. This can be very misleading. After all, it is only an aspect on one side of a polarity.

The Current Transformation

Be aware that, at this time, the baby is defining its sex. Because the baby is defining its sex toward the Yin, it is very important to understand that this is the last hurrah of the Yang. In other words, The Light Field is losing its power over us. That is very important to understand. The Light Field is losing its power, and The Demon Realm is growing in power. Of course, using that terminology sounds really bad. Let's put it this way: Illusion is giving way to Form and fact. This is the transformation that is taking place.

Illusion, most of the time, can be much more pleasant than the truth and facts. The Light is easy to maintain. All of you who have embraced Human Design and who live in a Piscean age in a Piscean time covered with belief systems know the irony of that. So, if you have these Gates and you have a Dream and you have a conversation in that Dream, that conversation is the Gods in their play. This is the whole Personality, the Collective Personality of Humanity, the Collective Personality of all living things, which have a Personality Crystal over all the time that the Universe has existed. It is quite a thing. And it is filtering what we receive. In that Dream, conversation is that source.

Now, when you take Dreams away from the Personal, a great deal must be discovered. When you make them Personal, they are so delusional. People with many activations in the Light Field are people who awake in the morning, and they cannot fit into this world at all. There is just no place. It's ugly, and it's dark, and it's scary. This is the land of fairies. This is the possibility of hearing exactly the right words, so, suddenly, just everything is wonderful. This is the place of Joy. It is a sales pitch. After all, that is the nature of the dichotomy; you have the Personality on one hand saying, "It's Light, it's Light, it's Light." And you have the Design on the other side saying, "No, it's Form, it's Form, it's Form." That is why only in the Tao do you get to see what is really working, and only there is Mutation. No mutation comes out of The Light Field. These are the forces at work, and they are the whole world around us.

Channel 8/1

We start with the Channel 8/1. In the Design of Mammals, this is the channel of the Alpha. Of course, the nature of this channel within the Dream context is that this channel is the Alpha Archetype that the Personality Field wants us to accept. There is only one way to deal with Darkness; you can only deal with Darkness through Joy. And it is only Joy in the Light and in the promise of the Light that can get you through the Darkness. Do you want me to do my Baptist imitation now? Because that's exactly what that is, please understand that. If you, in your Identity, the 1st Gate, the Self, want to penetrate the world because there is a Contribution you have to make in Manifestation, in the 8th Gate, you have to enter into the Darkness and bring your Joy, and you will find Love. "Jesus will protect you," whatever the case may be, that's what the Personality Field wants us to comprehend.

Now, look, they are both into propaganda. Remember that at the Dream Level, they have a much easier way of programming us than at the Waking Level. We're much more resistant at the Waking Level. Aside from that, in Waking Life, there is no separation between Personality filtering and Design filtering in the sense that they don't separately affect what is our awake Personality or our awake process. They only have that possibility when we are in the Dream State, and the Waking Personality has been turned off. In other words, *the Dream State represents a very, very important time.* Now, it goes on all day long, obviously. The Sleeping/Waking process in the way in which the Earth works, is an ongoing battle.

Isn't it fun mechanically to see the roots of our mythologies, the ongoing battle between good and evil, between God and the Devil, and all this stuff? It's just the simple Mechanic of what is there. The way we anthropomorphize is that we make it Personal. Death is not hell. But, after all, from the Design Crystal's point of view, if you paint that as the Dark Realm and the Devil, then you are all going to hell. If you are a Personality and you are up there in a Bundle, you could think that is heaven down here. But there is nothing up there. It is just a Hum. All our mythologies come out of this very, very basic dichotomy that we have in our Dream Life. The Dream Life has set up all of the heavy spiritual differences between this and that because that is where the battle takes place. The battle of good and evil and all that stuff takes place while you are asleep.

And, you see, *you are not the Warriors. You are the Battlefield.* Oh, please, grasp that deeply. You are not the warriors in that battle. You are just the battlefield.

What happens to us is that we have people who are more programmed on one side than on the other. Of course, that is what we have in the world. We have Dreamers who are heavily programmed at The Light Field end, and we have what brings to their Waking Life perception about the nature of the world around them. We have people who are heavily programmed on the other side in The Demon Realm. There is a great complexity as in anything. The mixing of those Realms, as we all see in Design, gives a little bit of this and a little bit of that. The Transits are so important as a result of this complexity. And, of course, we also have those who dominate at The Earth Plane. In other words, we really have very, very basic divisions here.

Gate 1: Joy

The 1st Gate is Joy. Joy is about imposing Direction and the ability to impose Direction. Remember, this is the Alpha, to become the Example. The Light always seeks Examples to shine as representatives of the Light. The way that Examples shine is Acoustic. Have you ever met a dumb guru? A guru who can't speak? Do you know any dumb prophets? That is one of the great jokes. The Acoustic Field within us is programmed in the Dream Life by the Light. This is the basic hypocrisy of life. The Dream Field programs us to be nice and we are not necessarily nice.

Gate 8: Darkness

When you get to the 8th Gate, you get to Darkness. This is what I deal with in my own Dream Life. In my Waking Rave and my Solar DreamRave, I have the 1st Gate, but I don't have the 8th Gate; in my Lunar DreamRave, I have the 8th Gate, so I have the whole Channel 8/1 Defined. The Personality, despite whatever it would like everyone to believe, recognizes that one has to live in Form. There is nothing to do about that, and you can't escape it. The inspiration of Buddha is that in Buddha's Dream, Form is bad, and Freedom is great. In the end, there is nothing but the desire to escape the Cycle of Life itself, to get out of the Form, to transcend it, and to finally be one with the Field of Light. I won't give Buddha a hard time today. He deserves a hard time, but I won't give it to him. No fault, no blame, no choice.

Darkness represents entering into the world. It is about entering into the world as an Example. It is about entering into the world as an Example of Light. I'm glad it happened in my Dream Life and that I don't remember. It is the only time, with this little bit of information about this channel, this Gate, that you really understand its name. The 8th Gate is Holding Together. We get trapped in the Vehicle, and this is the place where we hate the Vehicle. This is the place where we hate the Body. This is the place where we know that all we can do is imbue the Body as the Vehicle with as much Light as possible to endure it.

Most Personality Crystals never come into Form. Form is a hideous trip if you've never come into Form. It is not nice. I mean, it just isn't. The Body is quite a thing. Life is quite a thing. The vast majority of Personality Crystals are just in the Hum of the Acoustic Light Field. They don't want to be trapped in the Vehicle. The Vehicle is a price they pay to increase Wisdom. It is a price they pay to honor the Laws of Evolution, but it is a price to be paid.

I'm giving this information to you about the 8th Gate from a slanted perspective. The battle between Light and Dark never ends with any great victory. It is important for somebody with the 8th Gate in their Dream Life to understand what the role of that Gate is. You see, after all, it ends with very, very, very little shift of the scales. At the same time, the fundamental balance must always be there, always. We cannot be without Love in that sense. We will not be allowed to be without Love. That Light Field remains competitive in its struggle with the other side. At the same time, there is a sense of how arduous it is. It is the 8th Gate that is used as a propaganda tool by the Personality Field to let the person know that it is not about the body. "Give unto Caesar what is Caesar's." It is not about the body, i.e., the body is just a pain that you have to go through. If you have faith, if you have Love, if you have this, if you have that, you have joy, it's okay. The rest of it doesn't matter.

You get your reward when you leave the body. You get rid of all the heavy equipment. You don't have to worry about eating. You go into the Hum. If heaven were a place where you could have a decent conversation and a cup of coffee, you'd be okay, but mechanical heaven is a desperately boring place because nothing is going on. There are just Personality Crystals rubbing against each other and Humming. That is my joke, i.e., if you could get up real close, you put the stethoscope to the Personality Crystals, and you could hear them go, "I am, I am, I'm, I'm, I'm." So what? And the Neutrino program goes through that and continues – you see, you can only appreciate what that is if you realize that we are one thing in one life that spans vast, vast, vast concepts of time. As soon as you can see it in that way, you can understand that this is all an incredible process.

Channel 20/57

Do you notice something about these Three Divisions in the DreamRave? Look at the Earth Plane. The Earth Plane is a Splenic Generator connected to the G Center (Identity). Look at The Demon Realm. You see that the Demon Realm is a Splenic Root Generator. In other words, both the Earth Plane and the Demon Realm are Generative Fields, and because they are Generative Fields, they carry a great deal of energy in terms of how they impact the Dreaming Life. We've already seen that with the intensity of The Earth Plane.

Look at the Light Field. It is the Projection Field. It calls for recognition. If you look at The Light Field, you'll also see that it is the only Field with such concentration on the Throat Center. The Light

Field has three Gates in the Throat Center and three verbal Gates. What is very important in the way you measure this Field in your own process is that when there are Transits coming to The Light Field, pay attention to the difference in the audio in your Dream. You are going to find that the audio is very different, the quality of it and the substance of it. There is much interesting information to look at; experimentally, it is very important for you to go through the process and experiment with it.

With the presence of Channel 20/57, you have a direct movement from the Fear of Tomorrow to its actualization in the sense of being in the Now and recognizing that there is no need to be afraid. The 57th Gate is the Gate of Attunement. Look at its mirror in The Demon Realm. Its mirror in The Demon Realm is Dying (Gate 42). The Demon Realm teaches us that all things are corruptible. That is why we honor the Form. It is temporary. All things are corruptible. In the Light Realm, that is not true.

Personality Crystals are, for the most part, indestructible. Now, that is not to say that they cannot be destroyed. However, for the most part, they are basically what we would call Eternal. The Crystals of Consciousness that are in all of us here in this room are at least 15 billion years old. They have been around quite a while.

The 57th Gate is about being attuned to the beauty of Immortality. The 57th Gate gives us Immortality Dreams. These are forever places. It is one of the most extraordinary things about the 57th Gate; at this Dreaming level, there is never a tomorrow. Therefore, there is no Fear of tomorrow. There is this endless Now, with the possibility of no Dying (Gate 42). Of course, we are all caught up in that in our lives. By being disposable, we know that there will always be a desire in us, envy, or a dream, that we can live longer, healthier, blah, blah, blah, all this stuff. I don't know about Immortality. I find that idea rather boring, but, nonetheless, we would all like to extend all of that.

The vast majority of Personality Crystals know nothing about death or life, for that matter. In other words, Personality Crystals are not encumbered by that process. It is a promise that they bring us all the time so that we accept death. The propaganda is good and bad. It is like the old Chinese saying, "Good news, bad news, who knows?" The 57th Gate, Attunement to the possibility of immortality, of endlessness, we need all that. We need that as a balance to the Form recognition that it is all terminal, that we come into the world with a terminal ticket, and that there is nothing we can do about it. The 57th Gate is the balance on the other side. It does not mean that you will become immortal.

The joke is, and I love this joke, which is why propaganda can be so cruel that the Personality Crystal says, "Look, to become immortal, die." Isn't that a wonderful joke? Isn't that a cruel joke? That is the promise. "When you die, you will rise up into the great spirit, and it will take you," "the dog doo-doo will take you," whatever the case may be. Isn't that a wonderful joke? Die first, then you get it. You do not get another life in that sense. You get what is beyond being in Form. After all, not being in Form is really full of Light. It's great. There is no skin to get in the way of the shine. The gods have known how stupid we are for a very long time. I think it still annoys them that we gain any intelligence. I mean that.

Gate 20: Sight

The 20th Gate wakes you up instantly. It is one of the most powerful alarm clocks to shatter you out of the Dream into wakefulness. The 20th Gate has the inherent capacity in its power to literally wrench you into the Now. In those moments, you abruptly awake. We all know these moments from our Dream Process, i.e., that sudden awakening gives you a great deal of access to the Dream you just left. It is very important. In that moment, something wonderful happens. It is a Translation Process. What you hear in the Dream is actually just hearing, i.e., Acoustic, regardless of what you think you are seeing in this Light Field. But in the 20th Gate, there is the possibility for that hearing to jump across Consciousness into the Waking Field, where it can become sight.

Translation in Gate 20: Acoustic to Visual

In other words, an awareness opens up in the Dream Realm that can actually become something you can literally see in the Waking World. This happens in the sense that you can understand how it works, or you know what can happen. People have premonitions in their dreams. This is a very powerful moment of a "shock jump." It is a moment in which the Acoustic Phenomena can take on a quality in that allows translation to the awakening awareness as Sight. What it means to the Dreamer on the inside, inside of the DreamRave, is the perception that the Dreamer must be speaking. This is a very, very important Voice to hear when it is the Dreamer's Voice.

I live with a certain kind of magic because of my Design. The things I talk about here, they are just things that process through me. I don't really know how that operates. The same thing is very true of the 20th Gate. The dreamer who is speaking, who has the 20th Gate in their Design or by Transit, becomes the Voice of something. They are literally the Voice of something. It is not like the Acoustic Phenomena in the rest of this grouping in which that Voice is just a simple translation of a chorus of Voices; it can be very, very specific in the moment. When it becomes specific you can get information in that sense. Now, that information, remember, can never be trusted. *The only Dream experience the Dreamer can trust comes through the Earth Plane* because the Earth Plane is the only Realm that really relates to the Dreamer in terms of the Tao, i.e., what is really balanced between the opposing forces. So, it is very, very risky. In other words, again, the Dream World cannot be taken Personally. It is just that each and every one of us can speak for many, many forces. I want you to understand how that holds for each and every one of us. It doesn't matter whether you have the 20th Gate or not. You get it in the Transits.

There are many, many, many more Crystals out of incarnation than in incarnation. Each of us represents a party line of Voices that would like to get through and express themselves to us. As I express it like that, please do not anthropomorphize that as if they know they want to get that information to us or they know they are participating in that. They are not. They are just Crystals. But the Neutrino Field goes through those Crystals.

We are all caught up in Fractal Geometry. You have a Fractal connection to people who are alive with Crystals aligned to your Crystal, and you have a Fractal connection to Crystals that have gone out of Form and who have never been in Form. You are aligned with them as well. Through the 20th Gate are those moments in which unique expressions from The Light Field come through. I have met and have known at a personal level about five or six legitimate channels, although I really don't know what that means in their way of describing it. I only understand it mechanically. All of them had the 20th Gate, and most of them had the Channel 20/34 on the Rave Design side.

One thing to recognize about this 20th Gate is that it carries a certain kind of personalized Authority that can be very confusing if you take it personally. In other words, you get very specific input through that Dreaming Field, yet it's Not Personal. Let's create a hypothetical situation. Let us say that Einstein would like to talk to me. Einstein may talk to me through Tom. That is, Tom may have a Transit or that 20th Gate, and this information is going to him. He is the one who can receive it because he has the Fractal, and then he may end up giving that information to me. It would never be of any value to him. If he had tried to spend all his time analyzing why he got that specific message, it would have driven him crazy. So, it's still Not Personal. But it's different in the way in which it comes through. So, the 20th Gate is a very, very interesting Gate. It will be something very interesting for us to explore in that sense.

Gate 62: Love

In Design, Gate 62: A preponderance of the Small is the Gate of Detail. It is an extraordinary Cross-Species Gate. It is the only way that Mammals can connect to Human Mental Consciousness. Any of you who have ever experienced a Mammal as a personal companion know that you are able to transfer to that Mammal all kinds of things that are not necessarily natural to its nature: how to open and close the door, how to use the litter box in the bathroom. One of the most important things about our relationship with Mammals is that Mammals are not just simply here to connect to us on the emotional plane, "Ah, sweet doggie." Mammals are here to connect to us in a way in which we enlighten them. It's obviously not up to them. They don't have an Ajna Center. They do not possess a neocortex. They do not in any way have the capacity a human being has to manipulate Consciousness at the Mental Plane. However, Mammals have a Cross-Species connection to that. They are open to that. They can be trained. The most straightforward description is the connection between a master who has Gate 17 and a pet who has Gate 62. This animal can be trained at an intellectual level. You can train the dog to count with its paws. You can do those tricks and blah, blah, blah. But it says something extraordinary about the 62nd Gate.

The 62nd Gate is Designed to Bridge directly to the Mind. Think about that. The Earth Plane bridges directly to the Emotions. The Demon Realm bridges directly to the Emotions. The Light Field bridges right to the Mental Plane.

Here's our dilemma: We are at a point in our evolutionary process where we have dealt with two-thirds of the battle. The first step was to Survive, Splenic Awareness, to honor Splenic Awareness, to Survive through Splenic Awareness. The second step was the flowering, the opening up of Mental Awareness. We are near the end of the process, coming to grips with the Mental Process. Finally, we are opening up. By the year 2027, we will open up to the next step, the opening of the flowering of Emotional Awareness as a completion of our evolutionary development in these Forms, and that is only in that sense for these Forms.

The Mental Plane

One of the first things about becoming yourself is giving up Mental Authority. I can talk all I like to you about Type and this and that, but I know the power of the Mental Plane. I know how we are all caught up in it, how we all analyze and deal with it, and how we all measure using it because that's what the Mental Plane is all about. It is all about Measuring. We know that one of the most difficult things as part of our process in living Design and bringing Design to other human beings is seeing how deeply identified they are with the Mental Plane and the Mental Conditioning they have received in their Not-Self Life. One of the things to understand about The Light Field is that The Light Field consistently reinforces the False Authority of the Mental Plane. It is one of its things, so we are always mentally in that sort of hopeful, dreamy state, "It might get better, it could get better," blah, blah, blah. This is about hope. It's not one of my favorite words, but I know people like it. If you are abstract, you have to have hope. So, I figure, "Let them have it." But this is about hope, and this Field has the propaganda of hope. If it's in your Design, hope can be very rewarding. If you are a 1/3 Profile and you are not abstract, hope is disgusting. All things are relative.

Aside from my sense of humor, this hopefulness is a Mental trip. If the hopefulness is a mental trip, it means that the Mental tries to condition us to make Love our Mental Authority. In other words, as an example of a mental concept, "Love thy neighbor," This is great Light Field mental propaganda. Make that your Authority, "Love thy neighbor." The Demon Realm doesn't say, "Hate thy neighbor." It doesn't say that at all. It says, "Is thy neighbor useful or useless?" That is all. If thy neighbor is useful, perhaps there is Love in that. If your neighbor is useless, perhaps there is hate in that. The two Realms have very different ways of looking at things. Now, obviously, we need the balance. We don't want to be coldly mammalian. Remember, this is a Mammalian Program as a Matrix. We are, in fact, Mammalian. Don't forget that. However, we don't want to be just coldly Mammalian. We do need balance, but we also need to see and understand that because The Light Field operates through the Mental Plane, it has a disproportional impact on life.

So many human beings give their mind Mental Authority. They end up suffering because as much as they say that they would like to love their neighbor, they happen to hate the person who lives next door; they find them a terrible bore, a nuisance, and so forth, and so on, and then they feel guilty and ashamed. Gate 62 is the Gate of Love, so let me get to the nice side without being too cruel to all of this. It is not like I'm opposed to any of that. It's in my Design, after all. My DreamRave has Channel 20/57 and Channel 8/1. It is not like I can escape all of that. That's why I know the propaganda so well. They are constantly trying to balance me out. "Fill him with Light, fill him with Light. He's too Dark, he's too Dark."

Anyway, Love is in the Detail. The Personality, no matter what it tries to do in trying to imbue us with the disproportionate way in which we can look at the pleasant side of life, never escapes the facts. It never escapes what programs Consciousness in Form. Love is in the Detail. It really is. The deepest of all loves is the Love that is rooted in understanding. There is no deeper love. There just can't be. One of the things that is clear is that the pursuit of knowledge is not alien to The Light Field. It is just that the Light Field would like to control what you can take out on your library card. If you have the 62nd Gate, remember it is a Portal (Bridging) Gate. Of course, this is the ability to bring that Love and to translate that Love outward. In other words, to bring it across the Portal to the Awake Personality. It comes across in the Voice, and it is not in the words, but it is in the Tone. The Tone changes. If you can purely, decently, say to somebody with really the right Tone that they should take a long walk off a short pier, they might be soothed by that Tone. That 62nd Gate Portal (Bridge) is that Tone. That is what it is about. It ranges from sanctimonious to honey-coated. But it is very powerful. You have to experiment with this phenomenon, and, of course, the best thing for us to do in this kind of experience is to body-mike you.

For example, let's say that Gate 62 in your DreamRave comes via a Transit. You awake, or whatever the configuration is. You don't notice because you live with yourself every day, and you talk all the time; what you don't notice is a subtle shift in your Tone after you have that Dream Portal (Bridge) connection. If we could body-mike you, we could actually measure differences in the way speech works and in its frequency; you would see the difference. There is suddenly this, to say it's "loving," I mean, yeah, it is, but it has another, je ne sais quoi, if you know what I mean. These are the words of Love that come into life, you see because the 62nd Gate distorts the Maya.

I have my Design Earth in the 62nd Gate. The Maya was created in the 62nd Gate, so it can be explained in the 62nd Gate. In the 62nd Gate, you give things their names. There is *no Maya without the naming of things*. It doesn't exist. Somebody like Osho, who had the 62nd Gate, went around giving people names. Somebody like me, with my 62nd Gate gives names to things, Personality Crystals, and Design Crystals, and all this stuff. It's part of the process of the 62nd Gate to be able to define for us what our Maya actually is so we have commonality in language. We can all say, "tree," and we all know what we mean. This Gate as a Portal (Bridge) has very important value because it brings new words. How do you like that? It brings new words and new expressions into the world. And it brings them from the Personality Realm.

Go into an esoteric bookshop. Go to the channeling section. My favorite, actually, was Gurdjieff because he had all these hilarious names for things, you know, "boogaloo goo, schawaloogoo, boo-boo." One of the most common things in mystics is that they have all these funny names for things. They get these funny names across this Portal (Bridge). This Bridge brings these names and tries to fool us into thinking that we are Love and that Light is there as something that we can hope for and Dream for. It is the only thing that is going to carry us and balance us against the Darkness with which we have to live.

There is this old story in the Bible about the confusion of tongues in Babylon. These people who speak in tongues can be a very spooky thing. Sometimes, little children all of a sudden start speaking in a language that they can't possibly know. Whatever the case may be, all of that is learned and bridged through the 62nd Gate. *All the languages that have ever been spoken, all the dialects, all the tongues, all of it, every name of everything that has ever existed, every name that we have ever applied to anything in any way, all move across this Portal/Bridge.* That is quite something. It keeps us in touch with the continuity. Out of the 62nd Gate, you get the Akashic records and the Global Incarnation Index. You get the storage of all of that. All the names are stored. In the case of the Global Incarnation Index, all the formulas are stored. All the formulas are accessible. It is possible to see all of the formulas. This information is what moves across this Portal/Bridge.

All of the pressure that comes from The Light Field on the Mental Plane shows that life itself is a burden, and we need to get past it. After all, that is what it is about. "Get through this." "Don't sit," "Don't fuck up your karma," "Get through this and you know you're going to get your jolly award on the other side. By the way, while you're going along that way, here are some wonderful mysteries we can give you because we're storing the mysteries." They don't really store them; it is a lie, but it is their lie. They filter them. It is all coming from further back in the chain, but they filter it.

The 62nd Gate has a lot of mystical qualities to it. It is a very unusual kind of Portal/Bridge. In terms of our research, it will be interesting over the years to see what that really means in terms of case studies so that we really see what that's about. I can give you the Mechanical Nature, but it is so beautiful to see how all that opens.

Digression on the Importance of the Scientific Work

Last night, I had the pleasure of watching Marvin put these cases up for you to see; I'm like a 15-year-old kid. It's like, "Oh, yeah, that's true. I see that. And don't forget that. And there's that over there. When you say that, no, no, there is that." There is this constant ongoing process of the scientific verification of Human Design that is so important. You see, I've waited a very, very long time, and truly, it is my relationship with Eleanor and Marvin and their cats who are really at the source of that. The three of us have in common a great appreciation of Mammalian Consciousness. Out of that appreciation comes this ability to get to a point where I can really release this information. The fact of the matter is that there is so much work to be done at the personal level in the Waking Life, so much work to be done. This material is not personal. Dreaming life is only going to work correctly when the waking personality is healthy. It is very important for us to begin this work because we need to scientifically verify this material to get to a point where we can really show it to people.

Shortly, we are going to release a DreamRave Ephemeris. We plan to give you a chance to Dream along with us and see how the whole operates. It is going to be one of the most exciting spiritual processes that you will be able to enter into, conscious and Aware, into a Realm in which you give up your Personal Identity just to see your involvement in the Whole. That is very exciting. All of that is very exciting.

Byron's Mystical Dream

When we deal with the 62nd Gate, it is particularly interesting to me. I know that this is very special regarding the kind of information that can be released, the Mystical Dream. My favorite is Byron's famous Dream. His description of his Dream and his words about it occupied Mystics for a long time. The Mystics of the 19th Century said, "That is the most mystical thing that has ever been said." I would love to see Byron's Design. I would love to see his DreamRave. This Dream is classic Gate 62. There is this mystery mantra that comes out, and then everybody tries to decipher what it is. It is a very interesting Gate. It is a very magical Gate in that context.

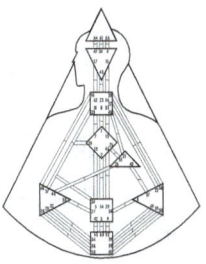

The Demon Realm

Environment

Okay, love. I am going to try not to be too friendly to The Demon Realm so I don't give a bad impression. I really should have changed these names around. I should have called it the "Demon Field" and filled it with Light. Love is in the Detail, we know that. Mutation comes through caution. So one of the things to understand is that Environment is about need, period. We need Environments. Remember, the Personality Crystal says, "We don't need anything. I don't have a body." They don't need anything. They are not into that.

The Demon Realm is the feed that comes from the Design side only. Design is only interested in one thing, Form. "Let's keep on evolving better and better Forms: a new Ford, a new frig, a new whatever." We are constantly in this Form process. It is the Environment. How is that expressed? "It is the Environment, stupid. It's the Environment." This Body is an Environment. A cell is an Environment. These are all Environments. This is what it's all about. We need the Environment. In the Mammal, this is Territory. The Mammal recognizes that without a secured Territory, there is no Survival and there is no mating. It is both about food resources and sexuality. But here, what we are dealing with is the even deeper sense that we need primary Territory. Primary Territory is actually having the ability to create a cell that holds itself together. The human cell is made up of things that were alive separately before the cell existed. The Environment, the creating of Environments, the developing of Environments, the expanding of Environments, the perfecting of Environments, all of those aspects are there in The Demon Realm. That is its Drive. That is its replacement for Love.

I want to tell you something. If you are in the right Environment in yourself and in the world around you, you are not looking for Love. It does not mean it is not nice. It does not mean you should not, could not, or cannot have it. You are not interested. It is the balance on the other side. Now, we can't let The Demon Realm say to us, "We don't need that Love at all," because that's not true. But remember, each side does its best to compete, to give you its perspective as the be-all and the end-all. The Light says, "All you need is Love," and the Demon side says, "All you need is a good room."

What did that guy get fired for? My wonderful trivia memory. In the Carter administration, some Georgian guy made some comments about blacks. He said that they liked "loose shoes, warm pussy" or "loose shoes, tight pussy, and a warm place to shit." Now, that's a black joke. No pun intended. That is an Environmental joke. That's what it's all about. Of course, the Light said, "That's politically incorrect, and you're fired." However, that is what that's about. You see, the environment of the Dark Side is everything. "Oh, let's have a better computer, yes. Let's have a better modem, yes. Let's keep on making it better, yes. New Form. Yes. Get rid of the fins or add the fins. Bring the things, da-da-da," you know, "Form, let's have it." That is everything on that side. "I love my new shoes. I don't love you. They are the perfect environment for my toes." It's all Environment.

This is what I came here to teach you. I come to teach Form. I know there are lots of Lights around. This is what this is all about to get you to recognize that. Look, for so long, we have been overwhelmed by the propaganda of the Light side. Now, there is nothing wrong with all that stuff. But it is disproportionate. That is all Yang over there and a Yin over here. It is this Yin that is going to carry us into the future, not the Yang, with all its promises. We are living in this transition as we move toward the end of the Piscean era toward the Aquarian Age. It is a theme that we are defining within the totality: what we are defining is our real sexuality. We are defining the ultimate balance between the Yin and the Yang in totality. There is a huge struggle going on. That is why the literature of the last four millenniums has all been Light and Darkness. They have all been mirrors of what has been going on, which, of course, in the Life of the Biverse, in the Life of the totality of 15 billion years, what is 4,000 years? For us, when we personalize it, "Boy, that's history." It is ongoing, and suddenly, we are aware of this through our Dream Consciousness Field.

Through the DreamRave, these concepts of heaven and hell have come into our lives. These Voices that speak to us from either side are forces that seem to move us from either side. One of the most important teachings will be our ability to bring the understanding that this is not Personal to the general public. *It is Not Personal.* It is what we all need to process. We need to get this and that in order to find the Tao in our lives. We are a combination of this and that. Human Design brings, in its Mechanics of the Maya, a rule that says, "Mind has no Inner Authority." This is The Demon Realm going, "Environment, environment, they win. We got it. We're better." And it's true. In other words, this is the shifting. It's one of my jokes, and I'm not the son of the father. I am a son of a bitch. I come from the other side. I know where my bread is buttered. My bread is buttered with Mama. This whole thing is going Yin. I'm no fool, and I'm not going to hang onto the Yang.

There is a difference between how The Light Field operates and how The Demon Realm operates in terms of how it tries to impact us. As you've seen, the Light Field impacts on us through the Mental Plane, so this is the only place where you really can deal with it. You have to be able to deal with it in the Mental World. When you deal with The Demon Realm, you deal with something that is quite different. First of all, you have Channel 28/38, so you have the direct connection between the Splenic Center and the Root Center, and then Channel 53/42, which is the Format Energy. Channel 53/42 is a Format energy that runs up from the Root Center to the Sacral Center. It is the nature of the Design of Mammals that this is the only Format. In other words, the Format of the Dreaming Life is here in The Demon Realm.

The Generative Capacity of both The Demon Realm and The Earth Plane really gives life its quality. In other words, these are generated, and they operate specifically in response. Remember that The Light Field is Yang. It tries to program us. Everything about The Demon Realm is about operating out of response to Form and the needs of Form or the need of the Environment. In other words, *the Dream itself is always a reflection of the demands of being in Form.* As such, Dreams tend to be less pleasant as subject matter than The Light Field, which gives them their bad reputation, you know, "Why do I have to Dream that shit? Why can't I dream about fairies and sweet things and nice stuff? Here I am, struggling with my dream." The Channel 28/38, classic Struggle.

Channel 28/38

I've had very few dreams that have had a direct relationship in terms of memory, but the ones that I have had were quite extraordinary. There is a Dream that I had in my early 30's. I was in the Dream, and in the Consciousness of the Dream, I was flying. I'm a feathered creature flying. I am astounded at the fact that I have feathers on my arms. I can feel the wings. I look down, and I see that my chest is covered with what looks like reptilian scales. I have no sexual organs. Everything is covered with these scales. I am busily looking at my lack of sexuality in the Dream as I'm flying; all of a sudden, I feel a yank, and I realize, as I look back, that my feet are chained and that there is a chain going all the way down into the Earth below. It is a beach, and there is a whole line of ants, people as it turns out, who are pulling on my damn chain. I'm struggling to fly up. Now, this is a Channel 28/38 Dream. It is really what it is all about. It is the Dream that does the pulling down. It is the pulling down to Earth. It says, "Come back down here into the Environment. Come down here into the Form. You're not finished with your Formwork."

Gate 28: Fear

The 28th Gate, the Gate of Fear, is a Gate that expresses fear at the deepest Form level. The Fear is that the Form will not properly support the Consciousness. I'll repeat that. It is a basic fear that the Form itself cannot support the Consciousness in the sense that the Form is not giving an advantage to the Consciousness. In Human Design, the 28th Gate, the Gate of the Fear of Death, is about whether life is going to be of Value or not, personal Value, whether one is of Value or not. This deep Fear can never be resolved unless the Form is correct. So, this is the Fear that you are in the wrong house; you are wearing the wrong kind of clothes; it is all kinds of Environmental things that can pop up around you. All of them are saying to you, "This is a disadvantage to your Consciousness." The perfecting of the Form is something that is absolutely essential in the drive that is here. Now, of course, that's one of the things to recognize about the Mammals. Mammals have no personal behavior. There is no 10th Gate in the Mammalian Matrix. Remember, we are not dealing with the personal here. We are dealing with all of the Design Crystals that have ever existed that are not in Form now. They pressured us to recognize that we had better pay attention to the form, period. If we do not pay attention to the Form, we are afraid.

Now, what's interesting about Channel 28/38 is that it mirrors Channel 39/55 in a Human, and at the Mammalian level, this is where Mammals have food problems. They have food problems because, of course, it is through Channel 28/38 that Hunting takes place. This channel is intensely Aggressive. It is the Struggle for life in that sense. One of the things about the 28th Gate and the 38th Gate is that the Form can also be one's own body, i.e., the struggle can be with trying to find the right Form; in other words, there can be food problems that are a direct result of difficulties which occur on the Dream Plane. Somebody with the 28/38 channel in their Dreaming Life can have resulting food problems in their Waking Life. There is a pressure that the Form is not right or the Form must be improved.

Of course, it is hard for me to describe to you how powerful a force is because that force works most deeply at your cellular level. As soon as I put Human Design in the seven-year program in you, I put a great Fear into your life. I have no choice, so it's not like I feel bad. At the cellular level, you transform. More goes on in your life at the cellular level than at the totality level of your being. Yet, there is an inherent Struggle between the Not-Self and the New Self at the cellular level going on in your body. You have one cell that is dying and being replaced by a new one in your Consciousness, while the one beside it is still an old one. Yes, it will die in the next fraction of a second, but, nonetheless, you have to see that this battle goes on all the time, and the Fear is deep at the cellular level.

This part of the Dream Life involves all kinds of assumptions about ailments, hypochondria, and the potential for hypochondria. "There is something wrong with me," says the Gate 28 Dreamer. I don't know what it is. There is something wrong with my Form. There is something wrong with me. There is something wrong with this Environment. There's something wrong." In other words, the personalization of this Fear acts as an agent of transformation. The personalization can end up with fearfulness and discomfort with Form. Everybody is selling "Change the Form." Don't you notice? Everything around us sells that. If you have a product and it's one year old, you change the box, you change the Form. You bring it out as "new and improved." You keep changing the Form all the time. Technologically, we have reached the point where people regularly change the Form of their bodies. They hack their noses and stuff their breasts, and they do all these things. We are constantly involved in changing the form. This is the power of the 28th Gate. Unfounded Risk-taking can be deeply part of the 28th Gate. People think that changing the nature of the nose they were born with will change how it feels to be in the world; this is part of the false propaganda of the Form side only.

Again, it's essential to see that only the Tao is a place where we can see the balance as it is lived out in the world through our Dream Life. We know no balance when we look at the mirror on either side. Yes, they both have their truth, but they only have their truth. They are only telling their side of the story.

This Fear can be very uncomfortable unless it is matched with Joy on the other side. There is hope on the other side that says, "Even though I do have a new nose, this person actually loves me for myself." There is still hope.

Gate 38: Aggression

Names, you know, that is my business. Names are my business, so I get into all these names. I realize how prejudiced people are about names. Write down a word like "aggression," and you know right away that that name that gives people a kind of slanted perspective. What we know about the 38th Gate from Design is that Gate 38 is a Gate of Struggle. It is really the Gate of the Fighter. Gate 38 is in a place where there is a tremendous amount of Stress and a tremendous amount of Adrenalized Pressure to Fight for things in life. At the Mammalian level, this is about Fierceness. Gate 38 creatures can be very, very, very Fierce. They have the potential in them to fight for what they need in this life. Please understand that the nature of this Aggression is that we are all here to fight to preserve the Form. To fight to preserve the Form means killing other Forms. The Light side cringes and says, "We are all one," and the black side says, "I've got to eat, honey. I'm in a body. I don't want to eat tree bark. That cow will do." Both sides of the story have their value. However, you have to see what happens. Imagine someone who is only slanted over to one side in their Dream Life. Imagine how hard that is. For us to take away that burden through understanding brings a relief of that burden. So here in the 38th Gate, yes, we do have Aggression. There's no question about that. We are conditioned by the Design Bundle to be Aggressive.

Have you ever seen a mother protect her young? Do you want to see something tough? Nothing is more Aggressive than the Yin in defense of Form and Life. On one side, we can say it's very ugly, as you know, "The hoo-toos killed the boo-toos because they want the hoo-toos' boo-toos." However, there is just the basic, "We have to eat, we're in Form." Aggression is inculcated in us. That can be frightening if it is not dealt with and if it is not understood.

One of my sons has five activations in the 38th Gate while he sleeps. He is in touch with stuff. He is very, very, very self-conscious about his Form. When he gets a bruise, he talks to me about that bruise until it's gone. "It's still there. You, see? It's a little smaller today." It's all about the protection of the Form. "Is it okay that it's there? Is it okay if it takes this long to go away? My Form needs to be protected."

We have to understand the Aggressiveness of Gate 38 as an essential ingredient for us. Look at its mirror in The Light Field. The mirror is the Darkness. The mirror in The Light Field says to you, "Sorry you have to go through this stuff. Yeah, it's messy, but it's all right. If you believe in Jesus, we'll get to the other side. It's okay." The Demon Realm side says, "Hey, baby, fight. It's all a fight. It's Survival of the fittest. It is a Struggle. Life's a Struggle. It's a burden. It's tough. You had better know that. You'd better be ready for it." Gate 38 is not a wimp Gate.

The channel itself, after all, is Individual. It is also Acoustic. One of the things to recognize about The Demon Realm is that The Demon Realm crosses both the Individual, the Collective, and the Tribal as Gate activation possibilities. In other words, it is very diverse in the way it impacts. Impacting the Individual process tells you something about how integration evolved into Individual Circuitry. Integration has Channel 20/57 and Channel 10/34. One of the things we learn in relationship analysis is that in Integration, one only cares for the other when Gate 28 or Gate 38 is present.

Understand about Channel 28/38 (Fear/Aggression) that the Fear is about the Environment and the Limitation of the Form. The Aggressiveness to defend the Environment and the Aggressiveness to go out and feed oneself pulls the individual out of aloneness into a much greater effort through which the individual can be a force for others. In other words, individuals become more caring in this way. The fact also points to something very clear. The Waking Life, the Waking Individual Personality, has to initiate this Survival process. In other words, Individual Mutation says, "Look, sitting in this tree pulling on these damn things all day and having to eat 14 hours a day is just not bloody efficient. So, let's go down there and kill those little buggers and eat them." That is what takes place there. There is this potential to Mutate the way the Form is maintained.

What also comes out of this is someone's ability to build a wall. I mean, this is, "Your home is your castle." The Environment gets bigger and bigger and bigger. Then your Village has to be protected. Then your Nation has to be protected. *Then* your Planet has to be protected. In other words, this is a very powerful force. At the same time, there are tremendous negative implications about what it means to build a wall because there are those inside and those left outside the wall. There are those who are fed on the inside and those who are not fed on the outside. One thing to understand about The Demon Realm is that, in the end, it is only about one thing: Food. *If you go to Sleep fully satisfied in your belly, you never have a bad Dream in The Demon Realm. Never go to sleep hungry.*

There are three billion people on Earth every day, and remember, while they are awake and we are asleep, we have their movie. They are hungry. When they go to sleep hungry, The Demon Realm has the deepest impact on them. The Demon Realm, in the end, recognizes something intrinsic: The Form is already in momentum, which is its evolution. No choice. It will evolve; it is evolving. It is about focusing our attention on that. Food, now, that's big business. Food keeps Form going day by day by day. Every living creature on earth spends time looking for food. All creatures. We take in this vibration.

There is something very funny and easy to do with people with Demon Realm activations who have bad nights, sleep problems, whatever. It is very important for them to have either a late dinner or a before bedtime snack. Now, honest to God, it's so simple because it is just a Mechanical, biological thing. Suppose they have a satisfied system and the system is busy working on churning over and digesting food. In that case, they don't get haunted by the fact that their Form is being destroyed from lack of nutrition or because the village across the way won't give them access to their fields or their crops or whatever the case may be.

Channel 53/42

Channel 53/42 is the only Format in the DreamRave Mammalian Matrix. You will notice that the kinship between the Earth Plane and the Demon Realm is much stronger than between the Earth Plane and the Light Field. Both the Earth Plane and the Demon Realm are Generative; they share that in common, while The Light Field is Projected. At the same time, this commonality exists in the movement in the power column of what is, in Human Design, the Abstract Circuit. In other words, you have the Channel 53/42 leading into the Channel 5/15. There is a basic deep relationship between the two. The Earth Plane, obviously, is deeply dependent on the success of the evolving Form in order for the Earth Plane to function properly. So, there is, obviously, this dynamic connection.

The Format Energy determines the quality of how Channel 5/15 works. This is the Power Column of the Mammalian Structure. It is the only way in which this continuity operates. We have Cycles of Rhythm. This is the true evolution. We have Cycles of Flow. That is why I can say to you, "Our time in these Vehicles will come to an end." There are Cycles of Being in the Flow in certain Forms as we evolve. That is the direct relationship between this Format and the Tantra. Remember that if you are looking at that Tantra in a human being with its natural Power Column being Channel 9/52, what you are going to have in that human being is someone for whom Being in the Flow is about being Focused and Concentrated. That is not true for the Dreaming Life because the Dreaming Life is not Personal. It is Cyclical. It is very different.

In looking at Format Energy, the first thing to recognize is that the job of this Format is to bring us recognition and acceptance of life in Form. For me, there is nothing that is more spiritual than that genetic gift as it finally works out in us. The fact of the matter is that because we have a Consciousness that recognizes that things live longer than we do, e.g., the Yew tree can live 1,800 years, some mushrooms can be 1,000 years old, and there is a part of us that yearns for that. When we are told about death, there is a part of us that has pain throughout our lives because we have to die, and that rotation, that in and out, and that movement seems senseless. The Demon Realm protects us from that pain. The Demon Realm says to us, "Forms are born obsolete." Have you recently bought a computer? They changed in that breath. Do you know what I mean?

We are born to die. That is the whole thing. The form says to us, "It's okay." Everybody knows that who gets the opportunity in life to die a natural death. There comes a moment in which it is all okay. It has been recorded over and over again in research. There comes a moment when it is just okay. That is what The Demon Realm teaches us. It says, "The machine you know is falling apart. Here's your chance to find out about the bullshit from the Light side. You can get a taste of that now. It's all okay.

You've been through it, and you made it. It's all right. But this is the way it's supposed to be. And don't worry, you are the kind that comes back." I don't know if that is such a nice send-off.

Gate 53: Flight

It begins with the 53rd Gate. Flight. "Let me run away." Flight. Everything about this channel is about what its name is in Design, which is Maturation. It is about the living process, the life process. Gate 53 represents the falling into Form completely. Falling into Form completely starts when we are very young. Falling into the running body. Falling into the Form. Everything is the Form. We Fall into loving the Form before we get to the difficulties of the Form. It is a part of us that is a seduction, after all. It is the propaganda of the Demon way that says, "It is going to be great to be in a body. Wow let's have some good times. See that? You have sex organs. Wow. Let's have some good times." It flies into the body. "You can eat and it tastes good. Oh, yes. Terrific." Now, of course, we don't know that flying into the body opens us to what is on the other side, which is death. Think about applying that in people's psychology if you have one or the other. Look at what you carry as Form information from the Design source, i.e., those who carry Gate 53 in their Dream Life want to be in the Form. You find more sex here than in Gate 50, which is called "sex." It's just part of all that. It's part of diving into the Form, being in the Form. This is where the Tantra as sex enlightenment comes from. It is all this diving in. It's like, "Wow, this is the best thing." The closest metaphor is the apple. "Come on, take a bite. Dive right in. Ain't going to tell you what it costs. Don't tell you how long you're going to pay. Dive in."

There is a kind of naivete, a kind of blind leaping that takes place in the 53rd Gate. Remember that in a Human Being or a Mammal, particularly in Mammals, Gate 53 is the Gate of Freedom. Don't chain dogs with Gate 53. The first chance they get, they will bite you. You can't do that to them; they want to be free. They don't want to be chained. They want to be free, to be able to have their own Environment and so forth and so on and all these things.

When looking at this Flight, remember that people with Gate 53 experience that. What they experience in their Dream Realm is deeply related to form. This Gate is where sexuality is so powerful in the Dream that an orgasm occurs upon awakening. In other words, you can be deeply inside of the Form. Violence is also very common in Gate 53.

This is where you get killed in a Dream. This is where you get slapped in a Dream. This is where you get hurt in a Dream. All these things can be felt with intensity because this is the deepest that the Dreamer gets into Form.

Within the Dream context, obviously, the body does not experience all those things. They filter the experiences as program themes that come through Dreams. We personalize that experience of being so deep in the Form that we wake up in that experience. By the way, sleepwalking takes place through the activation of Gate 53. In sleepwalking, you are so deep in the Form that you never really get out of it because you begin to function as if you are awake. This Gate can be a place where you are very lost. It can be very confusing when you come back to what is your natural balance and the domination of your mental perception on top of that.

Gate 42: Dying

The 42nd Gate is very different, with a name like "Dying." In Gate 42, things fall apart. The Tarot card, the sixteenth card, the Tower, this is the Tower. This Gate is where you see things shatter. This Gate is where you walk into a room, and the Forms are deformed, or faces are deformed. Those things are some of what comes through. There are many ways in which the Form can seem to present something wrong or where "there is something not right about it." This Gate is decaying. It's all about experiencing decay and recognizing that decay is part of the natural order.

When you meet these aspects in your Dream, and you personalize them, it is very frightening. People who have Gate 42 can wake up feeling like suddenly they are going to die, or there is something terrible that is about to happen to them, or whatever the case may be. These are people who awake and look at their hands to see if they are still there. There is something wrong, so they look around the room to see if the room is still what they thought it was. This Gate brings what Form is about.

Life works itself out through replicating Forms. Death is a necessary ingredient. We come in as a Form; we reproduce; we go out. Then, the next one carries on that chain. These Forms have evolved so Consciousness can reach this level. These Forms are terminal. They are terminal for only one reason: These Forms have egos. You cannot give an ego that kind of Consciousness. It is not meant for egos. All this is Not Personal. The ego is the world of "I" and "me." There is no ego in the DreamRave. There is no ego in the Mammalian Design.

There is ego in the human life. This Dying of Gate 42 is about seeing that it is correct to Decay. It is correct.

Gate 19: Environments

I told you that everything about this Demon Realm operates through a Theme of Food. It brings us to the Portal/Bridge, to the 19th Gate, to the Gate of Environments. This gate represents the need for an environment that can take in food. That is Number one. In other words, the Demon Realm says, "The body is the only thing." The Light Field says, "The body is not what it is about." The Demon Realm again says, "The body is the only thing. I must have a body." If you have the 19th Gate in your DreamRave, you are going to come back much sooner in an incarnation than somebody who doesn't have the 19th Gate. That is for all you mystical boo-boos who might like that one. It's a Portal/Bridge, after all.

Gate 19 operates as a Portal/Bridge when people eat. Think about that. In the future, therapy will develop through which to access DreamRave information from The Demon Realm. The work will occur with somebody while eating. Real magic exists the moment that people come together and break bread. That is why Channel 19/49 is a Mystical Channel. It is at the Source of our Mysticism. Those who come together Triblly share the same food, which is part of finding the "One" in the Personality Realm itself. What is so fascinating about the Demon Realm is that while people are eating, they get their data.

Let's say you are someone who has Gate 19 in your Design. We are talking about the Portal/Bridge. You have the 19th Gate in your Design. You had a Dream the night before. You awake in the morning. Nothing goes on with you in relation to that Dream. You don't remember it. You don't necessarily have a relationship to it. You go in, and you do your stuff, and then you sit down, and you have your breakfast. As you start to put the food into your mouth, then "click." It is one of those things to see. It is a very, very important mechanism. It is a simple mechanism. It is a Food Mechanism. It is the kind of thing where if you are a therapist and somebody comes into your office, you have some cookies. You don't have to invite them out for filet mignon. Have some cookies, have a little snack, and have something. Offer them something to put in their mouth. It's very important. It is a real doorway to getting into their Demon Realm. You break down their barriers that way, and then they open up to that within themselves.

Again, by researching this material, we will have a lot of fun because these things are fascinating things to learn. Tremendous information is there. The information there involves the ability to recognize the forms that we will need in the future. Prophecy is not prophecy in the sense of what the spirit will need but prophecy in the sense of what the Form will need to be available. The 12-year-old child who Dreams of a certain kind of machine ends up making it. In other words, there is this possibility here in this 19th Gate, not for a very, very mundane application but for new Forms to be revealed and for new Forms to be revealed to us. Gate 19 as a Portal/Bridge can be fascinating because what it brings out are new ways for us to come together as communities and new ways in which we can feed each other as communities.

Now, I did an excellent job of glossing over all the deep, dark, nasty, horrible stuff that is part of The Demon Realm, but then again, I did not smash as much of The Light Field propaganda as

I could. I figure the two realms are even at this point. Remember that both sides are really subjective. Don't forget that.

As you begin your own process, one of the things that would be very nice for us would be for you to communicate anything you discover in your Dreaming process out of the information we are sharing with you. If you could give us an insight into some of the things you have experienced with this material, it would be great because, of course, we would love to have first-hand experiential/experimental feedback from you about each of the aspects we are discussing. Could you give us this feedback through e-mail to ehp@noblesciences.com? Now, of course, obviously, not all of you can, nor do all of you have the desire to do that; however, any of you who do would be terrific for us.

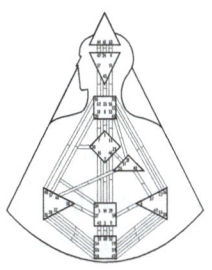

The Lines

In the time that's left, I want to walk you through the Lines. Remember that you will have to relate the Lines to the Three Divisions. In other words, we know that the Personality Side programs the Light Field, so those Lines are related to that specifically.

The Lower Trigram

Be clear regarding the Lower Trigram that we are talking about Profile when we refer to Lower Trigram Dreamers. In that sense, it is Right Angle or Right-Angle Dreamers who are the ones who have the most difficulty Depersonalizing. They are the ones who assume that Dreams really are for them. Dreams are obviously for them, but not in the sense that they assume. When you deal with the Lower Trigram, you are dealing with an involved process. The assumption is that the Dream is for them rather than that the Dream is for everyone. *Remember, do not discount what the Dreamer gets. But when we understand that what we receive on the Dream Plane is what we need to share with each other so we all grasp how the Whole operates, it's very different from* "That's my Personal Dream, and that was my message." *It is very different.*

Line 1: Secrets

The Lower Trigram begins with the 1st Line. The 1st Line in the DreamRave is called "Secrets." We know this is a Foundation. We know that this is the Line of Investigation. The 1st Line appearing in any of the DreamRave Gates allows for a really deep foundation material to arise. Psychologically, if the Waking Personality feels Insecure, then a 1st Line Profile Dreamer with many 1st Lines in the DreamRave may also feel tremendous Insecurity operating in the Dreamer's Life. This Dreamer feels discomfort because the Secrets are not there, and the Foundation is not there. This is also the being who can be obsessed with the fact that Secrets come from dreams. One of the most common words in the titles of Dream books is the word "secrets," e.g., "The Secrets of Dreams," "Dream Secrets," "The Secrets of Dreams Revealed," The Secrets of blah, blah, blah, they are never personal titles. They can be Personal in the sense that they can be applicable at the personal level, but they are always Fractal; they are always larger than any particular person.

Line 2: Possession

The 2nd Line is Possession. 2nd Line people are here to be Called. Yet 2nd Line people wish to be left alone. Of course, they wish to be left alone as a Waking Personality. The 2nd Line in the Dreamer shows that the Dreamer can be called through the 2nd Line. For example, somebody who has the 8th Gate 2nd Line is called into the Darkness Field; in the Dream, it is what possesses you. It overwhelms you. That means that the 2nd Line Transits are very powerful, particularly those 2nd Line Transits of the Moon that take place in the early morning hours when people are first awakening. These 2nd Line Transits bring out those moments when you get totally Possessed in an aspect of whatever it is you are dreaming, whatever level that is within your Design.

Remember, 2nd Lines can be paper tigers. In other words, what usually happens with Possession Dreams, in terms of the

Line itself, is that Possession Dreams keep taking Possession of you unless you surrender to them. You don't surrender to them if you think the Dream is personal because then it is frightening. 2nd Line Dreams always try to move away from other people. Wherever you are in the Dream Realm, you always try to find a place to be alone. These are dreams where you get lost or where you go out a door and suddenly go to a different place. You escape into something else. The 2nd Line always brings accents that are very, very strong and in which What Calls You overwhelms you in the context of the Dream. Many people consider 2nd Line Dreams very powerful nightmares because the Possession operating in The Demon Realm can be quite spooky. Suddenly, not only do you see Decay around you, but suddenly you see yourself Decaying. All that can be so shocking that it yanks you out of your Dream.

Line 3: Turmoil

I'm a great 3rd Line fan because this Martyr Pessimism Line is a difficult Line. It deals with Bonds Made and Broken. It is about Mistakes. It is about Trial and Error. Yet, it is the only Mutative Line we have, the only one that is Mutative. It is the only purely evolutionary Line. It is the only Line out of which real discovery takes place. Its name, Turmoil, comes out of that no matter where it is, particularly if it is associated with The Earth Plane. For example, you can be very uncomfortable if you have any of the Earth Plane Gates and the 3rd Line. It can be very uncomfortable because all of what breaks moves through you. All of what doesn't work moves through you. There can be enormous Turmoil.

Let's not trash 3rd Lines completely since 3rd Lines are where the most Profound Revelations come from. The 3rd Line is where Dream Revelation comes from. Now, when I say "Dream Revelation," again, let's not get into the tendency to glamorize that. That is, yes, it can be at a universal scale; all things work in a spectrum, but it is simply important to understand that out of Turmoil can come really deep discovery. Discovery can be revealed as revealed knowledge, revealed information, whether that is Form, whether that is the Light, whatever it may be.

It is obviously not going to be a common occurrence, and it is not going to be accessible to those people unless they are really actively involved in living out their own nature and their own design because then the Dream structure operates correctly. This means that everybody always has the potential for profound revelation. This is the kind of Dream where something goes wrong and everything goes right. It is one of the most dynamic themes of 3rd Line Dreams. It starts off, it can be frightening or a bad situation or whatever, and all of a sudden, everything changes. That moment of transition is the Discovery. Something deep has been discovered and depending on the Portal/Bridging Gate and where the Themes are, there is the possibility that that Portal/Bridge can be brought through so the Dreamer can have access to it in terms of the Waking Personality.

The Upper Trigram

Obviously, very few people know about this knowledge, and we'll do the best we can to let them know. Very few Human Design people know about this knowledge. In other words, all we can really do at this stage is let you know that you are the first generation of guinea pigs to watch the movie; you can see how all of that operates; we can learn from each other in that process. Those Dreamers whose Profiles are Upper Trigram and Left Angle have the potential to bridge and reach the largest number of people.

Line 4: Obsession

We know that 4th Line People are Fixed. The 4th Line is not simply about the recurring Dream but about the recurring Theme. Once a person has this kind of Dream, this same Dream keeps recurring. Looking at and analyzing 4th Line Dreaming carefully in terms of its basic themes, you will see that the 4th Line Dreamers always Dream the same Dream. That's why this Line is called "Obsession." It is not because they are Obsessed. It is because the Dreamer always Dreams the same Dream. Some people become frightened by the repeated Dream, and others don't recognize it. The very same Dream can have a different kind of look or feel, but it is still the same Dream. It is still the same story. It is still the same theme. It just goes on again and again and again. With a 4th Line activation in your DreamRave, you can map the times when a Gate in that area is activated because that is where you get your repeat themes. You know that repetitive DreamRave comes from the 4th Line activation.

Repetition is one of the most important things that we do. Do you know how many times basic instructions are repeated in your brain so that you can breathe? There is this endless repetition, and, as we know, Logic is Rooted in Repetition. It is Rooted in Repetition to get it right, to perfect it, all of that process. Obsession deals with Repetition, which is about teaching. It can be a cruel teacher. Wherever you have that 4th Line, it is going to limit you to more than the subject of that 4th Line. If you have Gate 53 in the 4th Line, you always fly into Form, but it is always the same Form. In other words, you keep getting the same thematic movie with which to deal. These people say, "That Dream must be telling me something." They've had it for ten years. "That Dream must be telling me something. I don't know what the hell it's telling me." It is not telling them anything. They have just tuned into an educational network and gotten into its loop. Until someone says to them, "Excuse me, do tell me about your Dream because I need to know what that is. I want to hear your Dream. Not so I can heal you, so I can find out what is going on. You are that venue for me." When you stop making the Dream Life Personal, it becomes Social and Transpersonal. The real magic will come someday down the road when we work Consciously, as a whole, with the Dream Life as we live it.

We can only do that work once we understand that the program has given us input. You tell me what you Dream, and I tell you what I Dream. We have different Dreams. We have different themes. It comes from the same program. Slowly, we begin to see what the program does. I get your message. You get my message. The Dream Life is the one place where, as yet, we have not fulfilled our potential as the ultimate communicating species. This arena is the last frontier for us in communication.

What we are doing here this weekend is rough. As I said, we will get to a point where Emotionally Defined children with Emotional Awareness will be able to tap into those fields in a way that we don't understand now. We have to begin setting the framework or the groundwork for what is possible in the future. We need to get these 4th Line Themes from people who have the 4th Line. We need to record these Dreams so other people can have access to them. As soon as they see that their Dreams are Not Personal, they stop being obsessed with them and are disturbed by them in their process. 4th Lines have Influence. Recurring Dreams disturb the Waking Life. If you have an odd dream that you don't remember or that you remember, but the next day, it's gone because there is another dream. A Dream that keeps Recurring eventually begins to haunt a person. It haunts their Waking Personality. As a result of this Obsession, they need to understand that they are just in an educational loop, and it is okay. They also need someone who is there for them with whom to share that information. This sharing process is very important.

One of the most sophisticated and advanced roles that will come out of Design will be the Dream Therapists who will come out of the Rave Life Sciences' work down the road. These people will be able to really work with people's Dream Lives, not to heal them or cure them because that's not what it is about, but to involve them in networking their Dream Awareness and understanding what it is that they are processing.

Line 5: Fantasy

As is always the case with the Structure of the Hexagram, the 1st Line tells you what it is, and the 5th Line tells you what it wants. This Structure holds in the Dream of the Dream which is kind of cute. The Dreamer Dreams of Dreams, or the Dreamer Dreams of – never mind. It goes on and on and on. There is nothing that carries more power than the Projection Field. Of course, the 5th Line is the heart of Projection. Two things are possible out of the 5th Line of Fantasy. Truly practical and valuable things can be discerned from anyone carrying a 5th Line in the DreamRave because that is always the potential of the 5th Line. It can bring what is Practical, to be the same, to be the Savior, to be all of those things. There is also tremendous pressure on the 5th Line to be the source of all that. Out of that comes a lot of Projected delusion, Fantasy. If a person has the 15th Gate of Chaos, where the order is compressed, and has the 5th Line, there is pressure on that person from the Dream Realm around them to solve the order right then and there. Of course, that order is solved either practically or delusionally if that is such a word.

Wherever you have the 5th Line, you are put under more Pressure in your Dream state than you are in your Waking state. The Pressure of the program works directly on your 5th Line potential. The fact that you work something out in a Dream under Pressure does not mean that it will work in reality. A common thing that comes out of the 5th Line in the Dream Life is writing that takes place that is not done by human hands. People suddenly write out a Beethoven sonata, or they suddenly start writing a book or a poem or whatever the case may be. The 5th Line in the Dream is where the Muse is. The Muse can touch all humanity. The muse that inspires us may only sometimes provide real solutions.

The 5th Line shows you clearly whether you are healthy or not, psychologically. If you are not respected in a Dream, it is something very important to understand. If you are in a Dream and someone says to you, "Hey, jerk," then you know right away, you have an immediate sign that there is something really wrong with your life, period. The 5th Line, the Projection Line, is always subject to problems with Reputation. If 5th Line people don't provide the necessary Solutions, then the Projected Field turns against them. In the Dream, if you already have a bad reputation, you are really in trouble, and you are really going to feel very, very uncomfortable.

We must experience everything, including what we experience in the Dream Life. It is all right. We have to have a taste of everything. It is about not making it Personal. While teaching Human Design all these years, I have dealt with the seriousness of Human Beings and how, Personally, they take their lives. I am personally involved in my life, but I Don't take it personally. I'm not in control of it. I'm helpless in all of that. Not taking things Personally is an enormous step. It is particularly important in the dream life. In many ways, the Dream State is where you can get Impersonal because it does not have the same quality as the Waking Rave. It is a great, great teaching. When we bring ourselves to the Impersonal Plane and recognize that we need to share what we experience at the Dream Plane with others, it is essential. "You tell me your Dream; I'll tell you mine. You tell me where your Dream comes from, and I'll tell you where mine comes from." This exchange is really what it is about.

Ultimately, we are going to see that that is going to be one of the most – yeah, I just had a flash. It will be one of those ways that people will meet each other in the future. It will be a way of greeting. It will be a way of recognizing that you belong together in the same thing. It will be about sharing your Dream. What you share from your Dream Life is going to be more important to a lot of people than what is shared from the mundane life. The mundane life is Personal, and that's you. "Yeah, I know that your kid is sick. What did your Dream say? Give me that. Let me hear what it is. It doesn't belong to you. You tell me." It's so beautiful. Please recognize that. You see, we need to come together as groups. Those people who do have that kind of recognition of their Dream Themes, their Dream Lives, need to come together so we get to share those things and so we get to find out what is really going on as soon as you see that through this Matrix, through the guide that is there in the Keynotes, you begin to recognize that each Dream expresses a Universal Language that is available to everybody else and is of value to them. You just have to learn how to take it in, that's all.

Line 6: Vision

The 6th Line is Vision. If you have a 6th Line Profile, then your Dream Life, your Sleeping Life, like your Waking Life, is conditioned by Three Phases. The first 28.6 years are filled with the intensity of the Dreaming Life. Then, there is a Plateau when one goes up onto the roof, during which time the Dreaming Life stabilizes. During this time, there may still be a high frequency of Dreaming, but there is not the same instability; dreams seem more familiar, so the Dreamer seems comfortable with the Dream Life. One even seems able to get some authority from it; one can talk about one's dreams and their impact on others or talk about what one has dealt with in one's Dreams and translate it to others.

The 6th Line is Vision. If you have a 6th Line Profile, then your Dream Life, your Sleeping Life, like your Waking Life, is conditioned by Three Phases. The first 28.6 years are filled with the intensity of the Dreaming Life. Then, there is a Plateau when one goes up onto the roof, during which time the Dreaming Life stabilizes. During this time, there may still be a high frequency of Dreaming, but there is not the same instability; dreams seem more familiar, so the Dreamer seems comfortable with the Dream Life. One even seems able to get some Authority from it; one can talk about one's Dreams and their impact on others or talk about what one has dealt with in one's Dream and translate it to others.

The Chiron Return marks the Descent from the Roof and the Re-Entry into the intense Field of the Dreaming World or of the Dreaming Life. The nature Vision in the 6th Line is always a potential for Wisdom, after all. Enormous Potential for Wisdom is possible through the 6th Line Activations in any aspect of the DreamRave.

If there is a way for a Portal/Bridge to get the information across, if there is a way to get the person to Depersonalize it, and to give the capacity to interpret it and read it, then you have very valuable information and valuable material. Dreams only disturb us if we Personalize. They are not going to do anything else. This 6th Line Vision has Real Wisdom available. When I say that, the Wisdom of the Personality and the Wisdom of the Design are relative. *We are the Matrix. It is us. It is us and it is all the other living things all together in combination within the program.*

Conclusion

This step of introducing Dreamwork and the DreamRave gets you away or gets those who are at the core of studying Design away from their own individual process. They can begin to grasp how each and every one of us, how everyone is Connected in the Whole and has a place. The DreamRave is very important because it is a way in which we can find a new community of understanding between each other in an area of life that we have rarely had an opportunity to share or understand in any given way. But this is another phase.

You have to see that this knowledge is the knowledge that is important to somebody entering into Design. It isn't important to somebody who does not know Design. What is important to them is the opportunity to discover their own nature, to discover themselves, and to begin their process. We need to set the Foundation for the future of what this knowledge can bring and what it means. What we are doing here is part of that process, that ultimately, down the road, when the books come out of all of this, somewhere down the road, there is a very large audience who will benefit from our experience together and be able to share this knowledge. It was fun for me to do this. I've waited a long time just to see what would come out. It is very interesting stuff. There is a lifetime of work that is possible out of all of that. I can retire and leave it up to Eleanor.

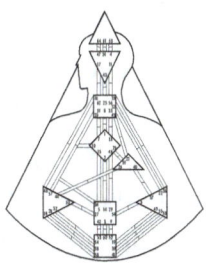

Clinical Applications
Introduction: Overview

Reviewing the physiology and the Stages of Sleep helps put the DreamRave and its information in a context that helps clarify how the program operates within you. A sequence operates throughout the night in accord with the physiology of the body rhythm. These components give a sense of the interplay between the WakingRave and the DreamRaves (Sleeping Raves). Appendix I includes some technical information on the Physiology of Sleep).

The DreamRave is our experience with the program. It is the experience of The Program because we sleep Horizontally instead of Vertically. Thus, we receive the Neutrino Program differently when we are awake than when we are asleep. This configuration makes us unique as a Species. Animals are always programmed Horizontally. We, however, have the uniqueness of being programmed both Vertically and Horizontally.

In addition to receiving our programming both ways, we also tap into other dimensions through the cross-species gates that allow us to experience being both human and mammalian. Our Mammalian experience has no activation, specifically in the human Gates. When we are Vertical in our Waking Consciousness, we have a neocortex. The neocortex allows us to interpret, at the mental level, a capacity that sets us apart from other animals.

Animals exist in the Now; they experience who they are as a Species in touch with the Archetypal Realm. The psychological literature focuses a great deal on interpreting Archetypes. It interprets Archetypes by giving Authority to the Mental level. The DreamRave revolutionizes our understanding and exploration of Archetypes and describes our connection with the totality. The totality gives us the capacity to operate within multiple dimensions as well as the ability to experience ourselves as Humans and mammals.

If we give the Mind Authority, we take capacity away from our true selves because we give power to the Not-Self. This very critical awareness emerges when we tap into the DreamRave as an experience; from the DreamRave experience, we can watch the experiment of what goes on within ourselves without the neocortex operating and without the Vertical programming that conditions us when we are awake.

The Circadian Timing System

The Circadian Timing System depends on the Earth's 24-hour rotation. It is extremely stable within human beings and other animals. On Earth, we all go through Cycles. *Sleep is critical for health*. It is also critical for a sleeping person to go through all of the phases of the Sleep Cycle, especially the Delta Phase, Stage 4 Deep Sleep.

Sleep is a primary drive of nature, like hunger. In the same way, when we go long enough without eating, we need food and can think of nothing else; when we have a sleep debt, we think only of getting sleep. Dement (1999, pp. 56-57) says, "Your sleep drive keeps an exact tally of accumulated waking hours. All wakefulness is sleep deprivation. Generally, people need to sleep one hour for every two hours awake."

Without Sleep, an individual's health suffers. Experiments deprived healthy people in a lab of Sleep by awakening them every time they began to go into Deep Slow-Wave Delta Sleep. After a very short time, healthy, Sleep-deprived people developed all kinds of symptoms. Studies demonstrate that even two nights of poor sleep, i.e., not restful Sleep, results in a deficiency in the immune system, making people more vulnerable to colds, flu, and other illnesses. Sleep plays a critical role in our health.

In light of the way we receive our programming and the unification of the planetary Consciousness, the importance of Sleep becomes even more significant. When we are in the Delta Stage of Sleep, we are being Unified as a Species with everyone else on the planet. In the Sleeping State, within our time zone, there is a Synchronization of the Cycle of the majority of Humans in that zone, so our rest is synchronized with others in our Auric Field. This awareness of how we are programmed may very well explain why people who are on the "graveyard shift" have more difficulty and, over time, when that Cycle is disrupted, have more problems.

Recognize in looking at the Circadian Rhythm that at any given time within a time zone, there are people who are awake and people who are Sleeping. Take a look at when you tend to awaken during your nighttime sleep; some people who have sleep disturbances are suddenly awake at 5:00 in the morning. Other people awaken regularly at 3:00 in the morning.

An interesting experiment for all of you would be to look at where people are on the planet when you feel disturbed at that time of the day. You might get a sense of who you are programmed, by what population you tend to be programmed, and where in your sleep cycle that disturbance occurs. Throughout the Sleep Cycle, different disturbances occur. Some people suddenly come out of the sleep phase disturbed, so their sleep cycle is interrupted.

Understanding the nature of time zones and societies' influence on each other unconsciously is fascinating. Think about what really goes on; for example, North America has a deep impact on the sleeping life of Asia, while the sleeping life of Asia has a deep impact on North American consciousness. Think about what they get in Asia from us here in North America while we live our daily lives. Think about what that Program is for them.

The Primary Influences occur on the Earth Plane. On the other hand, you can see both sides' fascination with each other. Constant programming comes from the other side. So many people in North America want to go East, thinking that that is where their "answer" is. And all these other Asian people awake each morning and say, "I want to go West." It is very important to see that we profoundly impact those on the other side of the globe.

If you get up alert at 2:30 in the morning, ask yourself, "What is on the other side of the Globe that brings this to me?" Read the newspapers, look at television, see what is happening. Looking at things this way offers us incredible opportunities because it shows us the place where we merge into the Whole.

Remote Viewing

Remote viewing is the capacity that some individuals have to go into a deep state, beyond a normal meditative rhythm, where they can view what is happening in a different place on the planet. Remote viewing has been used extensively by the CIA. We all have that capacity. We are all doing that. We just are unaware that we are doing it.

When we begin to have awareness of the "experiment" at another level, then that Form of our Consciousness will be more accessible to us. What we are doing with the material we are looking at with DreamRaves brings it all to a more accessible Consciousness. We are coming into our own as a Species where the integration between the Waking and the Dreaming state becomes One. It becomes one in the same way that our Consciousness and the rest of humanity, the rest of the beings and plants, become One. Everything in the Universe is One. This design experiment is about the opportunity to be aware of many levels.

Sleep is a regular condition of rest for a living thing in which an individual becomes relatively quiescent and unaware of the Environment (Dement, 1999). We receive input from The Demon Realm, which has to do with Environments; it has to do with the Whole Plane of Environments, yet we have yet to learn of it. Realize the impeccable magnificence of our being in a State of Deep Rest, yet we are being Programmed.

Our physiology changes when we Sleep and get to a deep level of rest. We become Mammals in that State. We lose the functioning capacity of the neocortex in the deep Sleep States. In other words, the abilities that set us apart from other Mammals disappear. Adenosine is a chemical related to Wakefulness and Sleep. The brain center, activated or deactivated during our sleep, is part of the pituitary hypothalamic area of the brain. It releases adenosine. In the Human Design Body Graph, these brain areas correspond to the Ajna Center right at the point where it would have its connections to the Throat Center.

The hypothalamus is part of the brain. Below it is the pituitary. The hypothalamus and the pituitary are part of the hypothalamic-pituitary axis. These areas are connected neurologically and chemically via a specialized internal blood circulation system. So you have, for example, in the thyroid system, which seems essential, TRH released from the hypothalamus, which is called the thyrotropic-releasing hormone. TRH goes to the pituitary gland and activates the production of TSH, or thyroid-stimulating hormone, which then goes into the bloodstream and makes the thyroid gland produce thyroid hormone.

The neocortex is uniquely Human. Subcortical structures lead down into the spinal cord. Note that all Mammals breathe and digest without being Conscious of breathing and digesting food. Those aspects of ongoing functions operate at the lower centers of the hindbrain or primitive brain, which is common to all Mammals. This area controls our hearts as well. Higher levels of the brain turn off when we sleep, and our lower brain centers continue to function so we stay alive.

When the higher brain centers turn off during rest and Sleep, the Mental Authority (the Ajna Center and Head Center) that we are programmed to give Authority over the body also turns off. The Anxiety coming from the Mental Plane, the interpretation of Personal Events, all of those things that affect respiration and blood pressure diminish.

Regarding Design, the Ajna Center directly relates to the pituitary glands. Planets affect both the anterior and posterior pituitary through the rulership of Saturn and Jupiter. Traditionally, in astrology, the pituitary rules the inside and the outside of the Mind. One fascinating thing is the Personal Identification we feel with the body, both on the inside, "I have a pain, I have a hurt," or on the outside, "I'm in connection to the World around me." All of those Awarenesses disappear during Sleep. In other words, we become liberated into the larger Whole because we lose the identification with our own Form in that moment. The pituitary controls our orientation.

The 17th Gate connecting to the 62nd Gate is the only Gate that connects us to the neocortex in the DreamRave Matrix. It deactivates during Deep Sleep. It also connects to The Light Field. The actual Mutation of the neocortex takes place in the 11th Gate. However, the ability of the neocortex to function to our benefit goes entirely through Channel 17/62. When we awaken in the morning, all of the past stories we have told ourselves about the meaning of Dreams and the interpretation of Dreams come out of Channel 11/56. We explain our State of Sleep and Dreaming in that zone between Waking and Sleeping. The different Realms may be related to the Dream State and the different Phases and Cycles of where we are in the Sleeping or DreamRave State.

The in-depth case, using DH (page 129) as an example, is very interesting because all Three Realms, which demonstrate different levels of activity and integration, are present. When you look at your DreamRave, the *Cycles of Sleep also relate to and reflect the different Realms.*

Scientific research may show that a person's Sleep patterns compared to their DreamRave Patterns and the Gates activated in the Lunar DreamRave along with the Solar DreamRave show some kind of Pattern regarding what is activated and not activated. So we have an interesting play.

Sleep Architecture

The Sleep Cycles are called "Sleep Architecture." We Cycle through different distinct Stages of Sleep. Sleep Cycles are desynchronized or synchronized. In the Dreaming Cycles, the rhythm of the respiration changes, becoming a little bit more active, whereas in the slow, synchronized sleep, which is the more restful sleep, the rhythm of respiration remains slow and regular. The Sleep Architecture is a little bit complex. See William Dement's book The Promise of Sleep (1999) for a full description of Sleep and its Stages and physiology.

Sleep: Preliminary Calm Wakefulness
The Preliminary Stage of Sleep begins when you lie down and become relaxed; it is somewhat Meditative. This Phase of Sleep describes the Solar DreamRave. We lie down Horizontally. We enter a relaxed state, an Alpha State. We slow down. We are not quite in our Conscious Waking Human Design Rave with all the activity going on, but we are not in that restful, Deep Sleep where we are being programmed by the other Forces. We are open to them but still aware of the Environment.

Sleep: Stage 1
Stage 1 is Light Sleep. Note that Stage 1 makes up a higher percentage of nighttime Sleep than any other Stage of Sleep. We begin to go down deeper; we begin to get more into a Theta Rhythm of Brain Wave activity. As the Theta Waves of Stage 1 Sleep emerge,

a sensory curtain drops and isolates the mind from the outside World. We begin entering the DreamRave Realm.

Each State of Consciousness has its distinctive kind of Brain Wave activity. Alpha has a Slow Regular Wave; it denotes Calm Relaxation. The fastest-moving wave is the Beta. Beta is the smallest and fastest; it denotes Wakefulness. Waves that are taller and wider occur in the most profound aspects of Deep Sleep. Think of them as an electrical activity that hums.

Sleep: Stage 2

The Stage 2 Sleep Pattern shows Spindle-Shaped tracings on the EEG, which are called "Sleep Spindles." The K Complexes also appear. They are the high-voltage Complexes that come in before the appearance of Delta Waves, which start in Stage 3 Sleep. Stage 2 Brain Waves are small, uneven, and of varying Shapes. Stage 2 Sleep significantly changes how sensory information is processed in the brain.

Sleep: Stage 3

Stage 3 Sleep begins the first Stage of Slow-Wave Sleep. Brain Wave activity slows dramatically, respiration begins to decrease, and the body goes into a much more relaxed state. This stage marks the appearance of delta waves with the continued functioning of the sleep Spines and K complex waves, although these become more difficult to observe.

Sleep: Stage 4

Stage 4 Sleep describes the Deepest Level of Delta Sleep. Sleep Spindles, K-complexes, and Theta Waves become impossible to detect. During this Stage, it is difficult to awaken someone, and the muscles are almost completely relaxed. Consciousness seems absent. Deep Rest occurs. In this Stage, the Lunar DreamRave is fully functional, during which we are most deeply Programmed.

Sleep: Rapid Eye Movement (REM)

After Stage 4 Sleep, Stage 3 Sleep returns accompanied after about 10 minutes by Theta Waves, Sleep Spindles, K-Complexes, and bursts of Alpha and Beta Waves. The eyes move rapidly back and forth, showing the active Dreaming Process. During this stage, a true integration of the various Rave Designs and Communication of Information and its Programming occurs. We remember Dreams from this Stage as we emerge back into Consciousness.

Fibromyalgia

Fibromyalgia is an excellent clinical example of what occurs in Sleep Disturbances. It describes an autoimmune-mediated disorder in which patients have 11 out of 18 "tender points" in their bodies and a Sleep Disturbance.

So far, the statistical data we have collected and looked at proves what we are discussing in terms of Sleep. The in-depth case of DH (page 129) shows a person who has Fibromyalgia. By looking at her case, we can begin to understand the Whole dynamic of interaction between the different Rave Designs. We can also see why DH would have a Sleep Disturbance. The case combines Sleep Physiology, DreamRave, and statistical evidence from a group of Fibromyalgia patients we have used as an experimental group.

Intrusion of the Alpha Waves of Preliminary Stage Sleep into Delta Waves of Stage 4 Sleep occurs in Fibromyalgia patients. Thus, Fibromyalgia patients rarely feel rested, and they hurt. They also show sensitivity on the body in at least 11 out of 18 "tender points" corresponding to different acupuncture meridians. A Rheumatologist often diagnoses Fibromyalgia because the disease has much in common with arthritis symptoms. Joints hurt. Sometimes, Fibromyalgia patients jump when touched because their body hurts so badly all over. They never get deep rest. Groups of healthy subjects deprived of Sleep, i.e., when they went into

Delta sleep, they were awakened and, within a few days, developed symptoms of Fibromyalgia.

A profile of Fibromyalgia patients emerges from our statistical analysis. Fibromyalgia patients seem to have a predominance of Channel 5/15 in their Lunar DreamRave and a significantly higher frequency of the 38th Gate. We hypothesize that Fibromyalgia describes in part a cellular disturbance, a disease that is related to the channel that puts you in the Flow and keeps you in the Rhythm. As well as being in The Earth Plane, Channel 15/5 is also a channel related to the Mutative process of Humanity. Many new diseases we see are part of humanity's preparation for the Mutation.

One of the primary causes of Fibromyalgia is the inability of the Waking Personality to adapt to the stresses in their life. What happens to Fibromyalgia patients who carry Earth Plane activation, e.g., the Channel 15/5, is that the entrance into deep-stage sleep rouses them, so they want to get out of that level of Information Programming. Giving up a personal identity that has been a struggle at a deep level creates even more turmoil and struggle for these people.

When we look at Fibromyalgia patient data, we will find all Three Realms more frequently in Fibromyalgia patients than in other groups because of their conflict in the Integration of the Different Realms with the Waking state.

Fibromyalgia patients are very much in touch with the Archetypal elements even in their Waking state. This connection may be very deeply disturbing to them, especially when they Sleep and, thus, they have no way to Integrate the information.

Adenosine

The brain chemical Adenosine prepares the body physiologically by having receptors scattered throughout the body and the brain. Some researchers have found that only certain cell groups are essential for sleep. What is striking in the latest brain-body research is the knowledge that receptors for many endorphins and other chemicals occur in all body cells. The interplay between mind and body is united.

Mind/Body Connections

We don't just have a neocortex that functions or doesn't function; what goes into a program when we are a Waking Being gets into every cell of our body. As a Sleeping Entity, we also interface with the Waking Rave. We do that in two ways: Intracellularly because of who we are as Waking, Conscious being having been programmed Vertically, and the way the Sleep Cycle goes. We go into that deep layer of the Mammalian program and then surface up in Stages called "Emergence." We go through the stages of sleep, and after a certain amount of time in Stage 4 Delta sleep, we surface back up and go back down with REM dreaming, which occurs even during the different phases. Some Dreams occur at a very deep level, and some Dreams occur between the different levels. I would guess that we will find that there are more frequencies of the different Stages with different activations in the different Realms.

Some people may be more prone to having one kind of Sleep than another, or they may Dream more in some phases of their Sleep Cycle than others. That looks way down into the future because it is hard enough to begin to get the data on groups of people, and the Gates activated between the DreamRave Lunar and the DreamRave Solar. It is even more complicated to go into a laboratory and measure the EEGs to see which cycle we are dealing with. Eventually, we will have monitors that can be used on people when they sleep at home, and then, we will be able to get the data.

Psychoneuroendocrine Immunology

There is a field in healthcare called Psychoneuroendocrine immunology that is new to me as a healthcare professional. That is to say, there is, in fact, a department at UCLA with that name. The psyche or psychology or the emotional state, as we have thought about it, is, in fact, known to be connected to the neurological system, the brain, the spinal cord, and the endocrine system. We have already discussed how the brain connects through the hypothalamus and the pituitary, the master endocrine gland, and the immune health. Psychoneuroendocrine Immunology connects it all. Another way to look at it is to see the circulating immune cells as circulating Neurotransmitters. Ra mentioned yesterday that the primary cells that circulate frequently are the Lymphocytes. In a broader sense, the blood and lymph gland-related immune cells include cells of that line. There are also bone marrow sources. These cells provide us with protection and are carriers of substances called Cytokines, "kine" meaning to move, "cyto" meaning cell, and these can also be thought of as Neurotransmitters.

Now, one other brief point. People who have allergies very often have many Cytokines released locally in tissues. These people very often have central nervous system and psychological effects; they feel fatigued, have decreased learning capacity, and have mood disorders. They have systemic allergies, not just a localized nasal problem.

The Role of the Solar Plexus Center

The diseases related to these Neurotransmitters are Splenically mediated, not Solar Plexus mediated. We have yet to develop any diseases originating in the Biological Body Graph in the Solar Plexus Center; they all start somewhere else and are secondarily programmed into the Solar Plexus Center. Think about that in terms of being Mammals; it makes it an even more vital point that we can give the Solar Plexus Center Authority if it is in our Design in terms of Waiting out the Wave, but what we are doing in that is allowing ourselves to Sleep on the energy and to be reprogrammed.

The sleep cycle itself changes energy for us on a physiological level. It doesn't change physiologically in the Solar Plexus Center itself; it changes physiologically through the DreamRave Design in the other areas of our physiology. Then, we experience it secondarily in the Solar Plexus Center.

All of this information really shows the newness of the Solar Plexus System. After all, it is the Third Awareness Center. In terms of its capacity to be in Awareness, it is not even capable of Awareness yet. So, as soon we enter into the Mammalian matrix, you see that the Solar Plexus Center has no place there. It is like looking for the Heart Center. One of the most essential things to disappear during Sleep is your Ego. It is one of the most important things. It just simply disappears. The ego per se of the mammal is integrated into what we call the G Center, and mammals become something else. The reality is that the individual you meet, Ego and willpower, is something we relinquish during the Sleep State. Sleep turns off the Mental System. We eliminate the Turmoil of the naive Motor Awareness of our Solar Plexus System, and we eliminate the Willfulness and the Possessiveness of "This is me. This is mine." People are profoundly caught up in their human lives with all of these problems. They can end up profoundly resenting that they cannot retreat into Sleep because they keep meeting the same things.

When people who have problems in their lives and carry a lot of Earth Plane activation go into the Dreaming state, they suddenly get the whole Earth Plane thrown at them. It makes them jump out of that State of Consciousness because they cannot deal with it.

One of the most potent tools for fibromyalgia patients is Hypnosis, Self-Hypnosis. Hypnosis occurs in a different but related State of Consciousness than Sleep. Essentially, Hypnosis gives a relaxed kind of rhythm in the brain. It allows a suggestion from the neocortex through the Waking Rave. Usually, hypnosis is done by either reclining or lying down. It allows the person to be programmed through their Mental Plane into the DreamRave plane and helps a lot to deepen their Sleep and to give them the suggestion not to be disturbed.

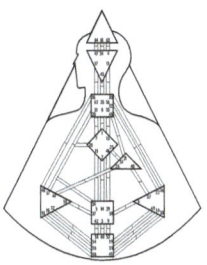

Transits to the DreamRave

Having been trained as a psychological analyst, I studied Freud and Jung extensively. Jung divided Dreams into four basic types: anticipatory, compensatory, complimentary, and narrative. The mistake that both Freud and Jung made in their Dream Interpretation was Personalizing the Dream and bringing in the Ego and Mental Explanation. However, we will find something very important if we take the structure of what they described. I was struck with this idea because I have been following my Dream Transits for several months, looking at them. When I first started following the Transits, I noticed that the Dream Transits explained the Structure and Content of Dreaming. It began to validate the Jungian Structure of Dreams. There were, depending on the Gates activated, times that I would understand why the kind of images I had in the night appeared based on the Gates activations. The Transits explained the Structure. Just take those four types of Dream breakdowns: compensatory, complimentary, narrative, and anticipatory, and think about them in terms of what we pick up on The Earth Plane and what we are programmed by from another time zone.

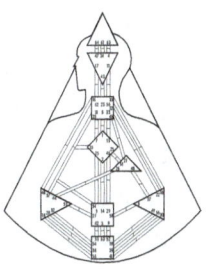

Archetypes in the DreamRave

The thing that is so interesting about the Jungian view of all of that is that we all come in on a Cross. We all come in with an Incarnation, and because that Incarnation is broken up, that is, the Cross is broken up into a million different subdivisions, we have about 700 plus Archetypes.

When you go into your DreamRave, not taking it personally doesn't mean there is no differentiation as to what you experience because there are different Designs for different Sleeping States. One of the things described in the DreamRave Keynotes is the vision of people sharing their Dreams, not from a Personal point of view but from what they are.

By recognizing that pattern, you get information about your particular archetype. That Archetypal Information then needs to be shared because it is a unique perspective in the Fractal of the Whole in that sense. As soon as you depersonalize it, you see it differently. Rather than this being who you are in the Maya, that "I" that you live in your Waking Life, you know that it is what your Archetypal role is within the Whole. That role is shared. You can share that Archetype and bring that Archetype out. You can explain or express that Archetype to others.

In that way, Jung was brilliant. He really grasped that Dreams were, in a sense, depersonalized. Dreams are Humans grasping onto deep mythological Archetypes that imbue all of us. What Jung should have seen was that we are the Archetypes. *Each one of us is an aspect of an Archetype.* Through the Dream, that aspect can emerge. All of the Archetypes need to be seen. We all have a chance to live our mythology. We all have a chance to recognize our mythological contribution to this life. The DreamRave is the closest we ever get to seeing how that functions. In that sense, Jung was correct.

The other side of that is Freud. He was not wrong; he just Personalized. Everybody speaks out of their Design. Here was Freud with a powerful Gate 50. "There's sex everywhere," he said. "It's everywhere, every time I go to sleep." He wasn't wrong, but he Personalized it.

When looking at the DreamRave and the Transits, it is very important to realize that what you are as you Sleep is the Archetype itself, and the Cosmos programmed it so that we have access to it. The Cross-Species Gates allows us to understand that and be more than just the Archetype itself. We also have a perspective on the Archetype. What makes us Human is the ability for Self-Reflection, self-consciousness, and Awareness. We can look at all these aspects and, through understanding and awareness, take them a step further and integrate them with the Waking Rave, which operates even while we Sleep.

As we emerge from Delta Sleep back up to Preliminary Stage Sleep, our WakingRave becomes fully activated. It gives us the capacity to understand what happened; the brilliance of that program is just awesome. We not only become the archetype itself, but we then move from that in a rhythm, just like the heartbeat, to understand and have a perspective on that World.

Let's further put things in perspective. There are 276,000

Individual Crosses in the Wheel. Think about that. There are 276,000 Individual Crosses in the Wheel. There are 6 billion of us on the planet. That means that for each of those Crosses, there are about 10, 12 variations, and 20 variations. There has never been knowledge that can take things down to this level. At this level, everyone lives out a unique Archetype. There are backups, so a couple of dozen people carry each of the energies of the Wheel. When you think about that Structure, you begin to understand your Contribution to the Whole. If 23 of the people die, we need you; otherwise, we have a deep genetic problem.

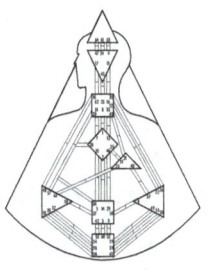

The Senoi

I want to mention the Senoi, a group from the South Pacific. They are very interested in dreams. The Senoi have been studied extensively in psychological anthropology because the Senoi believe that the Dream State is as valid as the Waking State and as accurate. When they awake in the morning, they tell their Dreams like they are another reality. Then, they rewrite the Dreams and use the rewritten version of the Dream when they go to Sleep at night to reprogram themselves and the deeper layers. This technique has merit regarding what we are now looking at in Dreams.

The DreamRave Lunar and the DreamRave Solar, taken in conjunction with the Waking Rave, show the Interconnectedness of all people. Someone has a Dream; they rewrite it and reprogram it through the neocortex. They are reprogramming the people they got it from who are now Sleeping. When they return to Sleep, what comes into them is now filtered differently. So, the Senoi have been using Dreams in an Impersonal way. They don't take Dreams as Personal; they never have. It is, just for them, part of the Program that they can then reshuffle and input differently with their humanity, and they have the Dream replay itself differently.

When I worked analytically, I used the Senoi technique with patients because often, what they interpreted very Personally seemed to make them worse rather than better. I always like to take a much more positive approach and allow people to use their Minds to reprogram what they interpret. I always worked from that standpoint. For example, somebody would write their Dream down; let's say it was a violent Dream; they would rewrite that Dream as not violent. It would transform before it became violent. When we were talking yesterday, the Senoi came to mind. It's very interesting. I studied them maybe 30 years ago. So, anyhow, that is a little aside, which I'm just mentioning as a technique. How we would then use it, with Consciousness, is limitless.

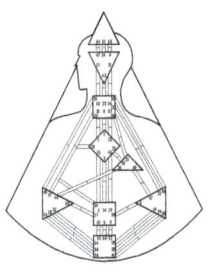

Reversals in the DreamRave Designs

Remember that in the DreamRave, there is a Reversal. The Design (Unconscious) functions like the Personality (Conscious) in the DreamRave. The Design (Unconscious) operates as the Personality (Conscious) would, so it is the Terrain. And the Personality (Conscious) in the DreamRave operates as the Tunnel (Unconscious).

This way of looking at things goes back to an ancient tradition in which the Dream World represents a World of Form that was seen to function in the opposite but parallel to the Waking World. In that world, what you hear on the surface, for example, is seen. It shows a rule of Polarity. In the DreamRave, the Design is Dominant, whereas the Personality becomes something that is Deep Beneath the Surface. The Roles have Reversed.

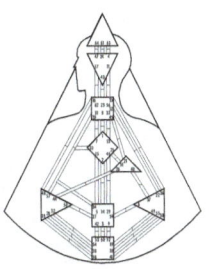

Case Studies

Case Study: DH

DH's Human Design and DreamRave Charts are shown on the following pages. Notice that she has a 2/4 Profile. I am not going to go into any depth about her Design. I want you to see it. DH is completing her Ph.D. (completed in June 2000) in Mind/Body research with a specialty in Fibromyalgia. She became ill when she was 16. She developed a sinus infection, which lingered on and on and on. For several years, she would get terrible sinus infections every winter, for which she needed antibiotics to resolve. Along with that, she developed a Sleep Disturbance and Fibromyalgia. She has been diligent: She limits her diet; she cut out most carbohydrates. To this day, she does not eat many carbohydrates; she does not eat bread; she does not eat pasta; she does not eat potatoes. She is very strict and very disciplined. By nature, she would have what you think would be a healthy Design. So the question is, what is really going on? I didn't consider using her DreamRave as an example until I reviewed the Sleep Stages with her since she has done extensive research on Sleep Stages. She said to me, "Well, I'm a perfect example. Why don't you use my case?" So, we have her permission to go in-depth. Her DreamRaves Solar and Lunar appear on the following page.

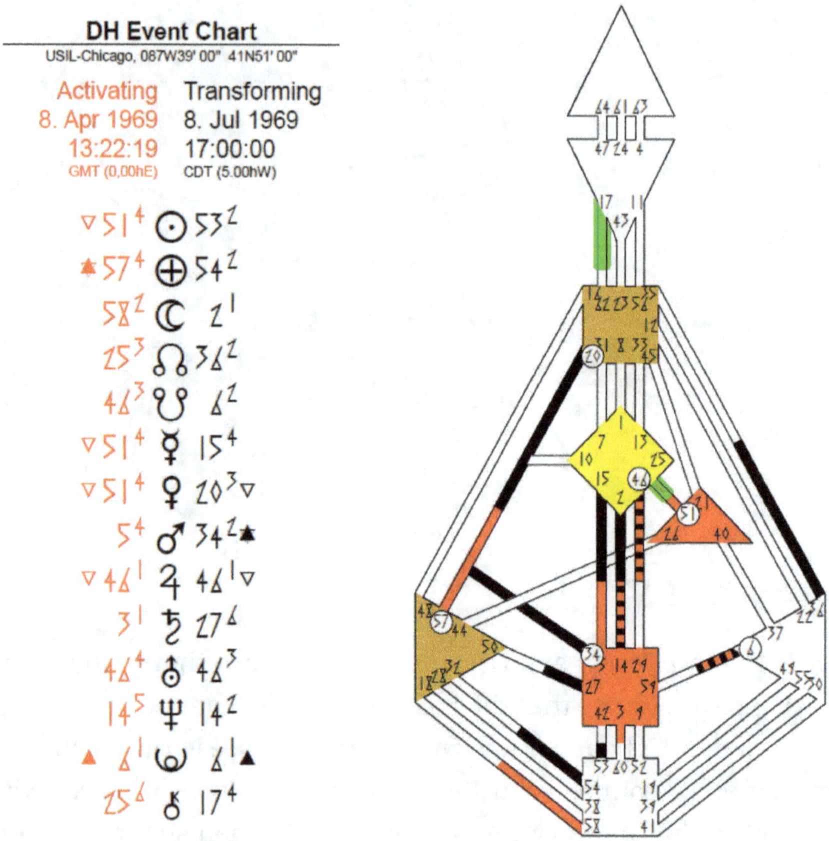

THE TRIPLE DESIGN MATRIX

Figure 1.4: DH's Human Design Chart

THE DREAMRAVE DESIGN SYSTEM

Solar Sleep Design

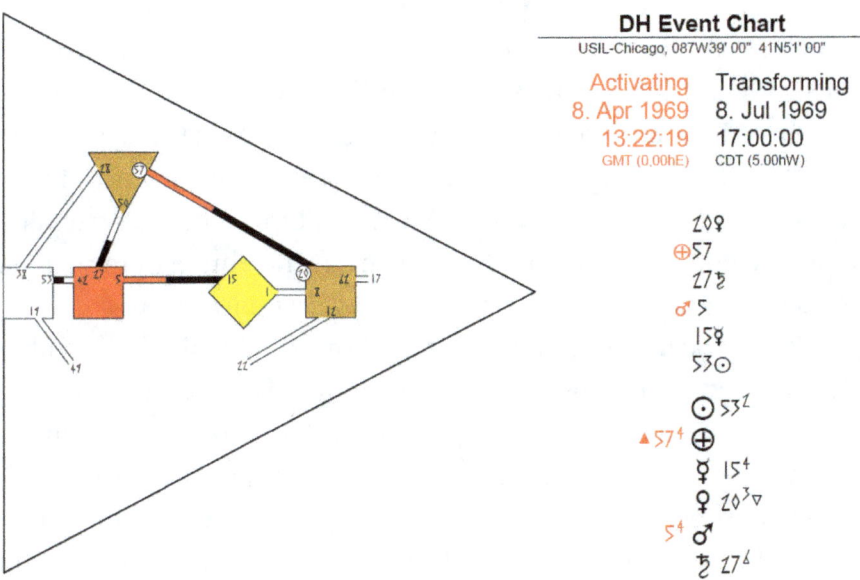

Lunar Sleep Design

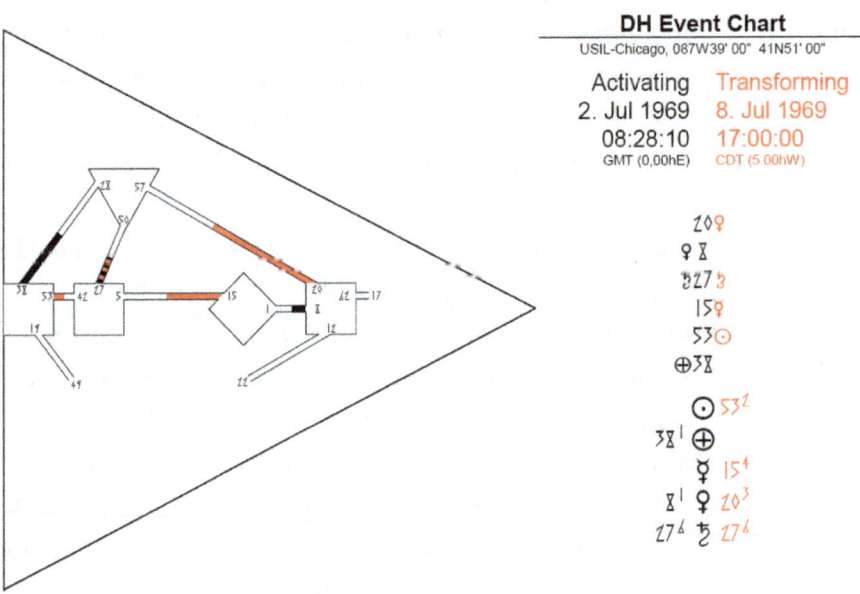

Figure 1.5: DH's Solar and Lunar Dream Design Charts

One of the exciting things that I presented in the last seminar is the difference between people when they are Defined in their Solar DreamRave and Undefined in the Lunar DreamRave and vice versa. We sometimes see the difference. Notice that DH has all Three Realms. She has The Light Field: the 20th Gate, 3rd Line, and the 8th Gate, 1st Line, both in Venus. She has The Earth Plane in Gate 15, Line 4, and Saturn in Gate 27, Line 6, both Personality and Design. In The Demon Realm, she has the Sun in Gate 53, Line 2, and the Earth in Gate 38, Line 1. It is very interesting.

Fibromyalgia, to reiterate, is a disease in which the body's Immune System is overactive; it is an autoimmune disease. The body protects itself beyond what it needs for its protection. One of the primary symptoms that DH had, which made a massive difference in her process, was that when she would start to go into Deep, Restful Sleep, she would have Alpha Interruption. Beyond that, she told me she would come up to the Alpha while sleeping. In that interruption, she would begin to interpret her Dreams in her Sleep so she would enter into something of her Waking State. Using the DreamRave language and giving it to you in that dimension, look at her Lunar and her Solar DreamRave. The Light Field would become more predominant during this Alpha Interruption. It would explain to her the meaning of what was going on even while she slept.

You can also see that how DH has activation on the Earth, in Channel 15/5, is very important. Look at Gate 15 and at the Keynote Chaos of that Gate. Remember that what chaos does is eliminate all the boundaries; it eliminates all the borders. In other words, what could appear to be an organization becomes very confusing because all the different layers get piled up onto each other. The other connection is in the way Gate 15 operates through the Channel. Going to Gate 27, also in The Earth Plane, takes in the Waking Side as We Dream. Pressure on that Gate occurs the moment that there is this sense that there is no proper order. All these layers of order make it impossible to see anything but Chaos, and then comes the deep need to Care. DH has caring as a 6th Line theme starting in the Waking Rave.

Caring is essential for a person with a 6th Line theme. It means that there is a deep need to find something to care about surfaces in the early part of life, in the first Saturn part of life. Imagine what it is like to suddenly enter into this Chaos and feel this drive deep within you. You have to care about it, which can pull you right up out of your Sleep with a need to come up with some Solution.

One of the things we found in Rave Life Sciences research is a predominance in Fibromyalgia patients of Channel 5/15, which you notice in the Solar DreamRave. DH has this channel, but in the Lunar DreamRave, she only has Gate 15, the Gate of Chaos. Without Gate 5, she doesn't have the Pattern, and because this Gate is in The Earth Plane, she also experiences the Chaos of the Collective. She also goes from Gate 15 to Gate 27, Line 6.

We hypothesize that Fibromyalgia is a Transpersonal disease. DH is someone who really needed to be Called Out. She is a 2/4 Profile. Look at the Lines in the DreamRave. It is fascinating.

The Demon Realm

I was going to take you first to The Demon Realm which is her Sun/Earth. The Sun/Earth in the Demon Realm are Design, meaning they are predominant for her. Here, she gets the program: 38 is Aggression, and she has Line 1. Both Personality and Design in The Demon Realm are 1st Lines, the Insecurity, the Introspection, and the need to bring what that is presenting as part of her own process. Then she is Called Out to The Earth Plane in a transpersonal way to translate through mutation what this disease is about. That is her Life Work. She has done a ground-breaking Ph.D. study on Fibromyalgia, which will revolutionize that field.

Gate 53: Flight

DH's Sun is in Gate 53, the Gate of Flight. Remember, this Gate is about racing into Forms. It is about the Potential of Transforming in the Form, of seeing the Form in different ways. It is about driving us to find the Form. You can see the ambition in that: to find the right form in order to comprehend, heal, or deal with it.

Yet, out of that, notice that with Gate 53, there is also the faulty Form. So it is out of the faulty Form that the integrity of the Form is driven. That is very important in terms of Gate 53, which is a Format. Gate 53 begins the Cycle going up to Channel 15/5 in the DreamRave. In DH, it is under the surface. Remember, Gate 15 in both her DreamRaves is a 4th Line, which is also important.

There is a magnificence in the connections between DH's Solar DreamRave and the Lunar DreamRave, as well as the integrity of the fit between the Line Profiles and the Realms in which they operate. When I was working with DH's Design in some detail, I was "blown away" by the integrity of the interface between the Solar DreamRave and the integration of that with who she is. In her Solar DreamRave, she has Gate 51: Shock. She has that whole channel, the 25/51, in her Waking Rave.

Gate 38: Aggression

To get back to The Demon Realm, let's go more into the 38th Gate, which is about Food. It is about protecting oneself and one's survival. Fibromyalgia is a disease in which there are many Food sensitivities and intolerances, so there is an inability to find a way to feed oneself, survive properly, and adequately protect oneself. Out of that Fear that it won't occur, there is a fault. You can see that DH in her DreamRave is a perfect candidate to carry the integrity of the Mutation for understanding and healing that disease because she has activations in The Light Field of the 20th Gate and of the 8th Gate.

The 8th Gate and the 38th Gate are significant because, as you can see, they are not there in the Solar DreamRave. They are only there in the Lunar DreamRave. That means that their presence is very significant. What we are particularly looking at, with her condition and her Struggle with Form, is the 8th Gate. The 8th Gate is the only Gate in The Light Field that says, "Sorry, but you have to be able to go through this Form. You have to deal with the body. You had better have your faith and hope, but you must deal with the body." So it is interesting. Also, note that this Gate is the Contribution, and the Gate is in Being in the Alpha. So many people afflicted by these conditions are great researchers in those areas.

Given her design, extraordinary intellectual potential, and totally open mind, she had to enter the Darkness (Gate 8). She launched herself into that Struggle. Interestingly, her Light Field brought this Struggle to her. It said, "Look, you must deal with the body. You are going to have to go through that."

Again, the 8th Gate is not one she has in her regular Human Design Rave, although she has Gate 38. We have found Gate 38 in many Fibromyalgia patients. But the 8th Gate is a different story. Along with Gate 38, Gate 8 is very critical. At her worst, DH has said, "I'm never going to come out of this." She has, at times, completely gone into the Darkness (Gate 8) and has been very upset with having to deal with this illness in her life because it is overwhelming. Yet, the brilliance of what she has done is very apparent, and in fact, she has been driven to do it.

DH attended the Rhode Island School of Design and received a degree in fashion design. She wanted no part of psychology or school. She disliked school. After doing fashion design for about six weeks, she said she didn't see the purpose in doing that. It had no spirituality. With some encouragement to follow her core response, she quit her job with a top designer and spent about a year catering because all she wanted to do was bake. She was driven, although she did not know why. She was driven about involving herself with Food (Gate 38). Gate 38 is about Feeding. She was cooking the things she could not eat. She was Feeding those Foods to other people.

Then DH decided to return to school to get her Ph.D. in mind/body connections in fibromyalgia. It came about in the same way she decided to do fashion design. One day, it came, "That's what I'm doing." And she has been absolutely focused on doing that.

Although we have probably seen close to a thousand patients with Fibromyalgia, maybe more, maybe less, DH is the one who is the most functional. I wouldn't say that she has cured her Fibromyalgia, but she has done amazingly well, and she still does the same exercises that are right for her because she is a true soldier in terms of how she performs. She stays on her diet, and she does all kinds of things in a persistent, Obsessive (Line 4) way, which is, in fact, what we would expect from her Design.

In her Lunar DreamRave, Gate 53 mirrors Gate 23, so there is a conflict in her. The way she has all Three Realms creates the conflict we discussed yesterday. There is a vying between The Light Field and The Demon Realm for control. The Light Field wants to explain why somebody goes through all this, and The Demon Realm says, "This just is, and this is the nature of things." DH does experience that conflict herself. But because she has the 8th and 20th Gate, she comes up with an Explanation and ultimately finds an Explanation and a purpose for what it is all about. Through that explanation and purpose, she can bring meaning to her patients' self-hypnosis sessions. Her patients receive her input and are impacted when they do their Self-Hypnosis sessions with the energies and understanding that they need to get through their illness at the Archetypal level.

One of the ways DH does the Hypnosis is by talking about all of the cells of the body being filled with Light, which comes out of her Light Field Awareness. She takes the Light Field Information and brings it down through the other layers. I believe that we will find that many Fibromyalgia patients do not have The Light Field Gates but are much more focused on The Earth Plane, which is why they come up out of The Demon Realm when they Sleep and get disturbed.

The 20th Gate is a Gate where you Awaken Suddenly, which was DH's pattern in her Dreams. I mentioned, in terms of her use of Hypnosis, that a significant turning point for DH was when she learned not to give Authority to that sudden waking; she stopped allowing it to take over by bringing her out into the interpretation, the meaning, the Explanation, and to stay in the Dream Realm where she could get Deep Rest. The key in Fibromyalgia, the critical factor, is that these people are in a hyper-aroused state, so they never fully rest. Deep rest is vital for the healing process and health for all of us.

The Integration

Gate 27, Line 6, is DH's Saturn. Saturn is the Teacher. It is also the Authority. It is also the Taskmaster. It is through her caring and transpersonal connection with her being a 2/4 profile that she brings together the realms. She makes sense of the Chaos through her understanding and the Mutation of her understanding. Her Waking Rave facilitates her gifts. You have to look at DH in the context of who she is first as a human being, with her purpose, her activation, and the strength of her regular design. Then, take that information into the Dream Realm. If she had a different Design in her Waking Rave state, the probability is that she would do other work. *It is essential always to bring the Designs into an integration.*

Whatever we talk about in terms of Human Design and DreamRaves, please understand the program's mechanism. The fact of the matter is that Gate 15, sitting there in an Undefined G Center, has no activation, no activation whatsoever, until something activates that G Center. The reality is that the program dictates that activation, particularly in that stage.

Case Study: Reflector

There are two other cases I just want to touch on briefly. Because we mentioned the Reflector, look at the Reflector (pages 140–141). This is the case of a very successful entrepreneurial businessman who is a Reflector. He has all three harmonics to the Cross-Species or Portal/Bridging Gates in his Waking Rave Design, all three. He has many activations, yet he is a Reflector. When he Sleeps, he has Channel 15/5 and nothing else. His Design is very, very interesting. It is interesting because when I looked at this initially, I had a hit and an understanding of the person, and there was no way I could have gotten it without looking at his DreamRave. I confirmed that when he awakens in the morning, he has a sense of Direction, a sense of himself that he would not otherwise have and does not have.

I know he wakes up at about 5:00 am every morning. At that hour, he goes and cooks for his animals and feeds them. He shows an example of *the importance of integrating the Waking Rave with the DreamRave.* This man has a very deep understanding and deep communication skills in business with major companies worldwide. The fact that he has the three Cross-Species Portal Gates tells me something very critical about how information integrates between the Lunar DreamRave and his Human Design as a Reflector with those Harmonics (Gates 17, 22, 49) to the Portal Gates (Gates 19, 62,12) constantly interacting.

We have someone who is very connected to all Species. He has a very Integrated Consciousness in terms of what he picks up. And then what he picks up when he sleeps is the boundlessness in a rhythm, pattern, and flow and the energy of the life form itself. It is a very Archetypal Design of a Human excitingly.

In the Waking Life, the Reflector is closest to the potential of the being without Personality. They are nothing but filters. And so they represent at the Biological level the possibility of recognizing the Whole in the Waking state. We know that also means Reflectors can be deeply confused by the conditioning/nurturing process they meet in terms of the Designs that are part of their life.

> The terms conditioning and programming have complex implications in the social science field. Instead of thinking of Reflectors as being conditioned or programmed, terms used in traditional Human Design, I like to think that Reflectors are open to all possibilities, and their challenge is the discernment of what aligns with them. The importance of integrating the Matrices indicates that no one design chart shows the whole of how someone functions.

Yet, because of the kind of Design this Reflector has in his DreamRave, he would be less vulnerable than someone else who did not have that Design. One of the fundamental differences that Dream Life gives him is the sense of Identity, which is only of value in the Waking life. Remember, there is no Personal meaning in the Dream. A fixed Identity in the Dream state adds a sense of the Rhythm of things, the Rhythm of all things. Quite an experience is possible when this Reflector steps back into the Waking state. There is a sense of Identity as a Whole that would not necessarily exist in somebody with an Undefined G Center in all Designs.

In other words, something is happening in the Dream State that gives him a Security of Direction that he would not ordinarily have in the Waking State because G Centers that are Undefined do not provide that Security. This Design is interesting, which is great because it is one of the things about understanding that Human Design teaches us that two-thirds of what we are entering into is a Whole new Realm.

In entering this Realm, we are dealing with this other aspect of life, a third of life that is important to how we Integrate as a Whole. The fact that there are fundamental differences in how that operates, like in this case, points toward both the complexity and the impact this understanding can have.

THE TRIPLE DESIGN MATRIX

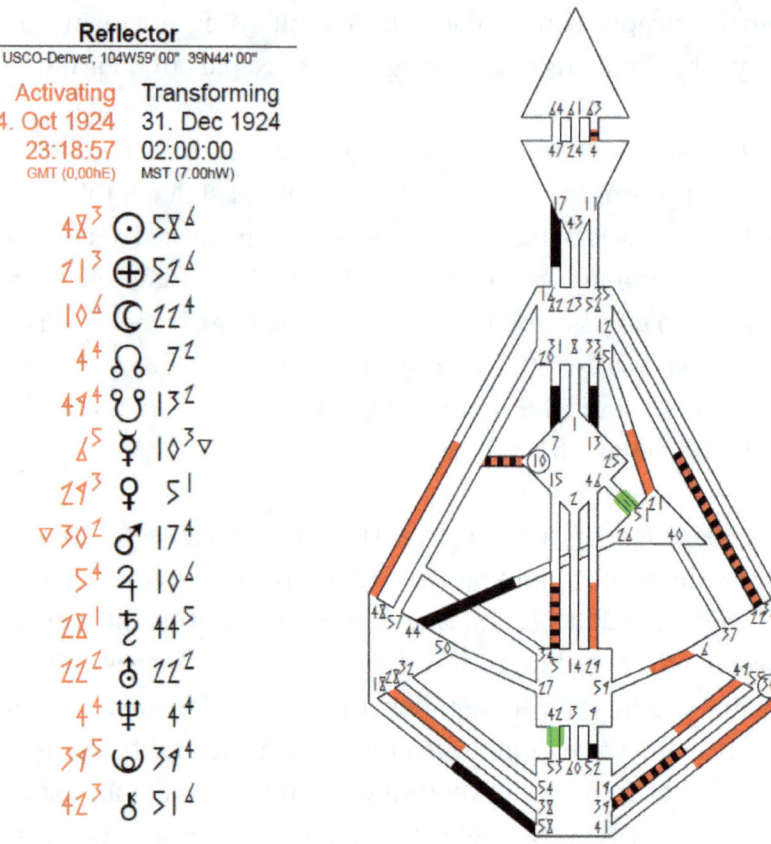

Figure 1.6: Example Reflector Human Design Chart

Solar Sleep Design

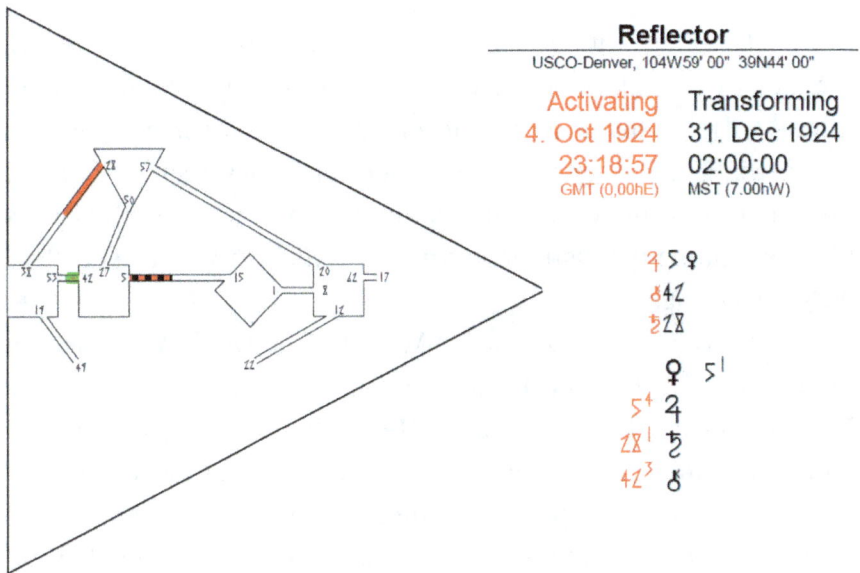

Lunar Sleep Design

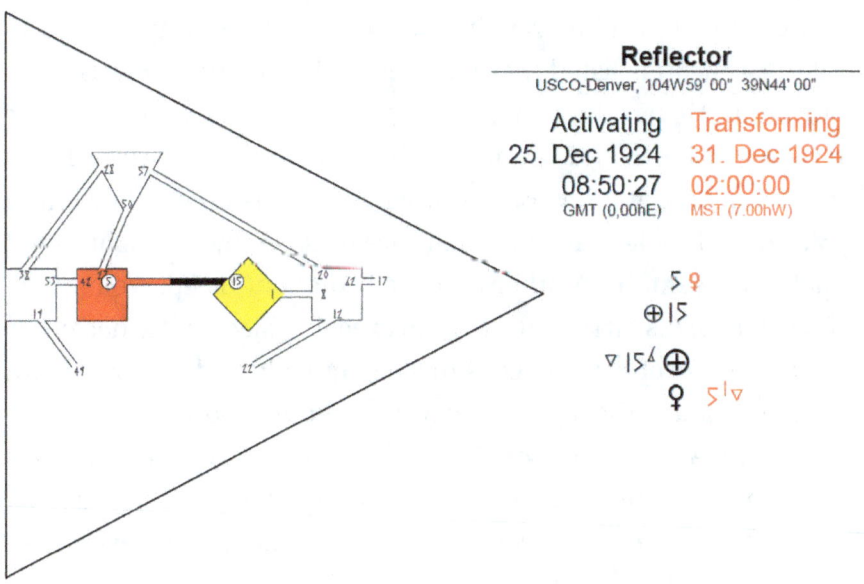

Figure 1.7: Reflector's Solar and Lunar Dream Design Charts

Case Study: NM

Now, let's delve into the unique case of NM (pages 143–144), a child with a Triple Split Definition and all four Motor Centers Defined. He is being raised according to his Design, a crucial aspect that his Mother, who also understands Design, incorporates into their daily life. We examined his Design immediately after his birth, revealing the distinct features that make NM's case particularly intriguing.

The interesting thing about NM is that he would have been a difficult child if he had not been raised according to his Design. He would be a behavior problem. He would be having temper tantrums. He would be willful. NM is the kind of child who could be raised in ways that would very much not be him, and he would be seen as a problem for being who he is. Instead, he is a delightful little boy who is always happy. Now, what is interesting in looking at him, and what I want to share with you, is that when we go to his Sleeping State, he becomes a very different being.

The only activations NM has in his Lunar DreamRave are in Gate 19. Chiron is listed there. I'm not using it, but he has Gate 19 four times. He has the Sun in Gate 19, Line 6, Mercury and Uranus in Gate 19, Line 2, and Uranus, both Personality and Design Fixed in Detriment. Gate 19 is Environment, which is very important to NM. When I looked at the Lunar DreamRave and thought about what to present, his Mother and I talked about Sleep. We have all noticed from his birth that NM is an excellent sleeper. He has never had a Sleep problem. He goes to sleep quickly and Sleeps deeply. He slept through the night when he was about a month old and was a preemie. All of his Motor Centers are turned off. When he gets ready to sleep, his mother says she sometimes puts him against her chest and lies down with him. She has had the experience of his Motor Centers turning off.

NM is very definitive about what he wants and needs to Eat. One of the most important things from his first Design reading was how

THE DREAMRAVE DESIGN SYSTEM

he needs to be fed. It is critical to how he has been raised. By the way, we are already starting to work with Biological Design, looking at different Patterns. The biological Body Graph makes it very obvious what eating patterns are for different people. So, we are already starting to look at some of that.

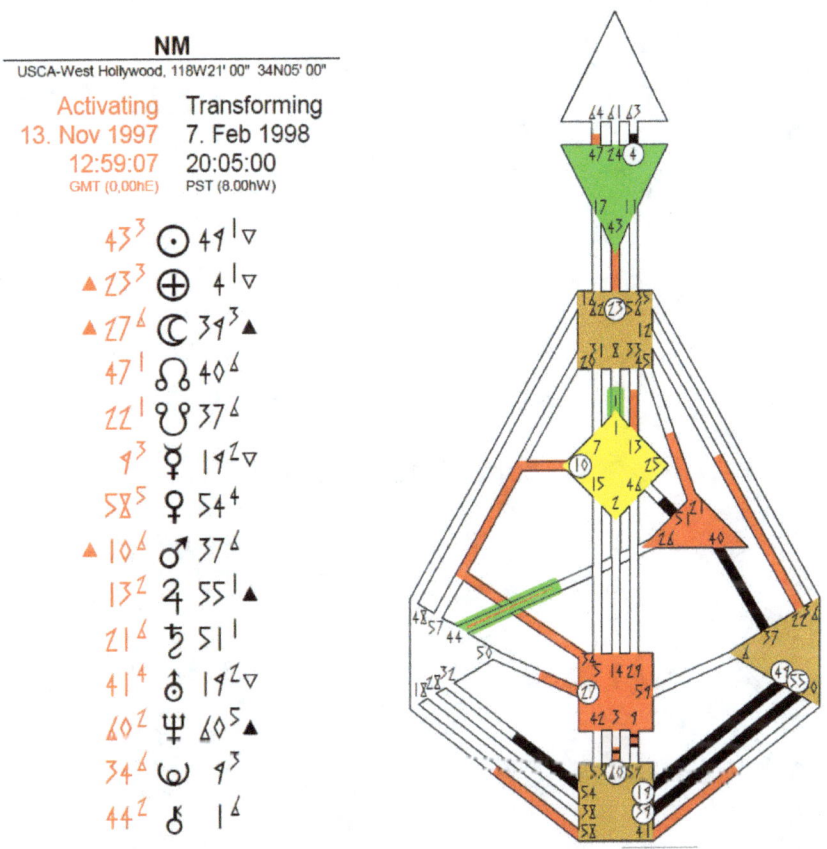

Figure 1.8: Example NM's Human Design Chart

Solar Sleep Design

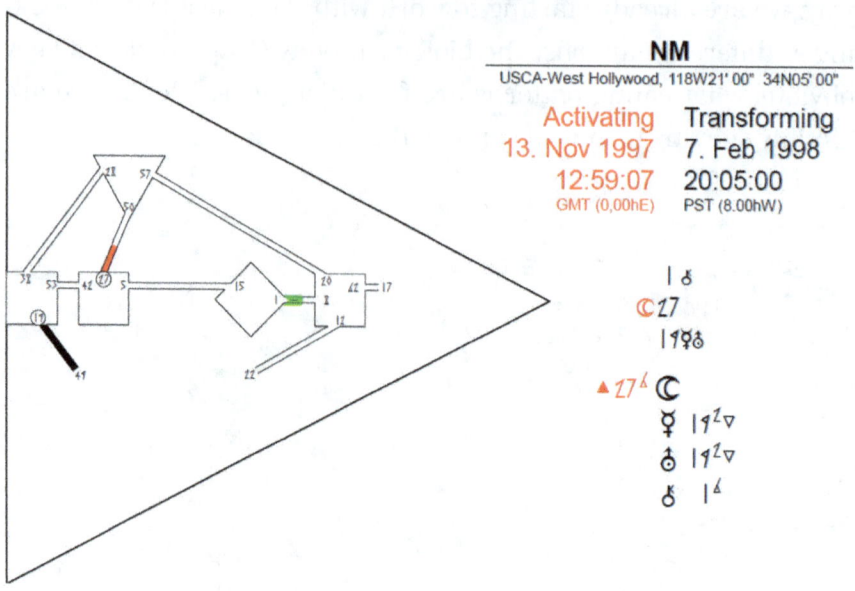

Lunar Sleep Design

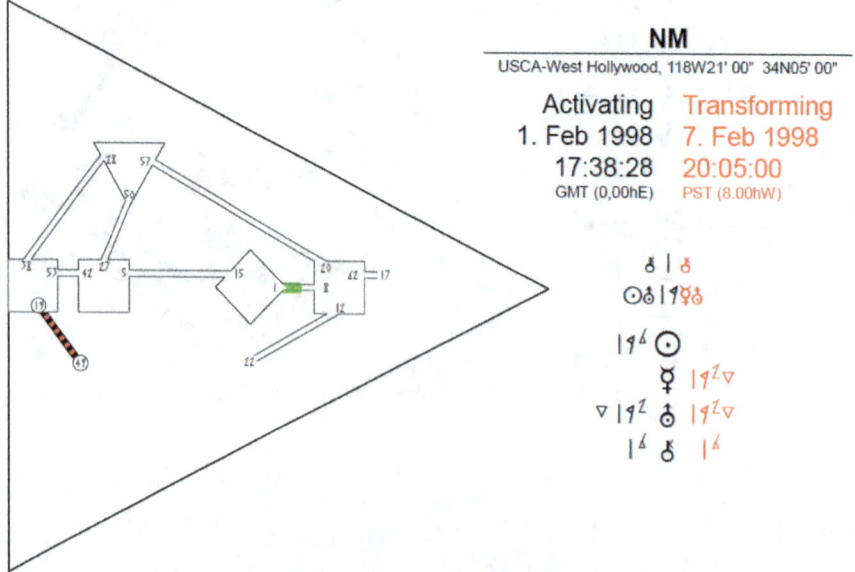

Figure 1.9: NM's Solar and Lunar Dream Design Charts

I have always been very specific about what I eat and what I am willing to eat, and I do not eat things that are not right for me. So, both of my children were brought up that way. With NM knowing his Design, his mother was very clear that she had to let him determine When, What, and How he ate. So, when he was eating any kind of solid Food, she would show it to him, and he would shake his head "yes" or "no" very definitively. Because he is Emotionally Defined, he is always asked more than once at intervals. He may say "no" the first time and change his mind as he moves through a Wave and wants to eat the food later. If he does not like it, he throws it down.

His mother had difficulty in her pregnancy, starting in the second trimester. She had a separation of the placenta. He was implanted very low, and there was a separation. So, even in utero, NM was a baby dealing with the Environment and the Environment on a Cellular level at the core of his identity and his ability to Incarnate. The obstetrician said to his mother, "Well, you're young, and if you miscarry, there will be other babies." His mother said, "This is my baby; I don't want another baby; I want this baby. I know who this baby is. I want this baby." And she was very definitive about that. The birth was also related to Environment and Food. She ate an orange and noticed that NM did not move around a lot, which he usually did after she ate an orange. So, she called me and said, "Something is wrong. He didn't react. He didn't respond when I ate the orange." I said, "Go to the doctor." Fortunately, she had an obstetrician who believed in the mother's intuition. Although NM was not in any fetal distress, he was not a happy baby. It was discovered that the mother was bleeding internally, and if she had not been that sensitive within 24 hours, both she and NM would have died. So, the Environment and her sensitivity and NM's sensitivity to the Environment is what saved him and her Gate 38 and Gate 53 of Survival and knowing when things are faulty for the Form.

It is especially interesting with NM that the Lunar DreamRave Sun is in Gate 19, Line 6, so it has a Transpersonal meaning. Also, in the early phase of life, it functions as a 3rd Line, and he has already been through quite a bit of Trial and Error coming into the World with things Bumping into him and having to deal.

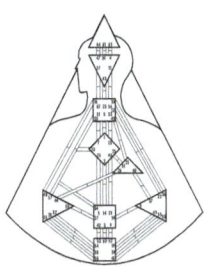

Conclusion

We are still in the early stages of our work with DreamRave and its integration into Design work. However, it is clear that using the Solar DreamRave and Lunar DreamRave in conjunction with the Waking Rave Design is an extremely valuable tool for understanding the Whole Person and the influences on that person's Consciousness.

> Since working with Ra on the DreamRave, my work has deepened and expanded considerably. Working with the Dream and Sleep Designs opened me up to considering the additional Matrix that Ra was told existed but was not given. I was given the Emotional/Angelic Matrix in 2002, a thirty-three Gate Matrix that helps transform Emotional reactive energy into Spiritual Knowing.

Book One References

Dement, W. C., and Vaughn, C. 1999. The Promise of Sleep. Random House: New York.

"Preliminary Research on the Human Design System and Health." Eleanor Haspel-Portner, PhD, et al., Rave Live Sciences, 2000)

"Revised Research Verifies 5 Types in the Human Design System." Eleanor Haspel-Portner, PhD. Rave Life Sciences. August 2001.

"The Triple Design Matrix: Type Statistically Verified Across the Matrix.: Eleanor Haspel-Portner, Ph.D. Rave Life Sciences. August 2001

BOOK TWO

DreamRave Keynotes & Clinical Applications

Seminar Transcript & Updates
Recorded March 25, 2001, Pacific Palisades, CA

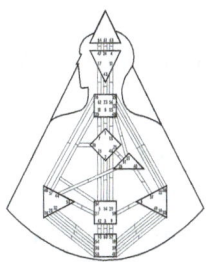

Foreword

This book introduces the Triple Design Matrix concept of the DreamRave Design System. The Triple Design Matrix emerged from the DreamRave work as it became clear that the different states of consciousness in which each Matrix functions integrate into a synthesis in the Rapid Eye Movement (REM) stage of sleep. During this phase of sleep, the Waking Rave Design, the Solar DreamRave, and the Lunar DreamRave are integrated. The Triple Design Matrix has scientific validation and reliably differentiates Type as the term is used in the Human Design System.

This book contains a transcription of "The DreamRave Keynotes and Clinical Applications" from a Seminar sponsored by Rave Life Sciences in Pacific Palisades, California, on March 25, 2001. It marks an integrated synthesis of our work with the material in its ongoing development.

Because of the time lapse between the presentation of the material and its publication as a transcript, Eleanor Haspel-Portner, Ph.D., annotated the material with updates clarifying some points, verifying some material, and revising other material. Since this is a work in progress, it is subject to change as new data becomes available, as is the case in all science.

We are extremely gratified, however, that this material to date has stood the test of stringent statistical analysis (cf. "The Triple Design Matrix: Type Statistically Verified Across the Matrix." By Eleanor Haspel- Portner, Ph.D. Rave Life Sciences. August 2001.), and that it adds a dimension to the clinical application of Design. The Triple Design Matrix is simple to learn yet remains practical and powerful at changing lives.

Because of the way this material was presented, it is not formal material. We have done the minimum editing to allow for the flavor of the speaker's style to remain apparent in the material, but we cleaned up some of the language by moving it from an oral presentation to a written one. We also used the editorial liberty of Capitalizing some Keywords for emphasis and to alert the reader to an important concept.

With the introduction of The Triple Design Matrix and its validation, a new tool that provides further access to our true nature has become available. This knowledge easily opens us up to the awareness of one world and one consciousness. In Living who you are, you are yourself, you are at one, and you are whole. It is your right.

> Since this book was published in March 2001, I have further developed the concepts and work presented in it. Noble Energy Maps® include the Dream and Sleep Designs and works with the integrated Matrices that consider the way humans and mammals function as they integrate the Four Worlds into their consciousness and life path. The material in this book is presented with commentary, but since it is source material, minimal editing has been done.

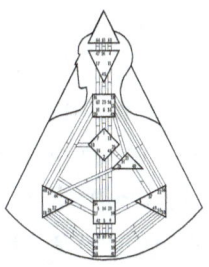

Preface: Triple Design Matrix

The DreamRaves

Work with the DreamRave has proved to be rather significant. Statistics verify that the Matrices differentiate reliable and valid constructs that hold across the Triple Design Matrix (cf. "The Triple Design Matrix: Type Verified across the Matrix," Eleanor Haspel-Portner, Ph.D., Rave Life Sciences. August 2001). The term DreamRave refers to a Design with a 15-Gate Matrix that functions when we are asleep. When we sleep, we move through different phases of consciousness. All living creatures, all Mammals, go through the Circadian Rhythm Cycle, a 24-hour Cycle based on the rotation of the Earth. Every living creature has a period in the course of a day when it sleeps. We know from research that sleep is restorative. Sleep is essential for health as well as for the immune system; it is essential for life itself. Any being deprived of sleep, even for a short period of time, gets sick. The sleep cycle moves through different phases.

We go from being awake and, as you know, when you are awake, you tend to be vertical, to being in a light sleep, which would be the beginning, the relaxation stage of sleep, the alpha, Stage 1 sleep.

Then, we move progressively into deeper sleep that cycles in the course of the period that we are sleeping. These cycles occur in blocks of about ninety minutes repeating 4-6 times a night. We always go down through to deep sleep, cycling up into a phase called "emergence," where we come back up to a lighter level of sleep, and then we go back down into deeper sleep. In the course of the night, we dream (Rapid Eye Movement (REM) sleep), and we also cycle into a non-dream state; we come back up where there is an integration, and we then cycle back down.

What I have come to in the work over the last few months with the DreamRave is that we cycle through our different Designs, in what we have begun to call the Triple Design Matrix (TDM). In the course of a night, as we cycle down into deep sleep and then come back up, we always function within the Waking Rave Design (WRD) that oversees everything. Then we cycle through to the Solar DreamRave (SDR), the Matrix based on our WRD in which the Design side is calculated at 88 Solar Degrees before birth. In the SDR, we have the regular 64 Gate Design Matrix functioning in a 15-Gate Design.

I believe that the SDR becomes functional when we are in the alpha rhythm, the relaxed sort of pre-sleep state, or in the stages where we come out of deep sleep and then emerge into a lighter sleep before we cycle back down. During this lighter sleep, the respirations are a little faster. It is more akin to a waking state than to deep sleep where respiration is very slow and where, we are, in essence, devoid of neo-cortex consciousness.

The Lunar DreamRave (LDR) is a Mammalian Design with the Design portion calculated at 88 Lunar Degrees before birth. I believe the LDR functions during deepest Sleep and is active during Dreaming. You will see how that operates; we will explain that in a lot more detail in the pages to come. Understand that what we have been describing is the "sleep architecture." It has a very specific structure that all mammals move through during the night.

At the time Ra and I presented this material, I had not yet calculated the Sleep Design of a Mammal. Thus, Ra was working only with the Solar DreamRave calculated at 88 Solar Degrees before birth and the Lunar DreamRave calculated at 88 Lunar Degrees before birth. After this presentation, I calculated the Lunar Minute DreamRave because I was certain that we were missing two critical chart calculations. I knew from having cats and kittens that cats both dream and sleep. Deep sleep is a different state of consciousness than the REM dream state. As an astrologer, it was logical to calculate using the Solar Degrees and the Solar Minutes to calculate the Waking Mental World Matrix and the Emotional/Angelic World Matrix. In addition, I calculated the Lunar DreamRave based on 88 Lunar Degrees before birth and at birth and I added the Lunar Minute Calculation so I could study deep sleep in my cats and dogs.

When I laid out the four designs based on these calculations, I recognized that the timing was scientifically documentable in early baby development psychologically and physiologically. In addition, the Lunar Minute calculation correlates to the way the physical body operates in daily life. I worked with my additions to the data presented in this book over the past 24 years. Noble Energy Maps® scientifically integrates the Human Design Body Graph information and documents it in the Four Worlds: Mental, Spiritual, Emotional, and Physical. This documentation confirms the synthesis with the Kabbalistic Tree of Life and psychologically documents stages of unfoldment in the process of individuation or self-actualization.

Some Brain Chemistry

There is also a very interesting phenomenon. A substance called "adenosine" is a chemical that has a very distinct action and binds to cells. It also functions throughout the body. Adenosine promotes sleep. What is really interesting is that if you look at where Adenosine is released in the brain, and you look at the Body Graph, you realize that it is released in the area that connects the Throat Center and the Ajna Center. In the DreamRaves (Matrices), those Centers are not active. The Head Center, the Ajna Center, the Solar Plexus Center and the Heart Center disappear during sleep. We have chemical substantiation for the fact that the chemistry during sleep and dreaming is different in our bodies than it is during our waking state. I put this scientific information out to you as some evidence that the scientific field already substantiates some aspects of the Matrix and its structure.

The part of the brain that leads down toward the spinal cord is like a little tail going down; then, it comes up and it's like a little bulge, which is called the "hindbrain." It is also called the "primitive brain." It is present in mammals and other "lower" life forms. What is different about humans is the cerebral cortex, the big bulge on the top of the brain. All animals have this cortex as well but the human cortex is much larger. Talking about the Mammalian Design or the Lunar Design is an example of how we become like our ancestral source animals during sleep. All of these Matrices operate independently of Consciousness. When we sleep, something breathes for us and something takes care of our heartbeat; our intestinal tract still functions and our body temperature stays the same; all of these functions operate through that lower part of the hindbrain. We only think we run the vehicle.

Mammalian awareness operates out of the Splenic Center. Understand that we all share Mammalian Awareness. We all share a Root Awareness together; it is the Splenic System. When we move into the horizontal position, in that horizontal state, we actually mimic the Mammalian world, and, in that sense, we go back to our source awareness. That source of awareness, our Immune System, is very primitive, very ancient, and yet, at the same time, it is responsible for our well-being.

We are at a very exciting moment in terms of Design; we have statistical verification for the validity of things like Type and Centers and things like that. But what we are also beginning to see is that the complexity of life is made up of us moving through various aspects of an overall Design; in other words, we move through these different stages. It is not an accident that the Dream World is something that is mysterious to us. In fact, we can look at the Dream World mystically or spiritually. One of the most important things to understand about sleep is that sleep is an impersonal world. In sleep what you actually do is make your contribution the Whole without the vanity of your Personality getting in the way and confusing all of that. Imagine if your Dreams were as tough as your life. We are not designed that way. It is interesting to see that we move through these different Structures in the process of a living day.

As we work with this material, we glean an increasing sense of how human beings are integrated in their geometry. As humans, we are unique from other species in that we do have these Centers that operate when we are awake. Other Species do not have these Centers in any state of consciousness. We have what we are calling the "Bridge Gates" or "the Portals," which we soon will explain to you. In looking at the DreamRave Matrix, we have the opportunity to see how we integrate from the archetypal mammalian realm and then bring the information into our waking consciousness for integration. Without looking at the DreamRave, we ignore a third of what programs us in our lives. So, you really must look at more than one Design; you have to look at all of them in order to have the true synthesis of the whole Design Matrix. The integrated matrix is called the Triple Design Matrix (TDM). It consists of the Waking Rave Design (WRD), the Solar DreamRave (SDR), and the Lunar DreamRave (LDR).

The Designs of Forms

The most fascinating aspect of Design information is that it is not exclusive to human beings. Other forms and the Design of other

Forms are known. Look at the illustration of the different Forms (Figure 2.1). Understand that the different Forms in Figure 2.1 are not all oriented to their proper geometry. They are all aligned together in the same vertical position so that you can see the similarities in the various forms of life. Look at the Design Matrix for insects. Look at the Design Matrix for birds, for reptiles, for fish. One of the things you notice in these Designs of Forms is that there is always a Cross-Species opportunity, i.e., Portal or Bridge Gates. The most fascinating of all is to look at plants.

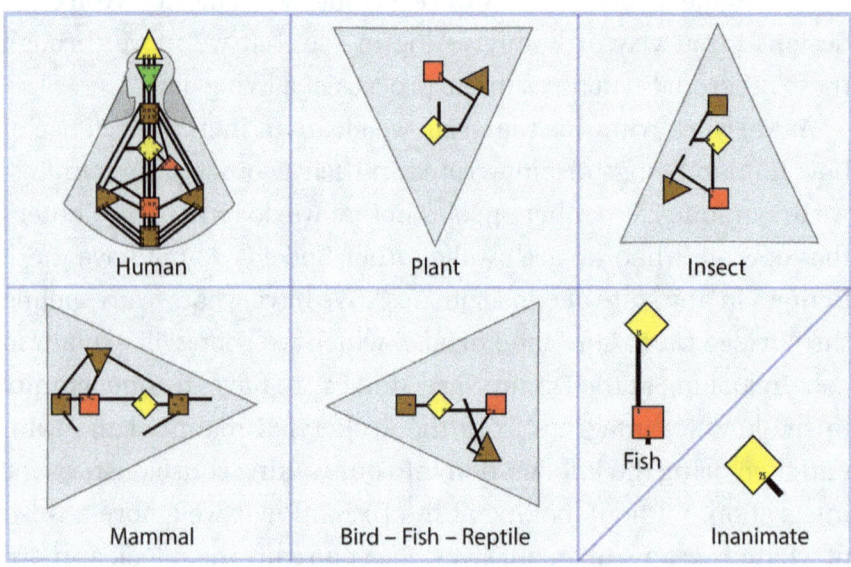

Figure 2.1: The Design of Forms

Channel 15/5

One of the things to notice about all these various forms of life, as well as about ourselves, is that it is all integrated to Channel 15/5. This channel has the deepest commonality in all forms of life and is actually the Design of the single cell itself. The single cell has Channel 15/5 with Gate 3. So, if you look at the Design of plants, you see that the plant doesn't have Gate 5; plants are open to other forms of life that have the 5th Gate. Gate 5 is the Gate of Establishing Patterns. Think about that.

The birds and fish can impact on the patterns of plants. Insects can impact on the patterns of plants. Mammals impact on the pattern of plants. In other words, plants are designed to interact with other forms of life, literally, in order to adapt to their needs and to have their pattern changed by their presence. Different forms of life have ways of integrating.

Human Beings have 64 Gates that are involved in the Matrix. By far we are the most complex in that sense. But, if you look at all the forms of life, you can see that the Mammalian Design is very sophisticated compared to the others and that the Mammalian Design is made up of a 15-Gate Matrix. You can see certain Centers that we have in common, and you can see Centers that are simply not there. There are three different ways that other Mammals can connect to us. They can connect through the Portal Gates: Gate 62, Gate 19, and Gate 12.

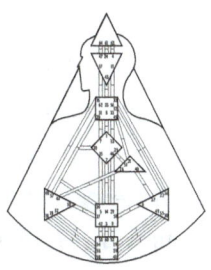

The Dynamics of the Triple Design Matrix

The Matrix as Programmed

Think about something. When you look at a human being, our Design is vertical. A Mammalian Design is oriented to the right position. Position in geometry is enormously important. We are all endowed with Crystals of Consciousness; we receive information via the neutrino stream that programs us. We are actually all programmed at various angles in the geometry. In human life, you can watch that when you have a child who tries to stand up. When that baby finally stands up it has a rush because it moves out of exclusively being in a Mammalian Matrix when in its aura only; it moves out of the horizontal 15-Gate Matrix and suddenly rises up into this 64-Gate Matrix.

Mammals receive their information differently from us. If we were to do the Design, of a plant, for example, we would see that they are upside down, at least in the way we look at things. In other words, we receive our neutrino information coming downward into us, actually at an 88-degree angle when we are vertical, but the plant gets that programming as the neutrino information comes through the earth first. In other words, we are all in a programming field. We are all in a programmed geometry, and we are receiving that in different ways. However, humans are very complex. We are not that far away from our mammalian roots.

How the programmed information changes

The moment we position ourselves horizontally we operate in the horizontal Matrix, whether a person lies down with his leg up or whether he goes to sleep. In deep sleep or if making love or not, as soon as a person gets into that position, the stream of incoming information changes. When the information comes in, in this horizontal position, it can only operate through the 15-Gate matrix even though everything else remains, and everything else is on the "hum;" it operates, but the new programming, the new information, comes in through this matrix.

I meet many people who do not know who they are. They lack purpose. Rave Life Sciences both authenticates and completes the opening up of all the areas where this knowledge is applicable. When the DreamRave Matrix information was given to me, I thought, "How cute. How nice it is that we are so dumb that most of the important things that we really do as a contribution to the totality are far beyond our ability to grasp it," and I thought, "How clever." Most of the time we are in our waking, vertical state with our 64-Gates and with all of the things that come with living the human process. We are very far away from living out our nature, which means eliminating that resistance to the deeper levels of our programming; we currently are fulfilling the program in the waking state, or at least in its surface potential.

> I do not use the word programming when talking about the psychological state of a person. All humans who live in a community learn to behave in ways appropriate for their group. When humans travel from one geographic area to another, they often experience what is called, "Culture Shock." It is this level of "programming" that Ra is describing. It is not classical Pavlovian conditioning or programming. What Ra refers to is learning to live among humans in the Mental World where you are expected to behave in certain ways and you learn to change your outward expressions to comply with what is acceptable in your cultural group.
>
> With information from the Tree of Life and the Integration of Noble Energy Maps®, we have a Body Energy Map that shows developmental sequences in you over the first three months of your life and it gives a roadmap for how you process information, consciously and unconsciously. In addition, it shows keys for transformations as you move through your process of individuation.

When we are asleep, that is when the work is actually done. It is a very beautiful thing because it is in the sleeping state that your personality disappears. There is no ego in the sleeping state. There is no possessive, "I," in that sleeping state. When you move into that phase, what goes on is very, very different. Not only that, but the way you are programmed is different. And, of course, the most fascinating thing about the DreamRave itself is that the DreamRave operates differently and has different kinds of programming depending on your activations.

> Rather than using the term programming, which removes the concept of choice from the equation, I speak about influences on you from outside your core energy field.

Understanding Terminology

The Solar DreamRave (SDR)
You need to understand the terminology of the Solar DreamRave (SDR) and the Lunar DreamRave (LDR). When we talk about a SDR, we are talking about your design, the way you have it in the Waking state, turned on its side with only those parts of the mammalian design active. In other words, it is your Design; it is actually the way it was originally calculated. The only difference is that the information is limited to the 15-Gate Matrix rather than to the 64-Gate matrix. That is the SDR. In other words, it is really your Waking Rave Design (WRD) just in that limitation.

The Lunar DreamRave (LDR)
The Lunar DreamRave (LDR) is very different. You see, all of this is a kind of serendipity. During my mystical experience, I had my dog with me. And my very questions, and they were not spoken questions, but, anyway, my need to know that there were other designs, that the dog was not being left out, actually led to my knowing about these designs of other Forms. The calculation for mammals was there because that was my need, I suppose. So, I know how to calculate a mammalian design.

And, a mammalian design was different only in one sense: it was ruled by the movement of the Moon; it had nothing to do with the Sun. In other words, when you do a mammalian calculation, you take the birth data and you go back 88 degrees of the Moon to find the design information; not 88 degrees of the Sun. That is the difference between 88 or 89 days [in the calculation for the Solar DreamRave that comes out to about three months] and 6 days [88 Degrees of the Moon comes out to be about 6 days]. In other words, in the mammalian realm, there is a difference in the amount of time necessary for the personality to get used to the vehicle. Think about that.

Humans have very complex vehicles. Our Personality Crystal comes in taking approximately three months just to get used to being in the vehicle before birth occurs. In a mammal, the need of that personality to accustom itself to the mechanism is less complex. It doesn't take as much time. So, the Personality Crystal comes in very quickly just before the birth, six days before the birth. When we calculate an LDR, that's what we are doing; we are calculating it from your birth date, but instead of going back to find the design 88 degrees of the Sun, we go back 88 degrees of the Moon. Of course, that changes the way activations work in your design. If we give you a mammalian calculation, all that design stuff that you have in your WRD or that you have in the SDR isn't there anymore. What you have is a new set of Design/Unconscious information.

An Example: A Reflector

The Moon drives us on the instinctive level. Often you will not see a dramatic difference between the SDR and the LDR. But the case in Figure 2.2 is extremely interesting. It shows the different Matrix Designs of a Reflector. We now know that Reflectors constitute only about 1 percent of the population in hard statistics. To have a Reflector and then to see that in the LDR, this Reflector becomes a Generator is very dramatic. It also can give you a little bit of a flavor for how important it is to look at what the configuration is in the Triple Design Matrix (TDM) (the WRD, the SDR, and the LDR).

In the SDR, again, what you are looking at is a different calculation. If you looked at this Reflector's normal chart, it would also be open, there would be no Centers defined. Of course, here, because you have a change in the Design calculation, you have the potential of new information in that Matrix, and, of course, you can end up in the actual LDR in the deepest dream state, with a different kind of design at work.

Recognize the importance of this material in terms of working with someone. Realize that if this person in the LDR remained a Reflector, this person would function very differently in his life than in this particular case where he becomes a Generator with a Defined G (Identity/Self) Center.

This Reflector is a slave to his dreams or a slave to her dreams. Think about what happens to someone who is normally a Reflector but who becomes a Generator during deep sleep. This person has an enormous amount of energy operating in their body; they receive an enormous amount of energy. They can wake incredibly energized, or they can actually wake up totally exhausted and feel like they've been working all night and being a slave all night, and that now they need to rest because they woke up. It is very, very different Programming.

Of course, people have no access to that information because they do not really know what is going on. We are not supposed to know. That is one of the whole things about the difficulty we have: The moment we start to talk about dreams, there seems to be the need for people to take the dream experience personally without really understanding that it is not personal. It is not about you interpreting your dream to find out what that dream meant. It is about recognizing that we all filter information in the dream state that is necessary to the way the totality functions.

> The Dream state of consciousness, at all levels of depth, activates the Splenic Side of the Body Graph. The Splenic side corresponds in the Tree of Life to the Pillar of Severity and the need to master Hod or the Splenic Center. The task here is to master the intellect and to discern truth and alignment from imbalance and Mental World reality. By using the Lunar Degrees and Lunar Minutes in calculating Noble Energy Maps®, it became possible to look at how you function in all Four Worlds as depicted in the Tree of Life and to recognize how you function Spiritually and what your life purpose is.

[Ed.Note: Research in clinical work has shown that the filters through the Triple and Quadruple Matrix actually filter the personality-level experiences of the Waking Consciousness and the Collective Archetypal Layers of Consciousness.]

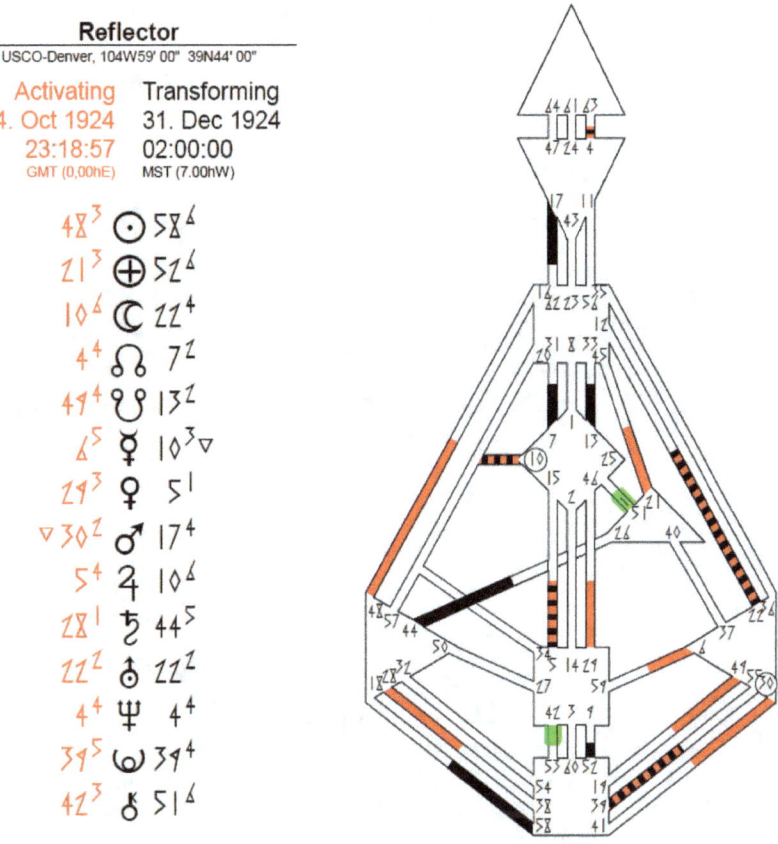

Figure 2.2: Example Reflector Human Design Chart

Solar Sleep Design

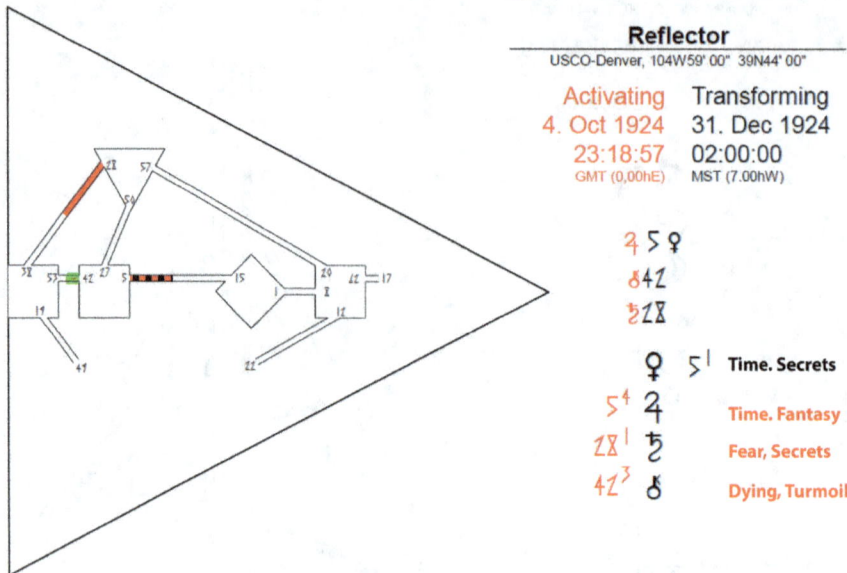

Lunar Sleep Design

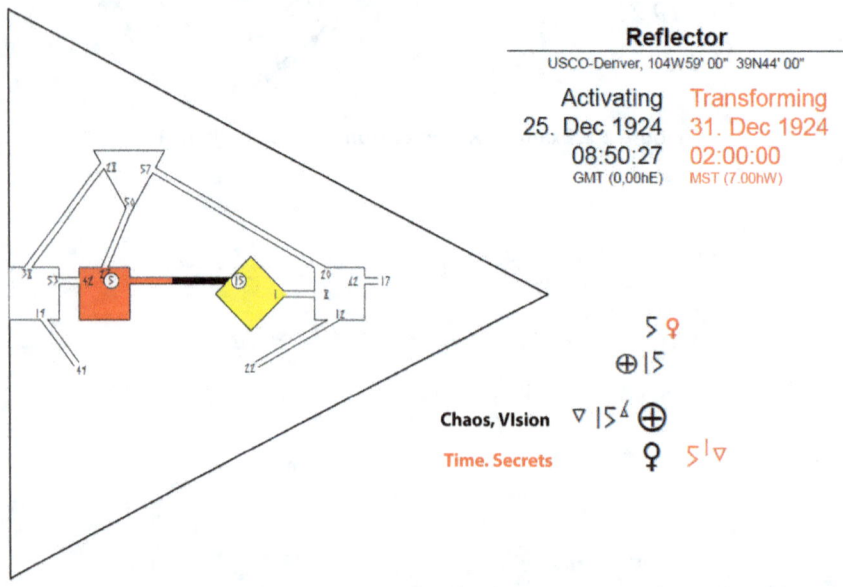

Figure 2.3: Reflector's Solar and Lunar Dream Design Charts

When you have some kind of an experience in your dream it may, in fact, be something that is taking place, as you will see, on the other side of the planet that has nothing to do with you. But you are in touch with the archetype of whatever that is. Remember, in a 15-Gate Matrix, we really have very powerful archetypes that are at work, and these are ways in which we can really see the way the program operates through us. You will see the kind of things that are involved in these Keynotes.

> When Ra talks here about the program, he is alluding to the neutrinos impacting us with energy that predisposes us to certain kinds of perceptions and feelings. The premise of the Body Graph is that we are impacted by the Neutrino Stream and our life expression is moved by its impact.

What happens to this Reflector is that he goes to sleep heavy, having done whatever he did in his day, and he wakes up in the morning with a very clear sense of direction and a clear sense of what he thinks his agenda is for the day. Now, this person is very tapped into his collective consciousness and is a very powerful person. He is also extremely connected to animals. One of the first tasks of his day is taking care of animals. This Reflector awakens with a keen sense of purpose and direction which he sustains throughout the day. From his description, sleep is very important to him and he goes to sleep early, and he wakes up early. He is definitely a Moon person.

> Ra made a false assumption in his statement about a Reflector being "heavy." Many Reflectors become Manifesting Generators in their Noble Energy Maps® Integrated Design. Even assuming only the Mental World of Human Design, you cannot assume that Type defines the way you express yourself in the World. Your energy bodies come together and integrate initiatory

> developmental tasks in your own unique way. Ra's generalizations are broad and should be taken as overstatements and oversimplifications of consciousness and personality expression.

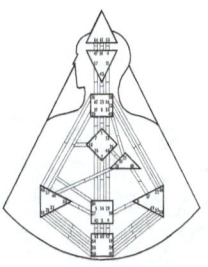

The Dream Keys Keynotes

Illustration 2.4 on the following page shows the DreamRave Keynotes. To talk about them, first, I have to talk to you about the way we are physically programmed. One of the things that you will notice here about how the Gate Keys are divided, is that there are three different blocks, i.e., the 15 Gates divide up into three groups of five each. Each of these groups is dominated by the Gate at the top, the Cross-Species, or the Portal Gate in a mammal. Here in the DreamRave, these Gates are called "Portals." In other words, they open up to different kinds of experiences, as you will see, or different kinds of information in the dream process. We have three different areas here that operate as circuits in the dream Matrix.

The Three Divisions have a very specific naming to them: The Light Field, The Earth Plane, and The Demon Realm. It is not that the Light Field is good and/or that the Demon Realm is bad. Let us not get into the morality of these names. Nonetheless, they carry a certain quality inherent in them that leads us in the right direction. It has to do with the way the programming operates when you are in this Matrix. The programming operates in three different ways. In other words, when you are in the horizontal state, depending on activations in your Design, you are going to receive three different sub-groups or sub-types of programming. It is very specific.

The DreamRave Keys

The Mechanics of the Sleeping Life

Secrets	Possession	Turmoil	Obesssion	Fantasy	Vision
1	2	3	4	5	6

The Light Field

| 62 Love |
| 20 Sight |
| 57 Attunement |
| 8 Darkness |
| 1 Joy |

The Earth Plane

| 12 Mutation |
| 27 Yearning |
| 50 Sex |
| 8 Time |
| 15 Chaos |

The Demon Realm

| 19 Environments |
| 53 Flight |
| 42 Dying |
| 38 Aggression |
| 28 Fear |

Figure 2.4: DreamRave Keys

There is a Crystal Field of consciousness of which we are a part. One of the things to recognize about the nature of the crystals of consciousness is that the crystals of consciousness, like the very binary that we are, are divided. So, we, literally, have a field of Personality Crystals, what you call yourself or what you think you call yourself. We have a field of Personality Crystals literally covering this planet. When I say, "covering this planet," I mean that it operates throughout the atmosphere and operates throughout the atmosphere in bundles. So, the little girl in Spain who sees the Virgin Mary or the little boy in California who sees a UFO, or somebody who chases after angels or whatever the case may be, these bundles are bundles of Personality Crystals that never incarnate. You see, it is your job to incarnate. Those who have come into bodies, those who are in bodies, are always coming into bodies. You don't get out of that job.

The vast majority of Crystals of Consciousness never incarnate into Form at all. Every single one of you, in the way you operate, each and every one of you has a Personality Crystal of Consciousness that connects to one of those bundles out there. When you die, that Crystal goes back into that Bundle. The ways the Neutrinos actually move through all of us integrate everything, all that information is integrated. Some people have contact with their Bundles. They call it "channeling." They give that cluster of potential Consciousness names and give it authority and all kinds of things. It is just simply the way Consciousness operates.

Look At The Light Field, The Demon Realm, and The Earth Plane

- **The Light Field** specifically programs the Personality Consciousness Field. Now, this is the dream world of Light. It is all about the possibilities of mysterious knowledge, of angels showing up, of all kinds of energy that we associate with the dream of consciousness and awareness. In many senses, we call that "positive" because it seems less threatening, and it seems interesting. Remember, Personality Consciousness has an agenda. It does. The yang without the yin is meaningless. On one side, we have this Light Field in which we have programming from the consciousness field around us, and on the other side, we have the Demon Realm.

- **The Design Crystals** bundle is one enormous bundle if you will. The Design Crystals bundle is within the Earth. Between the Personality Crystals bundled above and the Design Crystals below is where we get all of our terminology for "heaven" and "hell" and all of these things that operate in those mythologies. What the Design Crystal brings is Form. It brings the ability to grasp the essence of Form. The Light Field may bring you words that are whispered in your ear that may be, whatever. But what you are going to get from the Demon Realm is things that you really have to deal with, the things that are in the dark, the things that need to be exposed, the things that need to be grasped. It is also more difficult. Of course, we attach to that all kinds of difficulties because we are afraid of the Form Realm, and we are afraid of the dark forces. We do not recognize or understand them.

- **The middle division** is the most curious of all. When you come to the middle, you come to the Earth Plane. When I talk about the neutrino stream, understand it has been proven by science that the neutrino ocean has mass and that we are being penetrated by unbelievable numbers of particles that bear mass. We are in the programming field. That programming field is everywhere. The neutrinos that directly program my Crystal may be just going through my Crystal, but the fact of the matter is, the whole ocean of neutrinos goes through me, goes into you; you are going into me, there is this constant prana in this ocean of interconnecting.

When you have activation in any of those five Gates of the Earth Plane while you are asleep, what you are in contact with is not programming from above or programming from below; you are programmed by those who are awake. Now, think about that. The neutrino goes through the earth like a hot knife through butter. Nothing gets in the way of it; nothing stops it. The neutrinos that go through us now, that come down in the vertical, they go right through, and they get to the other side so fast that it is unbelievable. In other words, when you have activation in the Earth Plane, while you sleep here in America what you take in is the wakeful third world. Think about that. Think about what happens to them when they sleep, and they take in the living first world. It is amazing what gets put into the dream of humans by humans themselves. We program each other. So East dreams of West and West dreams of East.

In the circadian rhythm, that part of the physiology is based on the rotation of the earth, at any given time, half the world is asleep because of the 24-hour cycle. People are constantly going to sleep and others are constantly waking up. In this time zone, in the middle of the night, most of us are asleep. Go back and look at where on the planet people at that time are awake, you can begin to get a sense of how you are programmed [influenced]. When you begin to work with the DreamRave transits, you can actually monitor, at a particular time of the night if you wake up suddenly, where that programming comes from. (Ed. Note: remember that in the DreamRaves, the Design side functions as the Personality side functions in the Waking Rave, i.e., the Design side functions as the active consciousness and the Personality side functions as the unconscious dimension. Also, it has been our observation that because of this fact, the Transits for Waking Rave Design at 88 Lunar Degrees is a factor in considering the Triple Design Matrix Transits - this matter is to be considered in more depth in other papers).

Someone with very strong Earth Plane activations, someone, for example, with a definition, like Channel 50/27, knows how deeply connected they are with the other side. If you have Channel 50/27, and you go to sleep in America, remember that Channel 50/27, the Cauldron, and Nourishment face each other; this configuration is the cooking pot at its very basic level; it is about food and nourishment, looking after your children, caring for them; with this Channel 50/27 defined, you are going to have horrible dreams. [This statement has been clinically proven to be untrue.] With a defined Channel 50/27, you are dealing with the living world on the other side where there may be great want and lack of food and all of that stuff, and it can be deeply uncomfortable for you

[Ed. Note: Clinical research has not documented this pattern. So, in that sense, through any activation of the Earth Plane, you meet not the collective unconscious, you meet the collective conscious. That's the difference.]

Eleanor processed thousands of DreamRaves to grasp their significance and she bases her observations on the cases she studied. We are also beginning to see the statistical significance of the Triple Design Matrix (cf. The Triple Design Matrix: Type Verified Across the Matrix, Eleanor Haspel-Portner, Ph.D., Rave Life Sciences, August 2001). It is very important for us to understand the differences in the programming fields because they are really very different. Some people, who are only in the field of Light, wake up differently in the morning. They wake up with a certain feeling that is different because it is an illusionary field. It is not like it is necessarily what one should seek. It is just that they wake up with a different feeling.

> I have documented in 15,000 clinical cases that people who have Channel 50-27 in their Lunar DreamRave often awaken with a sense of angst. The angst comes from a feeling that there is something they are meant to do and they cannot quite identify what that is. As clients embrace their sensitivity and drive to be a help agent to others often their "mission" becomes clear. It is the Spiritual aspect of the Lunar DreamRave that tunes you into collective energy although the "angst" is not specifically a distressful feeling.

If you have a strong Demon Realm, you can wake up much heavier in the morning. It is a deeper force impacting on you. It doesn't have the same illusionary quality. It may lead to discomfort or worries or whatever the case may be. All this material needs verification. We are looking at sleep disturbances that we see, so we can begin to correlate between the various kinds of sleep problems and the kinds of activations in the charts.

What we offer you here is only the theory. It's like what we did when we started with Human Design: You can only offer the theory and then you get to see it in practice, and then you get to the point where you can verify it, where you can verify it statistically. So that is going to be a major step for us because, of course, we are really then going to be able to look at each of these three different aspects and understand how that programming impacts the whole. Remember the dream state is not personal.

As a matter of fact, to personalize it is to really create problems because it is not personal. The Dream State is the way we integrate with the whole; we are being used, in that sense, as a medium in the whole. We all have responsibilities in the dream state, all of us. One of those things to recognize is that we do have an incredible purpose in life, i.e., we maintain life. Because we have so much responsibility in maintaining life, most of that responsibility is taken away from any of our conscious dabbling. These Designs represent where we are being programmed. Recall the Rave that we looked at which suddenly went from a Reflector to a Generator; think about that person carrying that energy throughout the day. We carry the program we received in sleep throughout the day.

[Ed. Note: Thus, it is so crucial to always look at the charts for the TDM as a whole for a functioning individual. We are all programmed differently so the nuance of looking at somebody's chart becomes fascinating.]

In looking at the mammalian design, and in looking at other forms of life, we saw that there were Cross-Species Gates (Portals), this way of inter-connecting with the other. There is something very special about these Gates in the dream state. These Portals open up to different kinds of information and different kinds of "stuff" come through them.

Consequently, how they operate can be very special. Look at the Light Field, for example. Look at the Gates 1 and 8 or at Gates 57 and 20. If you look at those four Gates, and you look at them in terms of the basic Human Design Matrix, you can see that they are all very individual.

These Gates are about the Individual process. Therefore, these Gates are, by their very nature, Mutative. In other words, the Light Field is a Mutative Field. It can actually mean that much of what becomes mutation, i.e., much of what we get to see ultimately as mutation, may, in fact, be instigated or started while an individual is in the dream state (REM).

One of the things that we are going to find about the DreamRave is that the dream state itself may be a place where a lot of problems originate; in other words, we may find that certain kinds of diseases, certain kinds of disturbances, actually begin in that state itself rather than beginning in the Waking Rave. We are dealing with a mutative possibility. In the mammal, Channel 8-1 is about being an Alpha. It is about being able to express the Direction of Survival and the Direction of Mutation for other animals in the group. One of the things about the Light Field is that it is a mutative field; it provides us with information about direction as well as about where we can make a Contribution and bring the Contribution out into the world.

The 1st Gate is the Gate of Joy in the DreamRaves. In the Waking Rave Design, the 1st Gate describes the need for the individual to make a Contribution. In other words, through the 1st Gate in your sleep life, especially if you have a strong 1st Gate also in your Waking Rave, that need to make a Contribution is further instilled in you during the night. In other words, you wake up with that sense of "I need to make a contribution." Of course, when you look at Joy, the only Gate that we have in Waking Rave Design that really is close to that is the 58th Gate, the 58th Gate being "the Joyous." One of the things about the 58th Gate is that its Joy is in being able to provide energy for Challenge and Correction. It is just the Joy of being able to offer the energy. It is the same kind of thing here. In the DreamRaves, Gate 1 is real Joy in being able to offer one's Contribution.

You can also see the psychic dilemma of what happens with

somebody who is programmed in their sleep to make a Contribution, as an example, when that person awakens to their Waking Rave. They wake up into their Waking Rave Type. By the way, one of the most extraordinary things that we now have in the statistics is the verification of Type and its validity, (cf. Bibliography). An individual wakes up in the morning into their Type. If that person is a Generator who wakes up needing to make a Contribution and is not paying attention to Type, that individual may go roaring out into the world saying, "I need to make a contribution," only to end up being deeply frustrated, only to end up meeting resistance. Of course, that creates an imbalance in that person's process. This aspect is one of the things to realize anyway about the importance of Type. No matter how you operate and no matter what state of your process in any given 24 hours, if you are living out your Type, everything works out well for you. That is the whole thing about the basic mechanics of your nature.

> I have recently documented statistically that in Noble Energy Maps® Integrated Design, 99% of the general population are Manifesting Generators. What this means is that knowing the way your Four World Matrices operate informs your process and predisposing sensitivities to the energy around you. More details will be published soon.

What's interesting here is that the whole purpose of the Joy is to penetrate the Darkness. You are there to make the Contribution in order to eliminate the Darkness and to open up the Light, but it still means you have to go through the Darkness. One of the things to understand about Light programming is that Light programming says, "You must go through the Darkness. You must open the Darkness up; you must bring Light to the Darkness in order to make your Contribution." Now, you know how much of our mythology is attached to that kind of programming, programming that says, "The light will penetrate the Dark, it will open it up." And of course, it can become a deep force in one's life.

The Light Field: Ra's Triple Design Matrix Chart

I'm a Single Definition Individual Ego Manifestor (Figure 2.5). I have the 1st Gate. I do not have the 8th Gate. Yet when I sleep, when I am in my deepest state of sleep, I have this whole channel, the 8/1 (Figure 2.6). It is clear to me in my own process that my Contribution has been dictated to bring Light to the Darkness and to show people how the mechanics work, etc. But the interesting thing about seeing it as an ongoing sleep program is that I see that I am not somebody who has easy access to dreams. I do not. In this active sleep program, I am constantly being renewed in the programming that says, "Make your Contribution to bring Light to the Darkness." And, what fascinates me about the whole dream process is how we are given our marching orders while we sleep. Of course, that can create a deep conflict with the way we live out our conscious awake life.

When we get into the conscious awake realm, we get into a realm where there is relative responsibility, i.e., we are here to be aware. And, of course, we see how disturbed that realm actually is. It does not matter how correct your programming may be in the sleep state. Remember that in the sleep state, you are absolutely innocent. Remember that in the deepest stage of sleep, in Delta sleep, we are about as unconscious to the world as we can be and still be healthy. At that time, you are receiving your deepest layer of the archetypal program. You are not connected to the program the way you are when awake. At the same time, how you live in your waking state makes an enormous difference in whether or not you are comfortable with what takes place in your dream life.

I have Definitions in the Identity/Self (G) Center and the Throat Center in my Waking Rave Charts. These definitions change in the Matrices, i.e., I have Channel 8/1 in the DreamRave, whereas I have Channel 10/20 in the Waking Rave. I have both of these Centers Defined in my Rave Design Charts.

The Channel 8-1 is an Alpha. In other words, it fulfills the same thing that the mammalian Channel 8-1 fulfills. For example, if you have a group of wild dogs, the dog carrying the Channel 8-1, is the dog who is ultimately going to be the Alpha. That Dog provides the Direction for the others by making a selfish Contribution. That Dog is driven to make a Contribution that expresses the direction itself. So, of course, if you have Channel 8-1 as a program while you are asleep, you wake up with this sense of needing to make a Contribution, needing to act in order for others to follow, in order for others to see you.

Each Matrix in the Design Field has its process. After all, not everyone has the same kind of mix across the Matrices that represent different states of consciousness. Not everyone has a Definition from one Matrix to another. The definition in the DreamRave is not very common. It is a 15-gate Matrix, and it is a very different consciousness than the 64-gate Waking Matrix. The 64-Gate Matrix, with its neocortex, Heart (Ego) Center, and Solar Plexus Center, shows us what it is to be human.

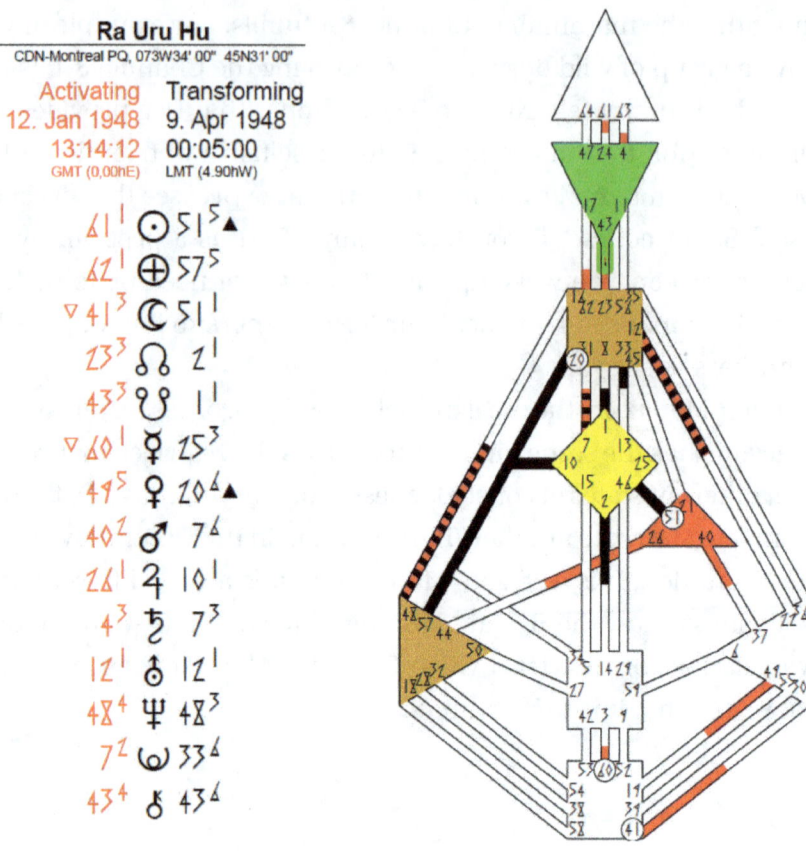

Figure 2.5: Ra Uru Hu's Human Design Chart

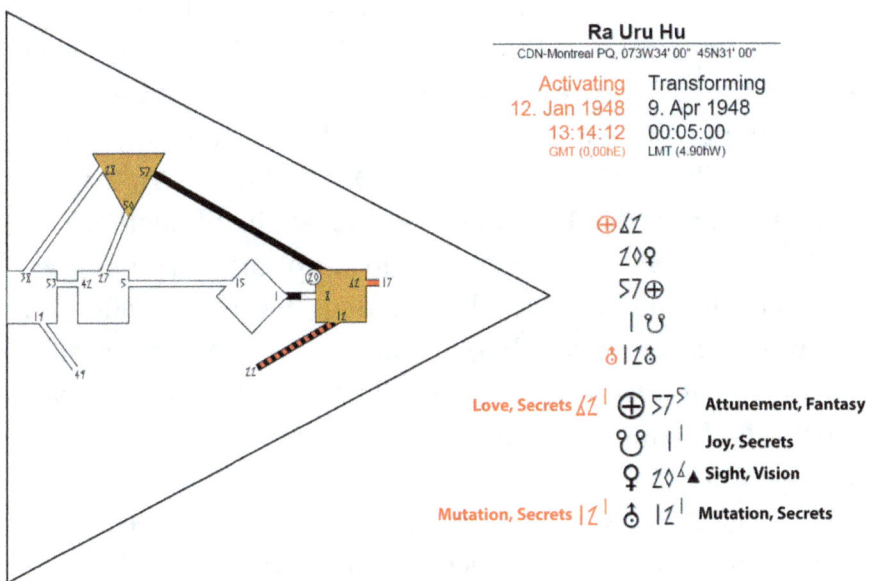

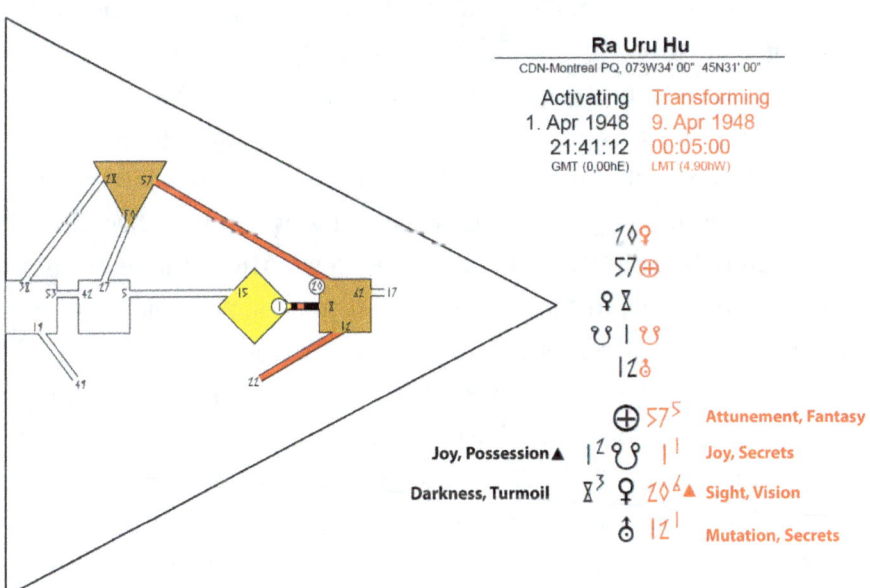

Figure 2.6: Ra Uru Hu's Solar and Lunar Dream Design Charts

In the DreamRaves, many more Gates are generally open than Activated or Defined, and the real nuances are actually in Gates that are different across the Matrices. Whole channels being different bring differences at a more gross level. When you look at this material in the way I'm describing it, note these kinds of differences. All four of those Gates are Defined in the Triple Design Matrix, so I have the Gates 20 and the Gate 57 in this Matrix. There is deep programming that goes on inside of me while I'm asleep which pushes me in a specific Direction. The real Direction is in my Waking Rave, where I have Channel 20-57. The primary difference is in how I can make an Individual Contribution, and that is what the DreamRaves point me to. It pulls me into dealing with the Darkness.

It's very important to always remember that the DreamRaves are not personal. When we look at the Triple Design Matrix in terms of the mammalian design, a Channel 8-1 animal would be an Alpha and would set direction, but it is much easier in many ways in an animal to see that it is not personal than it is in a human. When humans wake up in the morning, they immediately put their dreams through their personality filter, and they think that they have something to do with their dreams. The personality really doesn't create dreams (Ed. Note: The additional DreamRave calculation, which completes the Quadruple Design Matrix, actually has the information about what is being filtered through the personality layer of the Matrix and relates to the actual content of the Dreams. Thus, in this calculation, it may be possible to understand the why and what of the content of the dreams). [Since this was written in 2001, the work with the Quadruple Design Matrix became work with Prenatal, Natal, and Postnatal calculations. The eight calculations of the basic Matrices in the Four Worlds form Noble Energy Maps®, and when seen as an Integrated Body Map, show how a person functions and how the Worlds flow one into the other. This work, hypothesized by myself and Ra in 2001, has been scientifically validated on multiple levels.]

The most dangerous thing about being human is the very gift that makes us human, i.e., making up reasons. You spend most of your life making up reasons in order to get to a point where you do not have to make up reasons anymore. Of course, we always make up reasons; we make up reasons for everything. You wake up in the morning; it's not just "wake up in the morning." Right now, inside your head, the thought processes are moving through, and you make up a reason why they are there. You have no control over what is processed through you, none of us do. We make up reasons all the time for why a particular thought is in our head. Many people suffer from terrible mental anxiety in their lives. They suffer from terrible mental anxiety, and they have, for example, the 47th Gate or the 64th Gate; they are confused. The past haunts them. They awake in the morning with a buzz going by. They have all this information about something that happened yesterday, the year before, or the year before that. Now, it wasn't up to them for that to come through, and they did not pull it out. There is no reason. There is also no reason for going up and down on an emotional wave or for being melancholic as an individual. There is no reason. It is just passing through. But, in fact, we immediately make up a reason for everything: "I'm thinking about that, that means that I have to resolve that. It means that I have a chance to resolve that; otherwise, I wouldn't be thinking about it. And I'm thinking about it because there must be something in it that I need to know, need to fix." This is what the mind of human beings does.

> The dynamic interactions of the Four Matrices, when integrated with the Kabbalistic Tree of Life, address in the Paths of Intelligence the kinds of initiatory processes that are part of your process of Individuation or your path to Self-Actualization. The Tree of Life describes the process as a developmental process of conscious growth. Right thinking and discerning Mental processes are part of an early Path of Intelligence and relate to the Splenic Center awareness

> that anchors us along with the Sacral Center in our Spiritual Core. Ra's understanding of the way the Mind functions was unsophisticated and he did not account for the Emotional/Angelic Matrix although he knew from the Voice that it existed. I was given that Matrix and have validated its reliability across several fields. This Emotional/Angelic Matrix operates primarily on the Splenic side of the Body Map and carries a Portal to the Spiritual World. The Ajna and Crown in the Emotional/Angelic Matrix function to bring higher frequency thinking to consciousness in the service of transforming Mental World physical experiences into Spiritual awareness.

When you wake up in the morning with energy or direction inside you, the human tendency is to make up a reason for why it is there. When we do that, when we make an attachment like that, when we put a reason onto anything, we enter deep danger. That is when we are open to depression. That is when we are open to really crashing.

[Ed. Note: The DreamRave is unconscious in the sense that it has no direct conscious access to the personality. However, through the research of Rave Life Sciences, we know that the material programmed in the DreamRave is, in a sense, downloaded to the neurological mechanisms of the person during REM, and it is then accessible to them indirectly through that. In fact, that is what the general term "unconscious" means].

DreamRaves are unconscious in their deepest sense. It is the access to the personality and to the source of archetypal information that we now can begin to understand.

In my design, I wake up having had Channel 8-1 Defined all night. That impulse is deep inside me at a cellular level. Then, however, that impulse acts out in my life through my Waking Rave Design. Because it cannot go through Channel 8-1 anymore since Channel 8-1 is not there in my Waking Rave; when I get up in the morning when I jump up and into my vertical place, Channel 8-1 is not present. I have to work it out according to my Design, and according to my Type. We hypothesize that many sleep disturbances result from the consequences of the sleep state affecting the waking life because the Conscious being may not integrate the information well. It is possible that most of the integration has to do with Type. When I get up, I come back into my Type, and as long as I honor my Type, I am living out who I truly am. In my Design, Channel 8-1 will have to express itself through Gate 20, but, as a result of my Dream Design, it will be expressed in a different way than in someone else's Design. It will go back to my nature in that sense, but its expression will be correct because I am following the Design pattern.

> Ra did not have the Noble Energy Maps® Integrated Design when we worked together. Ra was incorrect in thinking that our Four World Matrices stop functioning when we awake in the morning. All Channels, Gates, and Centers are active in everyone all the time. If you consider a Reflector in the Basic Human Design, that person would according to what Ra said be a deeply disrupted person energetically. I have worked with very dynamic individuals whose basic Human Design Type was as a Reflector. Type is a predisposition, NOT a compelling way of being. Using your Higher Spiritual Mind is essential as an early initiation into conscious living. You must pass through this Path of Intelligence that teaches you to trust your Spirit over your Mental World experiences and constructs. Ra did not integrate the information from the Tree of Life into Human Design. In dealing with the Dream World, such integration and synthesis is essential.

That is why it is so critical to integrate the three Designs in the Triple Matrix. You cannot just look at any single one of them and make an assumption; you have to look at them in relationship to each other and to the whole person. For us to really look at the whole human process, we have to see very, very clearly that these three different matrices are always there for us at one level or another, and we are always dealing with them. It is like your computer: it has a hard drive that stores the information and uses many underlying codes to run the programs, none of which is actively in your awareness when you type into the computer. Your Waking Rave Design is akin to visible information on the computer. Now, all of it falls within the larger Body Graph, obviously. The strategies for us, and what actually keeps us healthy, depends on your Design.

In terms of doing what we are here to do in RLS, which is finding ways to heal people and help people with this knowledge, we are going see that many problems are about not being able to move from one matrix to the other or to integrate the information across matrices. That is the big issue. It is akin to a glitch in the hard drive of the computer. [Ra knew we needed to expand and integrate the Matrices. Now, in 2024, the integrated information is available through my work.]

This concept can begin to explain why one person might have an easier time than another person. If someone's Waking Rave is completely congruent, i.e., with no differential activations, with the DreamRaves, that is a very different kind of demand for integration than someone whose DreamRave has many activations that do not remain when they come back into the waking state. The tasks of individuals and how they can understand themselves will be very different depending on the DreamRaves.

Looking again at Channel 20-57, note that the 57th Gate is the only awareness Gate in the Design. The 57th Gate is a very complex awareness Gate because, of course, in Design, it opens up to the Integration Channels, i.e., the Gates 57, 34, 10, and 20. These Integration Gates make up a very complex four-gate inner system. In terms of Design, Integration is really the backbone of what it is to be human. It is our archetype to be able to survive, to follow our convictions, and ultimately to be ourselves in the now, which is the basis of what integration is about.

Within Gate 57 resides the deepest Fear that operates in mammalian life. The Fear of Gate 57 is the Fear of Tomorrow, the Fear of the Unknowable. In human beings, this fear drives us to know; it drives us to become the intelligent species we are. However, when you look at Gate 57 in the dream state, it changes. There Gate 57 is about being given information in order to attune to what is ahead. All of that attunement is Acoustic.

A very important thing about the Light Field is how it is impacted by the external sounds around it. For example, sleep disturbance in someone with many Light Field activations happens very easily if they are uncomfortable or hear disturbing sounds around. For example, in my Design, I have all four of those Gates in Definition in my dream state. I am someone who needs absolute silence in order to sleep. Without silence, it is very difficult for me. I am a pure individual. Thus, I am very sensitive to acoustics, making silence essential. The Light Field is disturbed by external sounds. With the Light Field activated, if you were to live on a busy street where the traffic never stopped, you might get into the sound flow, and it might be all right; it might not disturb you. But, if you are in an environment where someone drops their shoe, for instance, you would always wait for the unpredictable and proverbial shoe to drop; in that situation, with Light Field activations, you can be quite disturbed because of the acoustics.

The 20th Gate in the DreamRaves is Keynoted: Sight. The 20th Gate is the only purely existential Gate. In fact, the Light Field itself relates to getting very Now information. When I say, "now information," the Demon Realm does not relate that way. The Demon Realm brings you different kinds of information; in terms of the way we understand time, it may be the future time; it may be the past time.

People who have an experience of seeing the future, or people who experience things from the past, are receiving information that comes from the Form Realm. It comes from the Demon Realm. Here, in the Light Realm, the whole theme is to be right there, to be in the moment. Being in the Now can induce a very beautiful kind of sleep because a very deep restful sleep is congruent with the very existential state of being in the dream state itself. In other words, you are surrendered into that state. In that surrendered moment, many things are possible.

The 20th Gate is a Manifesting Gate. It is a Throat Center Gate. In the Throat Center, in the DreamRave, there is only one Gate in the Earth Plane, the 12th Gate. The other three Gates in the Throat Center in the DreamRave are Gates of the Light Field, the 62nd Gate, the 20th Gate, and the 8th Gate. Those three Gates are actually in the Throat Center. Now, that tells you something about the sleeper talking. We are going to find that people who talk in their sleep, people who say things in their sleep, are operating out of Throat Center Gates. [This information has not been documented.]

Ultimately, what you will be able to work with is the impact of transits on the Triple Design Matrix. Transits affect people while they are asleep. Think about somebody who does not have the 20th Gate in their Waking Rave Design, but the DreamRave has the 57th Gate without the 20th Gate. When they get into a deep sleep, their Lunar DreamRave suddenly activates the 20th Gate (or there could be a transit Activating in the 20th Gate). In other words, all of a sudden, they can have a disturbed night can be talking in their sleep; all of a sudden, their partner says to them, "Wow, that was strange last night. You were talking in your sleep." In other words, through that kind of data, we can see the many varied ways we are impacted in waking and sleeping states. Through the 20th Gate of Sight and the 62nd Gate of Love, things can be said in the dream that is very profound. In other words, they can be – I always have to be careful with such terms because people get carried away – they can be "revolutionary." They can express something very, very unusual. You can suddenly wake up with a mantra or a phrase or a concept or whatever the case may be, but, of course, that is one of the byproducts of the Light Field.

Apropos of the Transits, you can study them for yourselves through the Neutrino Through Windows Rave Life Sciences Module. In beginning to work with this material over the last six or eight months, I have noted some correspondence with Jungian dream analysis theory, with which most of you are fairly familiar. Jung mapped out four different kinds of dreams that relate very clearly to the activations of Transits in the DreamRave. We all come from a psychological background in this culture where dream interpretation has been made very personal. In terms of both the personal and the collective unconscious, when you begin to look at the DreamRave and how the Transits affect it, with the Solar and the Lunar and the Waking Raves, you can begin to see that with the dream theory Freud and Jung were really on the right track in terms of the structure and content, but they did not know that it wasn't personal. So, when you begin to take some of what they said in terms of the kinds of dreams, and you look at the Transits, you can see why somebody would have a compensatory dream or why someone would have a dream that is forecasting something. These could be processing something that is happening on the other side of the planet, and you begin to see those aspects in action both in real-time and in the archetypal realm.

In other words, what you are really seeing is the way the process works. After all, we live in a diverse binary environment; we are a binary ourselves. So, what you are looking at through these three different divisions is the basic binary, that is, the Light and the Dark, the yang and the yin. We get yang programming from the Light Field. We get yin programming from the Demon Realm. Then, we integrate them into the Tao. We integrate it all so all of us are always in tune with the Collective Consciousness through the Earth Plane. There is the drama of all of those people who are awake while we are asleep, and we take in all of that drama. But, of course, that is essential. As a matter of fact, we duplicate that on the surface as best we can with television and satellite and the web and all of these things in order to be connected to the collective consciousness; so, here with the Earth Plane, we have the Integrative field, the truly Integrative field.

The 62nd Gate, the Portal Gate in the Light Field, is the Gate of Love. In a mammal, Gate 62 is a very significant Gate. The 62nd

Gate: The Preponderance of the Small is a Gate of Detail. Of course, in a human being, this is the reasonable or unreasonable voice of Detail. Its voice expresses the logical process. One of the basic interrelationships between humans and mammals is a relationship in which we organize them by opening up their intelligence by teaching them patterns. In other words, a human being who has the 17th Gate can integrate with a mammal who has the 62nd Gate. Together, the 17th Gate teaches new Details and new things that can be learned until an old dog has no more time for new tricks.

The 62nd Gate of Love opens up to the most mysterious and mystical of possibilities. That Portal opens up to all kinds of different "opinions." It opens up all the different kinds of inspirational or conceptual information possibilities. In other words, if you anthropomorphize this energy, you can talk about it being someone you meet in your dream who tells you something very profound; it can become an encounter that you have with information that is outside of what you normally feel like you could get access to, all of that is possible there. However, one must beware of the Light Field. Just because it has a nice name does not mean that the information that you receive is of value to you. It does not mean it is true for you because it is not personal. In other words, you have to be very careful about the way you take in that information.

Human beings would be a lot better off if they never remembered their dreams; you do not remember your dreams the way you live them. Because you do not remember your dreams or gain access to your dreams in the way that you actually live them (you move from a 15 Gate to a 64 Gate Matrix), you do not really have any connection to the truth of the Dreams, and you can become very confused. You see, in order for us to actually be successful at the Dream Realm or in the Dream Plane, we need to allow it to happen, which is true of life anyway. If we allow it to happen, it's a lot better. But we have to be careful about the information we receive.

Think about somebody who has the 17th Gate in their Waking Rave Design but does not have the 62nd Gate. Think about this person. What this person has is opinions without Detail. Remember that is Opinion without Detail. I know many people who have the 17th Gate. I had a wonderful experience for years of touring with a person who had Gate 17.

The person with Gate 17 would say to me the night before, "Ra, we'll be ready to leave at 9:30." I'm tolerant. I'm willing to wait and see. And, of course, 9:30 would come, and I would be ready; my bags were packed. I was done. I sat there waiting. And, of course, the person with Gate 17 was not ready. This person's concept of time was distorted. It was not like they misled me intentionally; they would really have liked to be ready at 9:30. Not only that, they thought they were going to be ready at 9:30, but they were not ready. Some of the most unreasonably logical people are people who have the 17th Gate without the 62nd Gate; they really think that they have the Detail when they do not. All they have is an Opinion. [There is no substantiation for what Ra hypothesized about someone with Gate 17 having opinions and no details. Studies have not tested this hypothesis and since most of the specifics for the behavior of someone with a specific Gate has not held statistically, concluding such as Ra did here could be disempowering for a person with Gate 17.]

One has to be careful about the opinions one receives, particularly if that opinion is glossed in powerful illusion as you translate it through the dream state. Nevertheless, Gate 62 is a Portal to very interesting things that can then be spoken. What is so interesting about the Demon Realm is that the Demon Realm is the most difficult to bring out and to express because it has no natural voice in the Throat Center; consequently, it is very hard for the Demon Realm to find expression for itself.

When you look at the Light Field, there is a real joke in it. The Light Field is very powerful. You have the Identity/Self (G) Center connection to the Throat Center, and you have the Splenic Center connection to the Throat Center, but there is no Motor/Fuel Center involved. In other words, one of the jokes about what happens to us in our programming in the Light Field is that we receive programming by this "stuff," but that doesn't mean we can do anything about it. It brings us things to process, but we cannot actualize them because the Light Field has no direct connection to a Motor/Fuel Center. When you get to the Earth Plane, you get Generator power. Earth Plane activation is a very different kind of dream state activation than Light Field activation.

We also see physical vibration during sleep through the DreamRaves. Restlessness, in a simple way, probably connects to the energy Types. Their sleep may be very different than, for example, the sleep of someone who has the Light Field Gates only and is, thus, sleeping in a Projector Field. With a Projector Field, it means that in the Light Field, you can be recognized; you can have that kind of contact. It also means that you may wake up with a bitter taste in your mouth if that recognition did not take place. A Projector Field is energy-starved. [Ra's statements about Projectors being energy-starved have not been substantiated. Many Projectors are healers and channel energy. Consciousness and where you are in your Individuation process carry more weight psychologically than any specific Gate or Channel in your Body Graph. If a Projector knows that they are energy sensitive, they can use their sensitivity to maximize their perceptiveness and use it appropriately. Use Ra's blanket statements with careful discernment in each individual case.]

One of the important things for Projectors is that they do not sleep in a bed with somebody who turns them into a Generator. Everybody knows, at least those people who have ever had a reading with me, that I have told face-to-face thousands of people, couples, everybody that I can, "Don't sleep with your partner.

Give us all a break. Sleep in your own room. Sleep in your own space. It's not about love, and it's not about sex. When you begin to understand the DreamRave, you have to recognize how disturbing that is to have somebody in your aura while you are sleeping, changing the way in which the whole dream programming takes place in your body.

[Ed. Note: Ra has stated repeatedly that it is essential for people to sleep alone; research at RLS has not found this statement to bear up clinically or experientially. Eleanor and Marvin have found, medically and psychologically, especially with the research on the Triple Design Matrix, with its varied activations through the different Matrices of the SDR and Components in the combined TDM, that, in fact, it may serve well for certain people to sleep in their mutually combined auras. In addition, because dogs and cats function in the Mammalian Matrix, tuning their Humans into the Spiritual/Archetypal World, I recommend that you keep your pets with you when you sleep and meditate. They enhance your Spiritual/Archetypal connections.]

There is a time for us to socialize. There is a time for us to integrate in terms of the cycle of a day, and there are times not to socialize. We are, in this phase of our evolution, in this phase of our program, designed to be in the illusion of separateness because it is absolutely essential. In other words, each and every one of us needs to come to grips with our uniqueness. At the same time, we may need to make our own unique contribution. The sleep state is something that is so important for us because it is not personal. It is a way in which, as we expand this knowledge, we are going to be able to see a sense of our purpose and recognize how beautiful that state is (Eleanor has already documented that life's purpose can be read through the Triple Design Matrix). It is our contribution within that totality. That is what is necessary for all of us in this process. We are a collective species that needs to learn from each other in all of these things. We have to go through all of these processes. When you are asleep, you are so vulnerable; you are there to be in one of the most beautiful states you have in life.

The conscious life for most people, i.e., being awake in a body, is really an ordeal. They carry a burden and their problems, and they are not living out their natures; they are dealing with conditioning. When you go to sleep you really get back into why you are here and into the beauty of why you are here, to make your own unique contribution. It isn't about love, and it's not like you need that person beside you while you are unconscious, it's none of those things. I know that many people can feel rejection in that. They can feel like they are not wanted whatever the case may be. There are all kinds of stories people come up with. But it is an essential ingredient to be healthy in life. I mean, it is just essential. It is not a rule that cannot be broken. That's the other thing. It's not about the rigidity. It is about understanding as a principle, what is correct for you. It may, in fact, be beneficial for you when it is a natural byproduct of the intimacy in your life to end up spending a night with somebody and to have that, whatever that combination is, have an impact. But it is not about that being the way it should be it is very unhealthy for us (Ed. Note: This viewpoint represents Ra's view and not the view of Rave Life Sciences or its scientific research to date).

Understand our evolution. You can still see it alive in the world; go to the subcontinent, go to India, go see the way people are crammed together in their environment, and recognize that as one of the ways in which we are moving. The integrity of individual space is the greatest byproduct of wealth. There is nothing more extraordinary that has taken place than to see how many human beings now on the earth have the sanctity of their own environment where they do not have to live in a crowded space. The idea is that that is for the intimate part of your cycle each day, for the part of your cycle in which you are not consciously connected to what is going on around you, to have your aura protected. That is your right. Most people feel better when they awake in the morning, having been in their own protected space.

Real knowledge is not knowledge that says, "Here it is, go do it." It does not work that way. This is just information. We can describe to you your Type. We can tell you what the strategy is. You can recognize the Type and strategy intellectually and recognize that it is interesting and that it may, in fact, be of value to you. That does not mean you live it. It is one of the things about awareness. You have to be attuned to your strategy in order to take advantage of those moments where it is possible for you to taste the advantage of the strategy. If you are a Generator, you must find out what that is like to deal only with response in order to really see what you are in order to become healthy. Any disturbance that you have as a byproduct of, for example, not enjoying sleep is because you are not enjoying life. It is in your life itself, your waking life; you can fix that by simply being what you are. It is difficult for adults. I understand that. I know how deep the conditioning is. Yet, at the same time, the strategy is easy enough to follow. Each Type has an easy strategy. It is the miracle of what we have come to with this knowledge.

We just have the latest statistics, actually, the first really serious statistics. When you look at Type and when you look at the significance of Type, it is just extraordinary. There is very little difference in frequency of occurrence between the Manifesting Generator and the Generator statistically. All of the qualities of Type seem to stand up statistically. That means that Type is a mechanical aspect of being, it really is the real thing. If you follow the strategy of that, all of the things that we are talking about do not matter because it is for the deepening of intellectual understanding. We cannot change our structural energy Type. What it is to be a healthy human being starts with living your Type across the three Matrices, and then things in life change. They all change.

> At the time Ra and I taught this class, I had not yet done the calculations for the Emotional/Angelic Solar Minute or the Physical/Biological Lunar Minute Sleep Design Matrix, and I had not included the postnatal calculations. Each World's Body Graph shows a critical time in a baby's first three months of life when cosmic energies had a significant impact on their consciousness. Because I am a highly trained astrologer, I was able to use specific calculations to differentiate dream or REM sleep from a deep dreamless sleep. The calculations I used produced charts that exactly hit critical times in a baby's

> development and further documented that Ra was in error in his statement of "No Choice." At three months of age, babies begin to exert their preferences and make choices about toys to reach for, people to be held by, and toys that intrigue them.

The Demon Realm

The Demon Realm is very different. In the Demon Realm, you have Channel 28-38, in Design terms, it is the Channel of Struggle. In mammals, this is where you have the deepest Aggressiveness and the deepest Fierceness of the mammal because, of course, this is where the awareness that life is a Struggle originates. Channel 28-38 is about the trials and tribulations of dealing with life itself. Channel 53-42 is the Format Energy that operates between the Root Center and the Sacral Center. We are looking at a very different realm here than with the other divisions; we are looking at a Generating Realm. We are looking at an adrenalized Generating Realm with a deep connection to the Splenic System. It has, like the Light Field, a potential for spontaneous existential awareness.

The Portal Gate in the Demon Realm is the 19th Gate, and I will wait until I get there. It is very important to understand that the 19th Gate, like all Portal Gates, gives a general quality to its division in the Matrix. The Environment, in the sense of Territory, is one of the basic qualities of the Demon Realm. For example, the Demon Realm dream is often a dream full of rooms or places that you are in or approaching with doors that you are opening. It focuses on the Environment. Often, the Environment itself creates a great deal of potential fear, fear that one can be threatened. When you are in the Light Field, nothing in the Dream Realm appears to be threatening. Even though it can be threatening, there is no appearance of a threat. Yet, the moment you are in the Demon Realm, almost anything can be a threat. Just the fact that you are in some kind of strange room can instantaneously feel threatening. The Demon Realm always pulls you into your Form. It always pulls you into the dynamics of staying alive. Staying alive is the major theme of the Demon Realm.

The 38th Gate

The 38th Gate is Root Center Energy. It is a Gate of Opposition, Fighting, Fierceness, and Aggressiveness. It is the readiness for Aggression to achieve purpose. Yet, it cannot achieve purpose without confronting Fear. In other words, the Aggression of Gate 38 prepares one for dealing with Fear to achieve its purpose, which is ultimately Survival.

Channel 53-42, as a Format Energy, represents the Cyclical way. It is the only Format Energy in the Mammalian Design, and, thus, it is the only Format Energy of the DreamRaves. The Dream itself is Cyclical as a process. We cycle through our Dreams; we cycle through the various states of consciousness; we cycle through the day. All Cycles are part of Channel 53-42. Those of you who know basic design know that it is Channel 53-42 that establishes as a Format what we call our human experiential process, our unique evolutionary way. It is all Cyclical. And to begin the process, we deal with this basic aggression for survival.

If you have Gate 38 in your DreamRave, you might wake up in the morning feeling a heightened preparedness for no particular reason. You might wake up in the morning ready to Fight, yet there may be nothing to fight, and you may have no idea why you feel that kind of "ready to struggle" energy when you wake up. Again, it is one of those things that, if personalized, creates real trouble because it is not personal; just allow that energy to move through you because you can just live out your day according to the principles of your strategy. If you resist the way you come awake in the morning, you feel discomfort, e.g., many Demon Realm people resist the way they awake in the morning because they feel heavy, so they get up in the morning not wanting to feel they have to confront something. They may want to resist those feelings instead of recognizing that the feeling is natural for them in awakening. It is natural for them to come into the day ready with that kind of energy because it is the equipment that they will need during the course of that day.

The 38th Gate serves as the foundation for establishing the deepest possible thinking or knowing in any Form. Of course, mammals do not think, at least not in the way that we interpret thinking. But, the 38th Gate begins a process that ultimately ends up in humans in the 61st Gate, i.e., the need to know and the need to find inner truth. So, one of the things about the prompting of the Demon Realm is that the Demon Realm frightens you because of your ignorance. You will see about the Demon Realm and its impact on your life that the more grounded you are in your life process, the more equipped you feel, the more comfortable you are with the things that you have to do, the less impact the Demon Realm will have on your waking state. (Ed. Note: Since we now know that the synthesis of the Waking Rave, the Solar DreamRave, and the Lunar DreamRave in the REM state is crucial, it is also important to look at the influence of the Demon Realm in terms of activations that are present or absent from one realm to the other. When, for example, an individual has Gate 38 in the Lunar DreamRave but not in the other Designs, Gate 38 has a different impact than if it is always present and is, thus, an energy that is consistent in all designs).

The 28th Gate

The 28th Gate is the Gate of Fear. It is one of those very healthy fears. Of course, it does bring the potential of paranoia in the waking state. The Fear of Gate 28 keeps us alert. It is acoustic since it deals with individuality. One of the most frightening things for people in these dreams that come through Gate 28 are sounds in the dream itself. In other words, they hear a strange sound. This is often the moment they awake, and they actually think the sound is on the outside and that it is something in the outside environment that has awakened them. It is actually a sound on the inside that has awakened them.

Channel 28-38 is about heightened Alertness for Survival and about the defense mechanisms to be ready to deal with Survival and to be ready to Fight. People with Channel 28-38 activated can wake up very startled. Often, what happens to people who have that Channel is that before they go to sleep, they begin to have the Fear that they are going to be startled again, that they are going to have to meet that again, and that leads to all kinds of processes. If it is built into your design, you are going to meet it again. You are not going to be able to escape it. And the moment that you make it personal and say, "I've got a problem," and the moment somebody says, "Ah, yes, we know what this means," then you are really in trouble because it is not personal.

It is so important for us to grasp that dream content is not personal. Then, we can begin to see that what moves through us is archetypal programming energy and that it is highly generalized. Many of us process a specific Gate every night. We bring that formula, that information, into the waking world. And, of course, we bring that information into the world innocently. That is the beauty of it. The moment that we personalize it, we start interfering with our waking life, and our waking life is disturbed enough as it is. So, we really have to see that the basis of Human Design is living your Type. Everything else flows naturally out of that. I think research will show that many disturbances can be dispelled and dealt with by living your Type.

> I am currently documenting that the structure of the Four World Matrices, and the way energy flows through them has ramifications for physical/biological health. It is not just Type in the Mental World that determines who you are and your strategy. During the first three months of your life, you continued to be impacted by cosmic energy as you were in utero in the last three months of your gestation. When you were three months old you began to reach for objects and show preferences for things. At this time, you functioned as an Integrated being and all Worlds began to function in an integrated way in

> you. At three months of age, you knew who you were internally and began to have a sense of Self.

The Channel 53-42

The 53rd Gate is the Gate of Flight. In a mammal, this is the Gate of Freedom. This Gate carries the need to begin things, to start things. In my work in analysis, I remind people that one of the healthiest things to have in this life is the ability to be able to make clear decisions. Clear decisions are very important. Once you know your Type, and once you recognize your Authority or how you operate, then you can make clear decisions. Somebody who has the 53rd Gate, particularly the 53rd Gate, in their Lunar DreamRave, but who does not have the 53rd Gate in their Solar DreamRave, may be the kind of person who wakes up in the morning and says, "I've had enough with that. Today's the day that I start this," and this person will not know why that statement emerged. Such an event can be very, very disturbing because the 53rd Gate alone is always about the need to start something new. It is always about feeling trapped when you are in something old. It is always this sense that you cannot get out of something, and it can lead to a lot of depression. The 53rd Gate can cause someone to be very depressed; it creates a feeling of being locked in with no way out. These are prison dreams, dreams where you are trapped, dreams where people pull you back and hold you back; they are dreams in which you cannot get away and in which you cannot start something new.

> My research since 2001 has not shown that people with Gate 53 tend toward depression. These statements by Ra are unvalidated.

The 42nd Gate

The 42nd Gate, the Gate of Completion, is the Gate that brings processes fully through. This is the Gate of Dying. The Demon

Realm relates to facing things. It is about seeing that things are just shapes and objects; it is about seeing that they are just the room, the ground, and it is enough for us simply to be able to accept the patterns. I was given three different patterns. There are many ways that death operates in a human being. Natural death, i.e., what we call natural death, begins in the dream state. It actually starts there and goes through a specific lunar cycle in which certain Gates act as keys and can be turned on or off until the process is complete. The 42nd Gate is part of this process. It is part of the process of bringing death into our lives.

Dreams with Gate 42 activations are the kinds of dreams people are most haunted by because they bring dead people back to you. Suddenly your dead mother appears. I've had the experience where my dead father suddenly appeared in my dream. Gate 42 can bring those patterns back to you. It also always brings you to the acceptance of finality, the acceptance of transits; it brings the fact that these patterns are there and that we have to deal with them. Of course, that's a very heavy place for many people who awake to that place. They have this sense of dread, this fear of the trap of being in the box, or they may awake reveling in exactly the opposite. In the opposite feeling, they may say, "Whew, I'm glad I'm in the world with the sky and the sun and everything else;" of course, others can be very depressed by having those kinds of dreams, very depressed by having to meet continual closure all the time. Most important of all, Gate 42 dreams are about the integrity of your Form. These dreams tell you whether or not you are in the right place.

The Demon Realm needs to have a secure Environment. The Demon Realm needs to be clear that the Territory, your Territory, according to the program, is absolutely correct; in other words, that you operate correctly in the whole. What the Demon Realm tries to do is to give us this basic Form programming. Basic Form programming is that we need things, we go after those things, we get the food we need, we have partners, it is the dream realm that insists that we have God in our life, it insists that we have a partner, it insists that we have children and marriage and all of those things, and it is all being programmed by the Demon Realm so that we can stay in the Form principle.

The 19th Gate

The significance of the 19th Gate, the Portal Gate of the Demon Realm, is very important. The 19th Gate is very important for us in establishing basically what our needs are. Those needs go from the very mundane, i.e., the 19th Gate is the need for Territory, i.e., the need to have Territory; the need to have Resources; the need to have access to a partner; the need to have something larger than yourself, whether that be community or ultimately God; also, a deep understanding or capacity to recognize the spirit of life in other Forms. That pressure begins with the 19th Gate, the Gate of Approach. Animism is rooted in Gate 19. The 49th Gate is at the other end of Gate 19. Channel 19-49 is a Cross-Species Channel when it comes to animals and mammals. Human beings have the potential, obviously, of having the whole channel, of having the 49th Gate, a Gate that the mammal cannot have, and, thus, the mammal can only receive that Gate or have access to that Gate through its connection with a human. The 49th Gate is the Gate of Revolution. Gate 49 is the Gate of Establishing Principles. There is an irony in that because it is emotional, those principles are riding a wave of hope to pain. In sexuality, it is the Gate of Marriage and Divorce. It is the place through which we establish who we accept and who we reject.

| This statement of Ra's is not validated.

In terms of the relationship between humans and animals, it is through the 49th Gate and the 19th Gate that human beings were able to coordinate and bring together their live food resources; our ability to husband animals allowed humans as a species to eventually get to the point of breeding animals, of taming them, of keeping them in the backyard; all of those aspects allowed humans to know that when winter comes the animals are there and available so nobody has to go hungry.

Think of the bargain existing between Gate 49 and Gate 19; it is a fascinating bargain; everything about the tribe is a bargain. Gate 49 always promises the animal with Gate 19 the sanctity of Territory and the presence of Food Resources. It is the only way you get an animal to surrender its independence in those things. We establish a Territory; we put the sheep in a pen or a valley, whatever the case may be, and we make sure there is enough food so they are secure. We control them. In the Channel 19-49 are many different facets.

Because of that role, the 49th Gate creates and offers the Territory and food, but it can also result in the Sacrifice of that animal. At some point, the 49th Gate human selects which animal is to be slaughtered. That action is the beginning of a spiritual process in humanity. Anybody who has ever dealt with a mammal at any level of intimacy recognizes right away that there is something intrinsically conscious in animals. We make contact with the animal's Personality Crystal. In the moment of sacrificing an animal so that you can live, there is also the recognition that you are taking a life. One of the earliest things we did as humans was to celebrate the various animals that we conquered and that we ultimately ate. We put the cow and the sheep in the zodiac. Those kinds of things that we exalt, we turn into gods and godheads. We design idols to look like them. Such actions show the basis of our spirituality.

With the 19th Gate in the Demon Realm, you see also that, in the dream state, one of the things driving us is that we must find a Territory in which we fit and that place must provide us with the basic things we need. We need food, reasonable access to sexuality, and shelter. Those three things are intrinsic to the 19th Gate. One of the pressures we feel when we wake up from the Demon Realm is to be well-integrated into our community. If we are not well-integrated into our society, we may feel very uncomfortable. You wake up with the need to integrate into your community, to be able to have both your own Territory and to be able to see that Resources are available. At the same time, you need to feel secure so you can meet the other. Everything relating to the 19th Gate is about our neediness.

> None of Ra's statements about specific mindsets for specific Gates or about diseases associated with specific Gates held up to statistical analysis. Several diseases were tested in my Statistical analysis on 30,000 cases. For example, neediness may not be reliably predicted in Gate 19. All personality characteristics are multifactorial and should be handled as such.

Dreams of Gate 19 are dreams that become material tensions; we feel, for example, the material tension of waking up in the morning wondering whether or not there will be enough food in the refrigerator, whether there will be enough money in the bank account, whether there will be all of those things that are absolutely necessary for survival, and those tensions create pressure.

Remember, the pressure comes from the Light Field because it is the only Field that functions as a non-energy part of the Matrix. The Light Field is only projected. It, thus, does not have the same influence over the waking life as the Demon Realm, which has the Motors of the Dream Matrices. The projected element drives you in your dream and has to be recognized in your waking life. But when you deal with the Demon Realm, you deal with a very powerful generating mechanism that is really there to insist that you deal with the material realm. After all, the only place where human beings are uncomfortable is with their material realm, whether it is their body, food, money, or job. The discomforts are all caught up in the same material dimension.

A fascinating nature of the 19th Gate is that the 19th Gate is a way of exploring the Russian doll. It is like a doll that you open up, and another doll is inside; when you open that doll up, there is another doll inside, and so forth. The most beautiful thing about the 19th Gate is that it knows how to penetrate a pattern very deeply to find the essence of the Territory. Territory is everything. When the Demon Realm dominates in your DreamRaves, your body is first and foremost the prime Territory. What you have in the defense of your body becomes very important to you; feeding your body becomes very important to you. It's just there. You have to be able to maintain the body. It also means that you have a lot of disturbance here when there isn't enough food when there isn't secure shelter and when there isn't a safe and secure Environment. People who have Demon Realm activations need, most importantly, during their waking life, to have a secure place to use as a base. They don't have to stay there; they just really need to have a secure environment in their waking life; otherwise, they feel very uncomfortable. Without a secure environment, they feel like there isn't anything that is really theirs. They feel like there isn't any place that they can call home or any place where they can be secure.

When we look at the Light Field and the Demon Realm, we are just looking at the yin/yang programming in us separately. The yang has its agenda, and the yin has its agenda. It is slanted on both sides. We become the place in which there is a genuine synthesis of all this information living itself out. In the context of the way we are programmed, the real synthetic feel is what we receive from our own species.

Through the Earth Plane, when we sleep, we receive, and take in the wakeful collective, and as others sleep, they take us in. It is one of the things to understand about the influence we have in life. It is hard to escape the fact that it is very difficult to bring about transformation, at least at speeds that we would like to see, because of how dense it all is. The reality is that the vast majority of the people on the planet, or 70 percent, are Generators and Manifesting Generators combined (cf. "Revised Research on Five Types in the Human Design System," Eleanor Haspel-Portner, Ph.D., Rave Life Sciences, 2001). At least 4.2 billion people on this planet are Generators or Manifesting Generators. Out of those 4.2 billion, maybe 150,000 know that they are a Type of Generator. When you think about that statistic, you understand the level of frustration on this planet. That level of frustration is put out to the sleeper on the other side of the globe, and they give the frustration back to us when we sleep.

> Ra's description of the collective unconscious communication, when you dream, is oversimplified and likely erroneous. Whether you are awake or asleep, you are a light body made up of electromagnetic frequencies. When you sleep, you lose the Crown and the Ajna Centers in deep sleep and are in the Lunar Minute Physical energy matrix. During this time, your conscious suggestion to your unconscious mind plays a role in how you filter information and energy frequencies to which you are exposed. Keep in mind that you always have choices. As guided by the Tree of Life Paths of Intelligence, Splenic intelligence that carries the frequency of the truth of your Soul and your Spiritual awareness should always carry the most weight in your decisions.

When living in the Earth Plane, you live in a place of deep frustration because that is the dominant theme of planet Earth. Until all of that Sacral Center energy, until all of that generative power operates correctly, the vibration we take in on the Earth Plane will not be exactly pleasant. [As you learn to transform Emotionally reactive energy into spiritual knowing and understanding, you will find challenges emotionally unbalancing. Once you surrender to higher consciousness and your inner Spiritual Core, your life flows more easily and with little stress and more joy.]

The whole thing about the Earth Plane is that it brings us into contact with the moment-by-moment, day-by-day reporting of how the programming impacts the whole because we are in contact during our sleep with a wide spread of personality consciousness of people who are awake. We take their consciousness in during the dream state. In fact, during sleep, we are measuring. We take that consciousness in during the dream state, and we see where the common denominator is in the energy, in the spirit of what goes on around us on the planet.

The Channel 15/5

What makes the Earth Plane especially important is that it begins with Channel 15-5. That is where we started with you in the various Designs of Forms (Figure 2.1). Look at those various Designs of Form; the most common pattern is the Channel 15-5, the Channel of Being in the Flow, and the Channel of Rhythm. Channel 15-5 operates at the basic level and the cellular level. An analogy may let you see what is happening at the dream level because, in many ways, a similar kind of phenomenon goes on inside of all of us. Think about a single cell, just a single cell. Remember for a moment that we have a lot of single cells in us. We have hundreds and hundreds of millions of single cells inside of us being born, going through their process, dying, being replaced, and on and on. Think about all those cells. Think about something very specific about those cells. Every single cell in your body has a Design Crystal, and it has a Magnetic Monopole. It has no personality. It is a living Form.

A single cell is a living Form. When you look inside a body in this way, you are looking at hundreds of millions of living Forms working together, coordinated into a larger pattern. That is us. There are millions of living Forms working together in an organized pattern. The difference is that we have a transcendent capacity in the total machinery to participate consciously and communicate to each other the nature of what appears to be this vast process. The single cell does not have that capacity.

In our ability to be transcendent, in terms of that level of consciousness, lies our deep vanity, a vanity that assumes that we are not just like that, but we are. Just because we can think and just because we can dream does not mean that we choose. This is one of the things that you have to come to grips with because if you do not come to grips with "no choice," you are never going to surrender. There is nothing that we are in charge of, nothing. We travel at over 440,000 kilometers an hour in space. Everything we process, everything we think, everything we say, and everything we do is initiated in the deep gray areas of the brain before we are conscious of it at all. You stick your hand up in the air, but before you stick your hand up in the air, that intention is processed; it is processed before you even know that your hand is going to go up in the air. Then, when your hand goes up in the air, you claim it: "I'm putting my hand up in the air because I have something to ask." Then you think you are in control of your life. You're not. It is not up to us whether we like being in the program or not, and it is not up to us whether we make a Contribution to the program or not. We have an opportunity to be aware, to watch it take place through us as a medium. That is called "being awake." It is called "being surrendered." It is called "non-interference." It is about you seeing that all of this happens, and it happens all the time. There is nothing you can do about any of it.

> Ra seems here to be addressing a deeper choice place within us than the Mental World mind. I agree that decisions and choices are made in a consciousness beyond the conscious mind, however, as a human being, you have a choice about what to pay attention to and what to ignore. You also may feel that you know what is aligned with your inner self and what is not, and you may choose one or the other way to operate in your life. You have a choice within the limits of your consciousness.

Marvin's statement earlier in the morning was incredibly profound. He described biologically that there is the dreamer in the dreaming space, but the vehicle, and everything about it, has to be maintained. Who's driving the car? We forget that we are just passengers in the vehicle and we are not able to take control of the direction of these vehicles, or how they operate, or anything else.

We cannot change any of that. We are passengers inside. In the dream state, there is less resistance. It is one of the reasons why it is difficult to wake up; it is difficult to come back into your body. It is difficult to come back into the world because, in the dream state, we are innocent, and we are in the program the way we should be. Our greatest conflict is awakening in the morning, thinking we are in charge of our lives, yet we are not. When we do not accept our lack of control, or when we think that what happened in our dream life is something that we caused, or something in our dream life tells us something we think we should do, we do not get to see the mythology lived out. None of it is personal.

Prophetic dreams are interesting. In dreams where something significant seems like it is going to happen in one's life if that's the dream, and then a month later or a few months later, or a year later, it actually happens just like it was in the dream, and it is actually the dreamer taking in the information on the dream plane. We take in information. Even though dreams are not personal, you can have the experience in which dream-like prophetic ones occur where eventually something, like described, happens or something very similar to it happens or even exactly happens. But, guaranteed that dream was a dream that many people had. It's actually a pattern that you attune to, and then you get to see that pattern take form.

The pattern is not personal. You can look at it and say, "Ah-ha, I was supposed to know that this was going to happen." But, in fact you actually know things are going to happen; it goes on in your dreams all the time, but you only remember the ones that have some remote connection to you. In fact, you are just processing that information. Many people, for example, have a dream in which they see something happen to somebody in that dream. It takes place elsewhere. The dreamer is picking up that information from somewhere else. It doesn't necessarily mean that it is personal for them in the sense that they need to know about it, that they need to know why it happened, or that they have any connection to it because, of course, at that level, we process all kinds of information.

The human mind does everything in its power to find meaning and reason. It will just do anything in its power to do that. Of course, the most comforting thing about something mysterious is to get a handle on it with the mind. "Okay, I dreamed that, and that happened," and then, it becomes a personal experience, but it really is not. It is just simply a gift. Each and every one of you, based on the Gates that you have in your Lunar DreamRave, actually have a gift of being attuned to what is going on in the greater environment. The way you relate to that when you awake is through familiar things. The problem with taking in energy that you are not normally designed to work with is that the mind cannot make sense of it and wants to make sense of everything.

My mystical experience, my thing of calling what I dealt with "a voice," even in describing what that felt like, or anything like that, all of that is just me trying to find some way to interpret or give a form to an energy that I do not really understand. What happens to us in the dream state is that we are much more peripheral; we are much broader in our scope and much more open. If you look at somebody's DreamRave, you see that most people are much more open when asleep than they ever are when awake. There are exceptions, obviously. But, as a general rule, you are going to see that. In other words, we take in tremendous amounts of information. We automatically tend to personalize the information in the same way we automatically tend to personalize our lives. "This was my choice, I failed." "That was your choice. . .," whatever the case may be, instead of seeing that as just a process working through us.

Channel 15-5, the Channel of Being in the Flow, is the foundation of how life works. Life is a variety of potential rhythms, all operating through selective patterns. The 5th Gate brings us Patterns. The 15th Gate changes the way we operate in any specific pattern, e.g., you may be slow in a pattern or a fast pattern. In the combination of the two, what we have is the basic pattern of what cellular life is. In the cell itself, the Cross-Species connection is through the 3rd Gate; it is open to Mutation. The pattern is always subject to change. However, you also have to see in looking at the nature of the Earth Plane, that the Earth Plane is expressed through a Portal that is purely Mutative (Gate 12). It is through the Earth Plane that we pick up Mutative changes in the totality. We pick up Mutative changes that take place in the planetary personality.

Logical and abstract, collective beings are generally very uncomfortable with Mutation because Mutation is unpredictable; it changes the Pattern or can change the Pattern. Eleanor talked about the circadian rhythm. When someone has the 5th Gate through Channel 15-5, that person is deeply linked to this circadian rhythm. Certainly, one of the things we have seen early in this work is what happens when there are discrepancies between Channel 15-5 in either Gate. Differences between the Solar DreamRave and/or the Lunar DreamRave and/or the Waking Rave Design in these Gates may result in problems in the correct timing pattern or in the way the sleep pattern works. It may even affect the way that the waking pattern works. Channel 15-5 establishes time inside of the body. But, because time is relative; only through the Earth Plane do we all really stay in the same time zone, at the same time in the dimensional field together.

Note that Pluto moved into Gate 5 in October 2000, where it remained until November 2002. This transit in Gate 5 affects everyone throughout their cycle of consciousness and all sleep cycles for this time period. When a transit further activates the channel through Gate 15, defining the whole Channel 15-5, the collective on Earth is affected as a whole. It is quite a phenomenon to contemplate once you understand its implications and pattern. This level of understanding through the DreamRaves and what Eleanor has termed the Triple Design Matrix is quite amazing.

The person with Channel 15-5 is a natural Generator. This channel says something very fascinating. The Generator responds. Channel 15-5 is the Channel of Being in the Flow. It is the ultimate symbol of being awake in what life really is. Life is a generating flow. It is a Pattern moving in Space. We are that. When you can let go, and when you see that you are just that pattern moving in space, then everything operates properly because you cannot get in the way of the flow, you cannot become the driver, you cannot control the pattern itself. [Ra is describing the Spiritual Core of the Self. In the Tree of Life, we are taught that the Spiritual Core activates in the Sacral Center (Yesod), and when we anchor our consciousness in manifesting our Spiritual Self, we can attain our fullest potential.]

The Earth Plane has a very strong Sacral definition. The Earth Plane has Channel 5-15, and it has Channel 27-50; the Earth Plane has the Channel of Custodianship (50-27); it has Gate 50, which is all about the Herding instinct; the Channel 50-27 is the sexual channel of mammals. In a mammal, the 27th Gate is like the 59th Gate in a human. The 27th Gate is the mammal's sexual strategy.

A mammal's sexual strategy is not based on intimacy. Human sexual strategy is based on intimacy, the Gate 59 looking for the Gate 6. The same is not true for a mammal. In its sexual strategy, a mammal looks for someone with whom it can herd. That strategy is very different from that of a human. In other words, the mammal looks for a way to stay within the group, to stay within the herd. A female in the herd mating with a roe male is very unlikely, even if she is not high up in the hierarchy, to go out and away with the roe male because it would be much more difficult for her to raise her young.

The Channel 50-27 is the Channel of Nourishment. Channel 50-27, through the Nurturing of Gate 27 and through the Rules and Values of Gate 50, gives human beings the capacity, once procreation through intimacy has occurred, to provide the necessary nourishment and protection to safely get children to a point where they can defend themselves and survive in the world. In the case of humans, one-quarter of Saturn's cycle, seven-and-a-half years, gets a human child to the point of relatively independent survival. So, in looking at that and seeing what Channel 50-27 is about, you understand that in a human being, this is the root of the whole sexual phenomena in the sleeping life.

There is something very funny about that sexual phenomenon in the sleeping life. I love having fun with Freud, although it is not that I, in any way, belittle him. People are always limited by what they have access to. Freud was a brilliant man. However, if you look at Freud's design (Figure 2.7), you see that Freud had a Split Definition.

Freud was an Individual Emotional Manifestor. Channel 12-22, the connection between the Throat Center and the Solar Plexus Center [Emotional/Angelic World], and Channel 8-1 show that he was there to make a Contribution. Those channels were cut off from Channel 50-27, the connection between the Splenic Center and the Sacral Center.

Freud, in his own life, had no access to his true sexuality. He had no access to his own Sacral Center, and he was a Split Definition.

All Split Definition people who want to be whole, enter into somebody else's aura. [Here Ra is talking about the Human Design Mental World Chart only. Because 99% of people are Single Definition Manifesting Generators in their Integrated Noble Energy Maps®, Ra's statement is likely invalid. 99% of the population are complete in themselves and relate to other people as a way of connecting and growing].

If you have a Split Definition and you want to be whole in a healthy way, go into a public place to have that aura hooked up. Think about the middle-class Victorian Viennese women who came into Freud's office and lay down on the sofa in his aura. In his aura, they connected up the two parts of him. Suddenly, he would be in contact with all of this sexual stuff, his sexual stuff. Now, look, this is the place where sexuality operates in the dream, but it is not human sexuality. It is not about "I need to have intimacy with that person." Many people find themselves naked in a dream with people looking at them. This kind of dream is a classic configuration of the Channel 50-27 impact. The dream says, "I belong in the herd. You can see me. You can smell me. You can touch me. I need to belong to the herd. I'm not here for one person. I'm not, I'm here for that one intimacy staring at me. I need to be in the right communal environment because that right communal environment creates the nurturing field that is necessary."

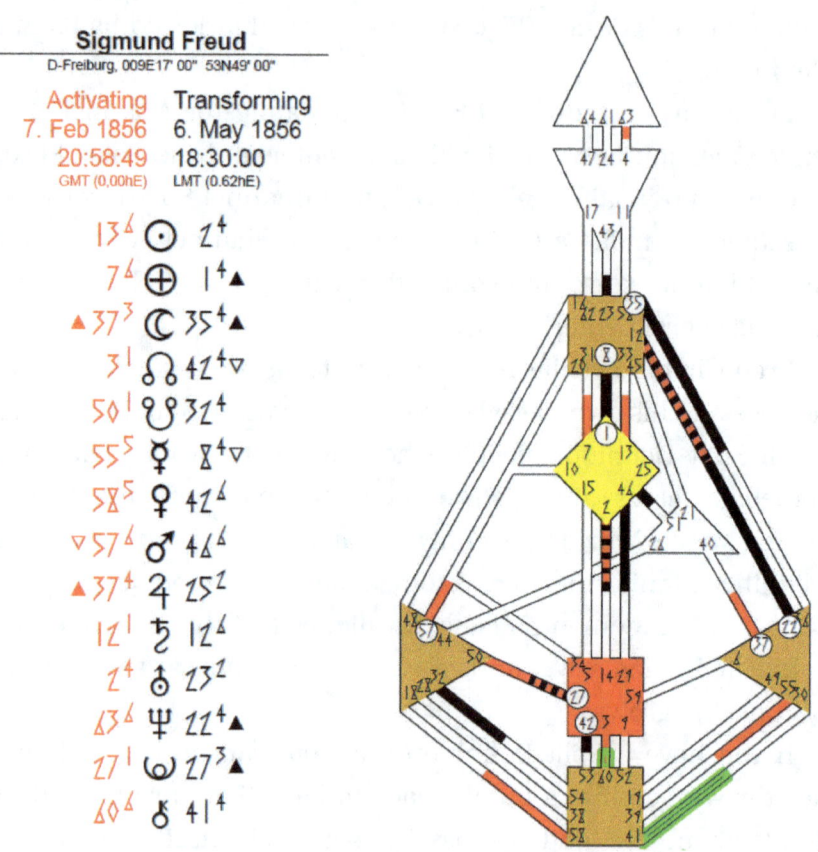

Figure 2.7: Freud's Human Design Chart

Solar Sleep Design

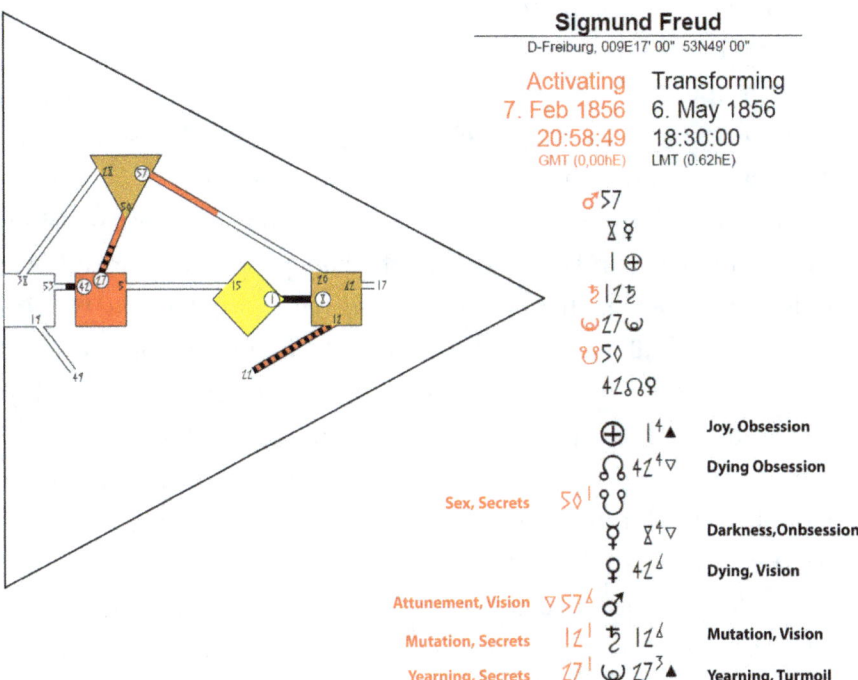

Lunar Sleep Design

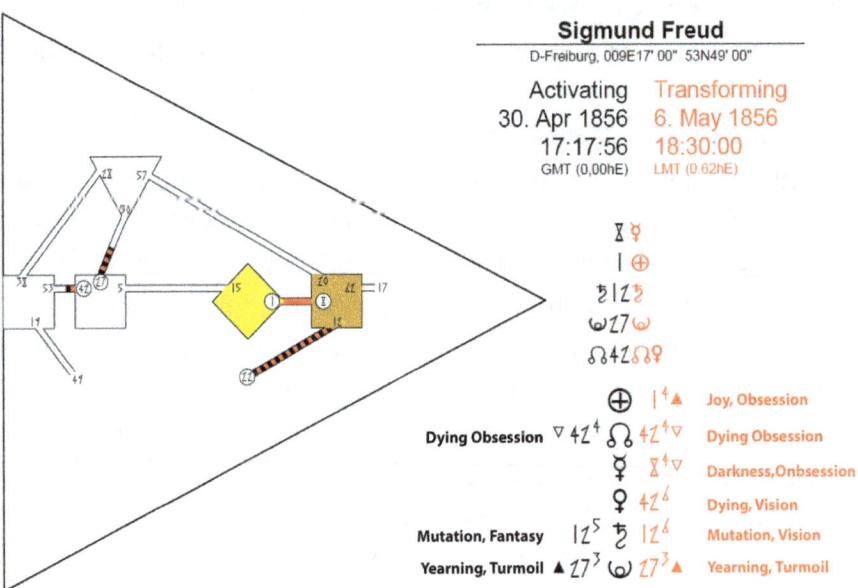

Figure 2.8: Freud's Solar and Lunar Dream Design Charts

When you look at the DreamRave, the Keynotes of the 27th Gate or the 50th Gate, and you see: "Yearning: Sex," please, do not interpret that within the context of how we, as humans, look at it. You have to see it operating at a different level in mammals. It operates at the non-personal level. The relationship in the herd, the selection of a mate to bond within that moment, is not personal; it is entirely genetic. It is directed at being able to produce the best possible genetic offspring and to have that offspring properly nurtured. For us as human beings that is all very cold, and we don't like it. We like romance and all that stuff. When you deal with the DreamRave, when you get down to that deep state, you get to a level of sexuality that we do not have any contact within our waking life. We get to a level of sexuality that is literally the sexual gene pool. It is the whole pool of who belongs together and of how healthy it is for us to be together. That is all there in Channel 27-50.

In addition, because the 27th Gate is a Nurturing Gate, and because everything in the nature of design is a duality, you have to see as well that to have Channel 27-50 in your DreamRave can also mean that your sleeping life is something that feels very disturbed. You may seem to have energy taken away from you. In the mystical books of the last century, they called this larva or larving; the term referred to people who fed off another's energy while they slept. The Earth Plane operates that way. The Earth Plane operates by programming the sleeping population by those who are awake. People who have the Channel 50-27 defined put out, if they have that channel in their DreamRave, a lot of nurturing, bonding energy, giving them the potential to be very tired in the morning.

For those people who have Channel 50-27 in their DreamRaves, they need to realize that in their waking life, they cannot afford to put enormous pressure on themselves to get up early and be ready for the world because they need a certain amount of recovery time when they wake up in the morning.

The 27th Gate is the Gate of Yearning. In Design, you see in human sexuality that one of the aspects of Desire, the 30th Gate, the

Clinging Fire, is keynoted in sexuality with this word, this longing, this burning, this Yearning. The Yearning is to fit in with the community or the herd. You are likely to be a humanitarian if you have a lot of Earth Plane activation because you feel the Yearning pain, the lack that exists in the awake world while you sleep because so much is lacking. [This statement is not validated.] Every 3.6 seconds, a child dies of starvation on this planet. You can imagine how many babies die while we go through our sleeping process. We have three billion people on this planet who go to bed hungry at night. We all take all of that in, particularly those of us who are in the West and who live in an affluent society. When we go to sleep, we take in so much of the world where poverty and hunger exist.

There is natural turmoil possible in taking the collective in because Channel 50-27 concerns the health of the genetic pool. Ultimately, Channel 50-27 is about the health of the herd as a whole. It is about the ability of the herd to stay together and function properly in a hierarchical structure. We become very tuned in to that. Channel 50-27 is the one place where you always meet the human condition. It is why Freud's personalization of the metaphors of sexuality, the dream metaphors of sexuality, created more problems than healing. Channel 50-27 does not deal with human sexuality. Therefore, its contents cannot be looked at in the same way. You cannot talk about it in the same language. It is not mixed up with ego. It does not have the quality of possession that human sexuality has, "You're mine." Animals aren't into that. The herd is not into that. The herd is concerned with the whole being healthy, fertile, and nourished. People who carry these aspects of the Earth Plane may wake up in the morning feeling very responsible for the condition of the world [This statement has been validated in my clinical reading of 15,000 Noble Energy Maps®.]; they may feel that they have to save the next tree they meet or that they have to provide for whoever is starving.

A big concern in investigating the DreamRave, despite its deep significance for us in terms of exploring the nature of well-being, has to do with how conditioned we have all been for so long in making up reasons. Most previous dream work has involved interpretations, so we have to be careful. The Jungian approach dealt with the nature of the archetype, the establishment of larger themes, and themes that populate the dream world; Jung's insights were very true. No need exists for us whatsoever to try to personalize our relationship to the archetype, rather, we need to accept the archetype moving through us. Why the archetype moves through you is not important. Acceptance of the archetype moving through you is important because every human being and every mammal is a filter. All of us provide an avenue or a vehicle for the program to operate. It is a beautiful thing.

At all of the various levels, there are 69,200 different birth crosses in the zodiac. Out of the 69,200 crosses, all have four variations. So, there are approximately 280,000 archetypal births in the wheel. If you compare that to 12 signs of the zodiac, you can see there is a real difference. If you look at that and divide that by the 6 billion people who live on Earth, you see that for each and every one of those primal archetypes, there are anywhere from 500 to 2,000 variations. That is not a large number, considering. With the archetype moving through you, you may be part of a group of 1,000 who are all aspects of one primal archetypal value. We could give each of those 69,000 plus the 280,000 archetypes the names of the gods, the demons, and forces associated with all of those archetypes. If you live out the nature of your design and if you allow yourself to let archetypes. If you live out the nature of your design and if you allow yourself to let the process come to you, you get to see that archetype. It is relaxing and releasing, but it is not personal.

It's not like you can say, "Wow, I'm great. I'm this." It would be like Ra saying, "Aren't I great because I have all this knowledge?" It wasn't up to him. Ra didn't work for it, earn it, or do anything for it. Ra is just alive. It is very nice. Ra accepts the mythology of what he is. He watches his process, but he is not attached to it. It's not like it is important to him that he make it personal because it isn't. Life is too short for all of that. It is the same thing with any of it.

Eleanor's excitement about the DreamRave was understood from a different place. It was clear that the dream process can be extremely disturbing for people because it is the only innocent process we have. We wake up with an innocent process, and it automatically meets the corruption of the unaware in life. It was obvious.

If you live out your Type, you do get to that place where you are surrendered. You do get to that place where you are awake. People think that that is big-time stuff. It isn't. It's supposed to be our right; we have that right every night when we close our eyes. It is already there for us. A third of our lives we all live as enlightened beings. That is the joke. Then we wake up, and we want to get rid of all of that. We wake up and we just jump into the confusion of being in control of life. We do not pay any attention to the fact that we didn't keep ourselves alive during that dream state. We were not aware of breathing, none of that stuff. It is such a joke about human beings

The Earth Plane

The 50th Gate

The 50th Gate is very profound because the 50th Gate is like the 6th Gate in the emotional system. The 6th Gate is where all of the potentials of emotional motors exist, i.e., where the potential for the various emotional waves that exist originate. What we call awareness, whether that be logical, tribal, or individual, all comes out of the 50th Gate. It is the source of awareness. That's why, in Human Design, Gate 50 is the Gate of the tribal lawmaker. Gate 50 is the Gate of Moses. Gate 50 lays down the laws for everybody. It determines the way the tribe, the herd, can live together and live together within bounds and within rules.

You also see that by labeling Gate 50: "Sex," how dangerous it is because people get carried away and think of that word in other terms. What is important is to realize that we cannot hold the group together without sex. That is the whole point. There is no way that the tribe can be maintained without sex. It means that restrictions on sex have to be a fine balance, which is what the 50th Gate does. The 50th Gate establishes the rules. So, someone with the 50th Gate says that males and females have to be circumcised. Another 50th Gate person says that females have to be locked up for a year after they menstruate. God knows there are all kinds of tribal rules established about how the herd can live together within a sexual environment without going crazy, without competing with each other to the point of hurting each other; in other words, all of these rules have to be established. So, in looking at sexuality here, please see that it is coming from a different perspective entirely. Many human beings who have Earth Plane activations wake up in the morning feeling sexual. There is a risk for those people in taking their dreams personally. In the highly sexually stimulating environment on the Earth Plane, you meet the sexual plane of what people call the "astral."

The sexual plane of planet Earth is really messy because of the simple fact that human beings don't live out their nature; they have not-self relationships. There are all kinds of difficulties in the way human beings live out their natures. There are all kinds of problems that people have with sexuality. These problems are all-pervasive. People who carry the 50th Gate want to change the way that works. They want to fix the rules, and they want to let people know, "This is the healthy way for us to be sexual so that we keep it together." Think about "baby boomers" and think about the sexual revolution as it impacted their parents. The actual comment that was pervasive was, "This sexual revolution is going to destroy the family."

When you change the way the sexual mores operate in the tribe, the continuity of the tribe immediately gets disturbed. There is an immediate fear that "We're not going to be able to continue the genetic process,' and as such, the tribe will slowly break apart. We no longer have families who are three generational. That configuration is a rarity now. For most of our history, it was one of the most common things. As a matter of fact, four- four-generational families were common for most of our human history.

So, out of the 50th Gate, there is something different at work. What is different at work is waking up and trying to figure out a way, in a sense, of keeping everybody together by keeping the sexual process balanced. Freud had that in his design.

The tribe only feels good when the tribe can watch its sons and daughters meet and come together under their scrutiny. What used to be the village dance, or whatever the case may be, makes the tribe happy. The gene pool is there. It is enclosed. There are no outsiders. The selection is there. Fertility is possible, and it can maintain and be maintained. The tribe has the traditions that hold that together. You can see that the way sexuality operates, now at the beginning of the century, shows a real dilemma in terms of sexuality. We are moving into a phase of deep infertility in humanity; we are moving toward a point in which reproduction is going to be an enormous challenge; we have a revolution going on trying to recreate life, whether in vitro or cloning or all other various techniques. We witness in the Channel 50/27 a part of this process.

Those people who have Channel 50/27 as part of their DreamRave action are very important in the collective's waking life because they serve as agents trying to keep the community together even though they do not know why. Genetically, it's so they can see the opportunities for sexual reproduction. The genes work in that way. It is also a way of trying to hold the community together.

The 12th Gate
The 12th Gate as a Portal is very important as the Gate of Mutation. As a Gate of Mutation through the Earth Plane, new things come into the world. Marvin's work about the nature of allergies gives much food for thought. What you are seeing if you look at the Throat Center, theoretically, is the basis of every kind of allergy.

There are 11 Gates moving out of the Throat Center, each Gate with Six Lines. We may find 66 basic allergies and prime allergies, with sub-themes below that. The 12th Gate is the Gate through which the Thyroid system itself mutates through that Gate 12. The 12th Gate is, in many ways, the most important Gate in the Throat Center because it carries with it the possibility of transforming the way manifestation takes place; it is deeply mutative because it can mutate or impact the emotional system. The 12th Gate, in Design, is a Gate of Articulation. It represents our capacity to articulate in language, to transform others, or to mutate others through what we say.

Earlier, we talked about how the Throat Center Gates in the DreamRave are very significant. Dreamers who speak in their dreams may be heard speaking outside while they are in that sleeping/dreaming state. It also means that communication within the dream is something that can be very special, e.g., many people have dream conversations in which they are told things they know nothing about, things in which they have no particular interest, but they are told things in detail, and then they try to figure out what those things are all about. What takes place in a dream like that is that information moves through them in the dream world: it moves through them, impacting others. They awake with a distorted memory of it all. They then try to personalize it. They may try to seek out what is meant. If we could collect recordings of all of the people who speak in their dreams or of all the people who sleep in the same zone, we would get a very complex message. This message programs information for the totality.

People who have the 12th Gate can be prophetic. The Gate 12.4, the 4th Line of the 12th Gate, is the Line of the Prophet or the Prophetess. It works two ways, i.e., it can be the voice of the wilderness, and nobody hears it, or it can be a voice that literally moves others, changes others, and mutates others. In a mystical sense, Prophecy, the ability to see into the future, the ability to catch that vibration, is the ability to be sensitive to a Mutation coming and to be sensitive to what that really is about. 12th Gate Prophecy is always about something that breaks the pattern. It is not about something happening in the pattern. It is the sensitivity to some kind of Mutative change.

The 12th Gate is a Gate of Caution. Caution creates difficulty for people who have the 12th Gate, a Cross-Species Gate that opens up to Gate 22. Think about the relationship of Gate 12 and Gate 22. Gate 12, connecting to Gate 22, is the only place where the relationship between a human and a mammal can begin. It is the only place where it can begin. Back 8,000 or 9,000 years when our major competitor was the wolf or the wild dog, the only way we were able to make an alliance with that animal was through this channel. The 12th Gate in the mammal is the Gate of Caution. It is a Gate of Caution in the face of temptation. This is a wary animal. The Solar Plexus Center represents something that every life form seeks because it represents the energy, we, as humans, call food. The Solar Plexus Center is a food hub. When the animal points to its 12th Gate, it cautiously looks at the human emotional field with all of its resources. There is food there.

The 22nd Gate

The 22nd Gate is the Gate of Grace. The Gate of Grace is the outstretched hand. The outstretched hand holds the big, thick, juicy slab of meat in it pointed outward toward that 12th Gate of Caution. The animal with Gate 12 moves very, very slowly and with great uncertainty, and that animal only approaches when it is hungry. It only risks approaching when it is starving. At that moment, human beings do their perfect job; human beings provide the resource; they provide the emotional resource; they have the Grace to provide the emotional resource, and in that resource, they form a social bond with the animal. Channel 12-22 gives an individual the social capacity to meet strangers, interact with strangers, and be able to give the stranger the potential of mutation. The 12th Gate opens up to all kinds of possibilities. It opens up the ability to move across and make connections with many things. But it goes deep, deep, deep into providing the Voice to describe what the vibration is out there.

Many people in Ra's life who were very busy dreamers fit the general description of what, in language, they called the "astral plane." The Earth Plane is where it all takes place. Those with the 12th Gate have a very special gift. They have the ability to pick up all of that Earth Plane stuff, and out of it, they can be a representative voice. Many people who carry this Gate 12 in their DreamRave wake up in the morning with the readiness to express something far beyond what they would normally think they are capable of or would want to express. It is through this Gate that they want to bring out what they have taken in. Without the 12th Gate, no one would ever talk about dreams. No one would talk about dreams. People wouldn't be talking about their dreams. Remember that the 12th Gate, as an individual process, takes that process in very deeply and very personally. This process creates a dilemma. The Earth Plane wants to tell you the dream but wants to tell you, "It's my dream. Let me tell you about my dream. Let me tell you what happened to me in my dream." This impulse is very strong in terms of the Earth Plane.

Review of Material

To reiterate, the Light Field cannot exist without the acceptance that Darkness is pervasive; the Light Field must deal with penetrating the Darkness. For the Light Field to make its Contribution it needs Joy, the energy to challenge life, in a sense, the energy to express oneself, to bring through one's own individual expression. Joy Lights up the Darkness. What that means is that the Light does not naturally frighten us; it does not create anxiety, yet, at the same time, the Light Field constantly points us into the Darkness. It constantly says, "Okay, there's the Darkness, go in there and bring Light." That is quite a task. The 8th Gate is really the yang's way of saying, "Let's go penetrate the yin." Penetrating the yin is what the yang always wants to do. "Let's turn on the lights, let's open this up, let's make our contribution by making it possible for everyone to see where the direction is." Of course, Channel 8-1 is the Alpha, and that's what the Alpha does. Remember something about the nature of the Alpha. The Alpha does not stand up and look at the rest of the animals in the herd and say, "Hey, I'm the alpha, follow me." The Alpha just turns its back and starts moving.

Everyone starts moving because that is the power of the Alpha. We see that it is only when the yang can get us to constantly penetrate the yin, constantly penetrate the darkness, that the yang is happy; it keeps us busy by doing that. That is its job. You can see how that has been deeply translated into our religious mythologies; how we have to live in a world of sin, that we have to be surrounded by darkness, and we have to bring the Light to it. We have to Light the way. The yang always demands it.

In the end, at a mechanical level, what the yang says is that life is about penetrating the Form. The yang doesn't care what the Form is. The yang just wants to figure out a way to penetrate the Form, to get inside of it, to make love to it, all of those things. The Demon Realm, the yin, is not interested in the yang. It's typical. It knows what the yang does. The yin is interested in us having the equipment to live within our Territory, i.e., our bodies, and in us operating properly within this Territory. The most confusing Field is the Light Field. The Earth Plane is the most painful Field in the sleep.

Through the Earth Plane, you can pick up the discomfort of the world around you – it's an uncomfortable thing. It's not like the Dark. It's not like being in that room in the dream realm where there is sudden anxiety. In the Demon Realm, even in anxiety, there is a curiosity because Form is like that. We want to know what the anxiety is all about. However, in the Earth Plane, the vibration is all too familiar. It is the world in which you are conscious. This probably leads to a very disturbing sleep. It may be more uncomfortable for people to come into awareness the morning from the Earth Plane than it is to come from any other Realm.

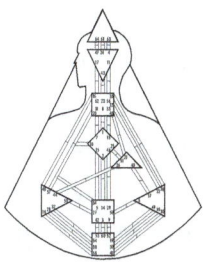

The Lines in the Hexagram

Introduction

Rave Life Sciences has a Gate Sheet that makes it easy to cross-reference Keynotes through the different Designs of Stages of Consciousness. As we move through various stages of consciousness in the day and life, as we move through these stages, there are subtleties in the way we look at a Channel or a Gate. Names or Keynotes make it easier for us to work with them analytically. In dealing with the Lines, remember that we have a difference always in the hexagram structure between the lower trigram and the upper trigram. The 1st to 3rd Lines involves a self-absorbed process. Also, for example, 1st, 2nd and 3rd Line people are impacted very heavily by the dream coming in, so to speak. In the upper trigram, the 4th to 6th Line people put out what might be called transpersonal. In other words, the program is a prana. There is always a prana. We have certain dreamers, for example, who are always passive. They always take in the dream information moving through them. The information goes through into the whole. We have dreamers who, as the information moves through them, put out specific additional information or add information, if you will, and put that out on the outside. There are two ways in which the energy flows. It is the same thing when you are dealing with a profile and when you look at somebody in their waking state. In terms of that prana, for example, the lower trigram person's geometry is of personal destiny. Lower trigram people are self-absorbed in their process.

In the upper trigram is a transpersonal process. For example, the 4th Line person may have a fixed fate. The 5th and 6th Line people are involved in transpersonal karma. You have a very different kind of dream experience depending on the Line. You must look at more than just a Gate. Interpretation depends on the Line with the subtlety of that configuration. Some aspects of your DreamRave make you an instrument putting out information, and other aspects of your DreamRave make you a receiver of information. You can see simply in the Line structure what happens. A primarily lower trigram Line person, someone with the 1st to the 3rd Lines, is in the receptive part of the dreaming process. A 4th to 6th Lines person has an active part in putting out information into the dream field. 4th to 6th Line people can be an active player in the dream process.

> My statistical analysis of Profiles shows that they are a mathematical configuration distributed with regularity in the Mandala of Synthesis®. This means that the number of individuals with each profile is mathematically determined. No interpretation of lines has been documented or tested in terms of characteristics or ways of relating in any of the Matrices. Be mindful to test your hypotheses regarding profile.

So often, people have the experience of a dream where somebody comes to them. Many people will come up to me and say, "You were in my dream last night." The fact of the matter is that in my design or the transit, there are transpersonal or karmic Lines in my dream life that put part of me out as a vibration field. It's not like

I know that. The other person may have a receptive configuration to mine that may be a harmony to my Line or a Resonance to my Line; the other person may have similar nodes in the same kind of geometrical positioning; they may receive that experience of what I'm putting out and personify that as me. It is not me; it's just what moves through me. I happen to be a transmitter in that situation. It's going on all the time. It is very important to see that when you are looking at the Line differentiation, you also look at differences in the way the prana works in the dreaming state.

It's not just, "All of everything is moving through me;" it's also, "Things move through me, and I simply experience them in the dream state. Things move through me, and they are transformed in me in the dream state and go back out." In other words, everyone has aspects that allow us to be an instrument of the continuing evolutionary programming. If human beings understood how important they are, they would hold themselves up to ransom.

The Lower Trigram Line

1: Secrets

The 1st Line is called "Secrets." The 1st Line is about Investigation. It finds the Foundation of things. All 1st Line activations in a DreamRave indicate Insecurity in the dream. If you associate that 1st Line, for example, with the 19th Gate, with Environments, you see that for those beings an essential thing is to find out the Secret in the Form. In that DreamRave the Secrets of the Form are possible. The Secrets of the Form come to them. A wonderful story is that you have a room that you go to when you dream. You go to that room and it's always the same boring, bloody experience. You go to the room and there's nothing to find, you don't know why you are in the room. There is always the possibility that all of a sudden, one day that door opens up. In other words, out of that 1st Line, Secrets are possible. And the Secrets are relative to getting the information, to getting it from the outside, but to getting it according to your Design. Remember it is not a personal Secret; it is information that finally gets a chance to come to the surface. 1st Line information is very important because it is Foundation information. If you have strong 1st Lines in your DreamRaves, you wake up in the morning with a sense of the basics that have to be dealt with. It also means this quality of Secrets. There is a level of discovery that is possible here.

Line 2: Possession

The 2nd Line dreamer is the most reticent dreamer. Because the theme of the 2nd Line is "leave me alone," the 2nd Line dreamer has barriers against being affected by the DreamRaves. They literally put up barriers. It doesn't mean that they do not respond because of that, but it does mean that they do not have an easy interaction with the dream world. Particularly, by the way, when you see the 2nd Line in the Earth Plane. The 2nd Line in the Earth Plane can be very difficult because these are people who really feel overwhelmed when sleeping. They feel like they are just not left alone. These people can actually wake up angry because they are just not left alone when they sleep. There are all these forces, however, they describe them in their experience.

Line 2 is a Line of Possession. It's such a funny word. It's very easy for people who have this to be "possessed." That is why they have to put up such a barrier. These are people who can be possessed by the same kind of dream, for example, taking them over and constantly being there. The only way that cycle can be broken is through the way they live their waking life. We are going to see the real problems, and we are going to be able to find all kinds of them that relate to the DreamRaves. The solution is still in the way you deal with waking life because that is the only way that you can attune yourself to what actually takes place in your dream life. You can actually get to a point where there is real harmony in the way you move through the world. (Ed. Note: Research has subsequently demonstrated that it is actually in the integrated field of the REM state that the mechanics of the attunement take place. How much Waking Rave Design consciousness affects the Triple Matrix is still to be determined. However, cross-cultural Samoan data suggests that input from the Waking Rave can affect the DreamRave integrated field, although probably not the Lunar DreamRave itself).

Line 3: Turmoil

The 3rd Line is perhaps the most difficult as all 3rd Lines are. The 3rd Line is about Trial and Error. When you deal with 3rd Line themes in your Design, look at the Sun and the Earth and see if you see a 3rd Line there. If a 3rd line is there, then you know that you have to deal with Trial and Error in your life; you have to deal with Bonds Made and Broken. You have to deal with disappointment, i.e., failure; you have to deal with mistakes; you end up feeling like a Martyr; you may feel very pessimistic about life unless you understand that that is positive – whenever I say that, I also watch people's faces. No lights turn on when I say that. It is deeply positive.

The whole thing about being a 3rd Line person is that you get to find out what does not work. Most people take that personally, "It's me that doesn't work. I'm no good. I'm no good at this. I'm no good at that. I wasn't good at the relationship," "blah, blah, blah," whatever the case may be, or the 3rd Line person blames the other person. It doesn't make any difference. It's all based on the same thing: It's not personal. As a matter of fact, it's fantastic. You see, human beings have been able to succeed by the very ability of being able to recognize what doesn't work, and eventually informing other human beings so we bypass those failures. That's how our evolutionary process really races along. We have this great ability to say, "No, no, no, don't go there.

That's bad." There are so many 3rd Line people who run around thinking of themselves as a failure and their lives as terrible because they have only seen all of these things that do not work. I always tell them the same thing: "No, no, no, it's not true. You're wonderful. Tell other people what doesn't work, save them the trouble. Get paid for it, by the way, it's nice. Save them the trouble and end up feeling good about yourself."

When you deal with the 3rd Line, you deal with Turmoil. That means that any time you see a 3rd Line in a Gate in the DreamRave, you know there is a tremendous amount of Inconsistency. Things come together, and they come apart. These are dreams where things really bump into you. These are dreams that can be frightening from that perspective. These are dreams where you get hit. These are dreams where you fall. These are dreams where things bang into you. These are dreams where you get surprised. There are all kinds of basic Turmoil in that. Of course, the beauty of the 3rd Line is Discovery. Out of the Turmoil can come fabulous things. Out of recognizing what does not work comes the most important information human beings require, i.e., Preparation: "Don't go there. That doesn't work. Take that road over there, everything is going to be easier," and then you eliminate all kinds of resistance. So, please, those of you who have 3rd Line themes, or those of you who look at your children, or friends, or lover, or whatever, and you see those 3rd Line themes, understand that you can transform that pessimism and transform it into what it is, i.e., wisdom – it is wisdom. It is wisdom to see what does not work and what fails. That is a great wisdom. When you see that, you begin to honor yourself for having that wisdom and begin to recognize that that is where you put your energy with other people to guide them away from those things that don't work so that you can be rewarded through things that do work. The program wants you to do that. With 3rd Lines, there is a lot of experimentation, if I can put it that way. Experimentation takes place in the 3rd Line.

The Upper Trigram

In the upper trigram, you have something very different than in the lower trigram. The upper trigram gives the natural ability to deal with the other. The dream state is also about dealing with the other. The dream state is about us being in the program, operating correctly within the program with no ego involved, with no emotions involved, in other words, no mind involved, just being there in the program.

Line 4: Obsession

The 4th Line, Obsession, is deeply influential because it is fixed. It also has the gift of Socializing. The 4th Line dreamer always meets people: "Last night, I saw George, Harry, Mary. I saw Hank; I haven't seen him in 20 years." They always meet people in their dreams. The fourth Line is a Line of Opportunity. Think about it this way: If you have lower trigram Lines, your relationship to the other in the dream plane is non-specific.

What happens to you can come from anywhere. It can bang into you from anywhere. You do not know from where it comes. You have no preparation for what happens in the dream world, so the lower trigram Lines make you much more insecure in your dream world than in your waking world because you are less prepared. The upper trigram is prepared. The upper trigram always knows that there is somebody else, always knows that there is another. The 4th Line in Design can be deeply influential. But, more than that, in medical terms, it is the great "infector." The 4th Line dreamer is the advertising department of the program, i.e., the 4th Line is not passive. The 4th Line takes the program in and processes it through. It has already become active. Line 4 people output an aspect of the program itself, influencing others.

Fads originate from the 4th Line dream phase. Fads go out into the astral. They go out into the dream plane. They go out into the Collective Personality Consciousness. Fads sit there. People always wonder about how simultaneous events work, i.e., there is a serendipity of creatures over here and over here discovering the same thing at the same time. It is because we all pick up the program together in the wave; we all get our marching orders in the dream state. Then, suddenly, in the course of the waking state, these things begin to emerge. Of course, the waking state takes responsibility. It says, "I did that," and, "It's my discovery." "No, I was first." Someone on the other side of the planet is saying, "No, I was first." These things go on all the time. The 4th Line is very influential in putting out information. It puts out information that impacts the collective. Certain themes start appearing in the collective. Jung recognized this phenomenon. Not only did he recognize that there was a collective archetype in all of these variations, but he also recognized that there was a rhythm to the archetypal energies and images. Certain archetypes emerge at certain times in the collective unconscious.

We see through the 4th Line that it is the 4th Line that brings these certain themes and prepares us for the acceptance of a symbol. Think about major corporations in the world creating a logo. It wants that logo to impact as many people as possible. Basically, what happens through the 4th Line is subliminal advertising. The logo is already in the collective. That is how the program works. It puts archetypes out innocently at the unconscious level. Nobody knows they are receiving the program. No one knows they are open to that logo. But when the logo appears, everyone recognizes it. I had that experience with the human body graph. I know that in the dream life of humanity before 1987 because I have had evidence of it, there were many people programmed to be ready to see this image of a human body graph. When people finally saw the body graph, it wasn't alien. I've had people say to me, and I've had that hundreds of times in these words, "I've been waiting for this. I knew this was out there somewhere." The program works in just this way. 4th Lines have a great impact. They put out very fixed information, and they can be very influential in creating a whole collective movement.

When we have those who are able to take this research to a social/geo-political level, we are going to see that certain philosophies, concepts, movements, and ideas flower. At a certain time, we are actually going to see the program and what sets it up at work. We will see that surface in the waking life, and suddenly, we will see it come into the general consciousness. It will get returned through the Earth Plane, in how it was processed by humanity, in how they are taken in that information. Then, in the dream life, we also process it again to see how it fits in, and how it is working. It's very extraordinary the way we are integrated into the whole and the way each one of us has a function within the whole.

Line 5: Fantasy

The 5th Line and 6th Lines are pure transpersonal, karmic Lines. Their connections in the dream life are specific. They are not surprised; they take in general information at the dream level; they interact with forces with which they have always interacted. It's kind of like an "old boy, old girl" network. They connect to all kinds of people within their geometric karmic field. One of the things about left-angle crosses, about people who are transpersonal at this level, is that they only interact in life with those with whom they have such a geometrical connection. For example, I am a 5/1. I'm a transpersonal being. My karma is transpersonal. You may have no karma with me, but I have karma with all of you, and you wouldn't be here, and I wouldn't be talking to you unless there was that connection. The transpersonal being always has a karmic link, always has some kind of strings going out to different hooked-in connections.

This 5th Line of Fantasy is about the projected dream. Here, the dream of humanity within the dream is launched. Line 5 represents the longing for completion, the longing for beauty, the longing for peace, longing for all of those kinds of things. Line 5 does not necessarily have the ability to get there. But it carries the fantasy of getting there. We are in an evolving process that moves from the 1st Line to the 5th Line. The 1st Line is the basis. The 5th Line is where we all want to go. So, the dream of humanity, where humanity wants to go, not our personal dream, the dream of the spirit of our species, where the dream leads, is found in the 5th Line. Programming agents of the dream have always been there. The future has been mapped out. It's nothing new. We all have it inside of us. There are things inside of us that have always told us things we know about. We know them through the dream; we know them through the information pool that is established in the DreamRave through which we all have access and interact in that field.

Line 6: Vision

As in all 6th Lines, the 6th Line dreamer has a very peculiar cycle in their dream life. They have a lot of intensity and turmoil in their first 30 years as a dreamer; they reach a point in their aloofness, in the 6th Line sense, where they feel more distanced. During that phase, between 30 and 50 years of age, the 6th Line dreamer is of the greatest value to us. The 6th Line is here to attest to the progress and success of the other five Lines. The 6th Line is here to see that, to give it its blessing, and ultimately, to enter into the process because it realizes it can be a Role Model. All 6 Lines establish the Role Model looking to this Line of Vision. 6th Line dreamers are the most aloof of all dreamers. They are always spectators, creating the illusion of what is possible.

Most Americans have read Carlos Castaneda. Mythologies and stories exist about people who can stand aside in their dreams, be the observer in their dreams, watch the dream within their dreams, etc. This is a 6th Line trait. It is possible when the 6th Line reaches its Kiron return. The post-50-year-old 6th Line dreamer has an opportunity to be in the dream and not in the dream at the very same time. It can be a very special state. They are the ones who can tell what is going on in the Dream Realm. It is their job to observe it.

In exploring what goes on in the dreaming life, we expect to get a great deal of excellent information from people who have 6th Line aspects. People with the 6th Line aspect have a much broader and much clearer ability to describe the kind of themes that they process in their dreams than people with other Line aspects. Not only that, but because they are 6th Line people, they attract forces coming to them. Others share with 6th Line people to get their blessing, to get the 6th Line dreamer to say, "Yes, yes, this is the way, this is the vision, this is the process, this is where we have to go."

Whenever anything is established in the collective, it is the 6th Line that either gives it the ability to sustain itself and keep on going, or it is the 6th Line that shuts it down. Remember, the 6th Line, like the 5th Line is transpersonal; it is active in the way it operates within the dream. The 6th Line isn't just passively waiting for somebody to say, "Is everything okay?" The 6th Line is a beacon sitting up there saying, "That's all right. That isn't. That's okay. That isn't." The 6th Line people literally put out into the collective what everybody else takes in.

All the 6th Line people on earth, all of those who are asleep, half of them who are asleep at any given time, provide us with moment-by-moment judgment of how well things are going. Fortunately, the 6th Line is hopeful. One of the things we can understand about the nature of our ultimate position within this whole thing is this deep hopefulness in us that everything is going to be okay, that everything is going to work out. That hopefulness is what the 6th Line brings us. "I will tell you," says the 6th Line, "if there is something to trust. Because if you can trust it, then we can be hopeful that everything is okay." The 6th Line, in that sense, is a barometer, if you will, of what is going on in the whole structure. It is a barometer of what is actually healthy or not.

Whenever we see a 6th Line dreamer with problems with sleep life, with problems going to sleep, or with problems of disturbed sleep, we have some- things to consider collectively. If the disturbance is epidemic, if we have that going through a lot of 6th Line people, then we know that the whole is in trouble. The 6th Line is there to attest to whether or not our progress is good or not, and the 6th Line people inform us of that. We all receive the message.

Understand how profound the program is. Understand how limited we are in all of that. The limitation, however, is not in any way at the expense of the incredibleness of being alive and being in a body. As a matter of fact, the more you get to see how helpless you are, the more beautiful you see your own Self to be. You ultimately get to see your real Contribution. Your contribution is made all the time. The clearer you are, the more surrendered you are to your nature, the more it operates the way it should. We do not have to be actively involved any more than we have to be actively involved when we go to sleep about breathing. We continue to breathe during sleep. Things are okay, and they look after themselves in our Form. It is all right. Relax. Sit back. Look out the window. It's beautiful here. That's the whole thing. You can get very excited by understanding that your very being alive is something that is so deep, so profound, that your impact on everything, on life itself, is alive and doing well, and you are part of that. That is very special.

> Because Profiles turned out statistically to be a mathematically calculated distribution, I began instead to use the Sun/Earth and Moon/Shadow opposition to determine the Incarnation Cross or as I call it the Pattern of Orientation of the specific Chart. Since Noble Energy Maps® uses eight Body Graphs in nine calculations to get the Integrated Noble Energy Maps®, the Keywords show the evolving process of the Planetary positions at critical times in development. These describe the process of inner struggle or challenge that is part of the position of the Sun/Earth and Moon/Shadow. I have found this approach more powerful than using profiles to empower people.

When working with the DreamRaves, it is very important, as in the Waking Rave Design (WRD), to look at the planets for each of the Gates and each of the Lines. Look between the Waking Rave Design (WRD), the Solar DreamRave (SDR), and the Lunar DreamRave (LDR) to know which planetary changes have occurred. Sometimes, a Gate remains active, but the Line changes or the number of activations changes. I have seen that; it is very common in the SDR and the LDR. So, you really have to look at that comparative configuration in terms of planets, Lines, and Gates.

Remember that in looking at the LDR, the Conscious and Unconscious are reversed. It is reversed in the black and red on your Chart sheets as well.

We shared some preliminary powerful statistics yesterday, but in terms of the DreamRave, we have found some very significant things statistically. We have three groups. We have the Fibromyalgia group, which has 63 people in it. They have all been diagnosed as bona fide Fibromyalgia patients. We also have a group of people who were in an Addiction treatment center for alcohol and/or drugs. We have a matched sample of 63, matched by latitude, longitude, and birth year. In terms of astrological sampling, doing a sample that way meets the criteria for good control in astrological scientific study. We, thus, have a respectful sample of these three groups. In addition, we have a sample of 5,000 from a general population for norms against which to compare these populations, and the general sample has been matched by birth year to this subset.

Now, in looking at the SDR and LDR, what is absolutely fascinating, and I mentioned it this morning, is that Fibromyalgia as a syndrome is characterized in part by a sleep disturbance. The diagnosis of Fibromyalgia is at least 11 out of 18 tender points, and it is also characterized by increased allergy, immunologic problems, and sleep disturbance. Fibromyalgia patients are usually in chronic pain in multiple sites.

Characteristically, in Fibromyalgia, the sleep disturbance shows up with sudden waking, and there is, when the person enters slow wave sleep, an intrusion of alpha waves into that slow wave sleep. So, Fibromyalgia patients tend to wake up from sleep where the level that is healing is disturbed. When I did the statistics for the different Gates between these three populations, for the most part I didn't find great differences. I did find some differences in the regular Waking Rave at the .05 level of significance in the 6th Gate and in the 47th Gate. But what is really much more incredible is that in the Fibromyalgia group itself, I found a significance at the .01 level in the 38th Gate between the SDR and in the LDR as well as in the 53rd Gate at the .05 level of significance. What we have is confirmation of sleep disturbance in two very critical Gates related to survival in the Fibromyalgia population. This data is very preliminary and not confirmed in larger, more sophisticated statistics, but I am putting this out to you as evidence that SDR and LDR have the potential to show us the nature of different disorders, how they operate, and begin to differentiate within sub-populations.

Statistics Confirm Sleep Disturbances in Fibromyalgia Patients

We have already confirmed that there is great significance in how people are affected by collective consciousness. No one knows the cause of Fibromyalgia. If you have no idea what the cause is, whether it's immunologic, a sleep disorder, or emotionally based pain, and if you have a way of pointing the way, then you can do superior studies in that forum. You try to figure out what is happening with this condition. This data really, again points to sleep as being critical.

And simple things, just without getting into any deep speculation about all of this, but simply, we see, for example, that we have two Gates, the 53rd Gate and the 38th Gate, which in and of themselves carry a great deal of significance anyway. We see that the TDM certainly indicates a problem area or a source area, just in the simple way that we have talked about so far today. For example, the 53rd Gate needs freedom, it needs to begin things, it needs to start things. And you have a human being who, in their sleep process, has this energy in them to begin, to start. They wake up in the morning, and they still have their life, but they may not be able to start anything. That energy within them feels funny because it doesn't feel like it fits into their life. They feel like there may be an impetus there about which they have to do something. They could start waking up with dread, the dread that there is this energy in them to start something when, in fact, they do not know what that should be. They don't know what they should be doing. There are attributes at work while we are asleep, and those attributes create momentum in waking life.

The 38th Gate Struggles and Fights and is ready to be Fierce about only one thing: fulfilling its purpose in this life. People in an environment where their sense of usefulness or value is not respected or treated well may have the 38th Gate causing a disturbance. Gate 38 seeks nothing more than finding purpose in life. So often, the nature of our relationships and the people around us condition us deeper and deeper into our false inadequacies.

There is a beautiful structure in the significance of these Gates. We have the 38th Gate, Channel 53-42, and Channel 5-15, which form the Power Matrix in the DreamRave. Channel 53-42 is the only Format possible in the DreamRaves. It then connects up to the Channel 5-15. We have a beginning axis that is very critical in Survival. Fibromyalgia is an autoimmune disease, i.e., a disease in which one's own body attacks itself immunologically; it attacks the very nature of survival in these people.

In the two of them, just in terms of keynotes, what you are looking at is the Struggle with Cycles. Those two channels, the Channel of Struggle and the Channel of Maturation, represent Cyclical processes in life. Fibromyalgia is a struggle with Cycles. There is a struggle going into sleep, coming out of sleep, going into the waking state, coming out of the waking state. There is a Struggle built into the disease that is expressed in those Gates. There may be, in fact, a genetic relationship that actually makes it difficult to smoothly operate through those cycles. We will find out. But that's what those two Gates indicate as keynotes.

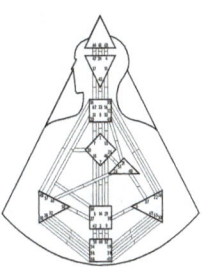

Clinical Application

Case Study: How to Work with the Triple Design Matrix (TDM)

In the case we present here (Figures 2.9–2.10), we want to paint broad strokes rather than very specific interpretative ones. For now, with work with the Triple Design Matrix in its early stages, it is enough to look at the patterns and to be able to understand their significance in the subtleties of Type for which we already have scientific validation. We are going to look at the differences in Type, the definitions and how they affect activations in each Design Matrix, the Lines, and their differences affecting profile and purpose in life. When you add in planetary configurations across the three designs, you begin to realize that to work with design without using the TDM is like working with only the Personality or the only Design side of a Waking Rave Body Graph and leaving out the information gleaned from the other view.

THE TRIPLE DESIGN MATRIX

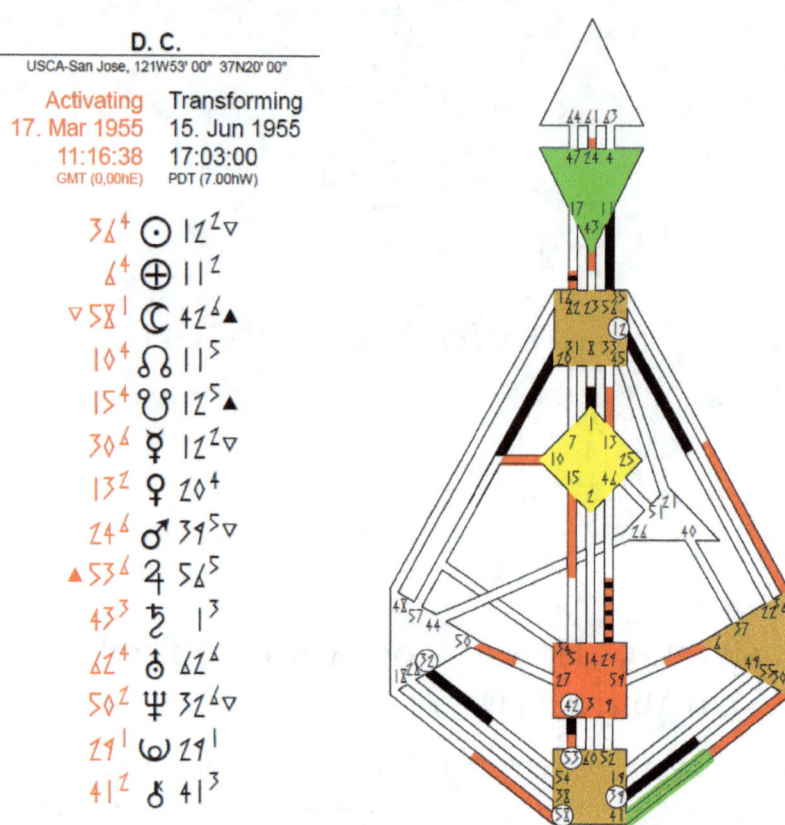

Figure 2.9: D.C's Human Design Chart

Solar Sleep Design

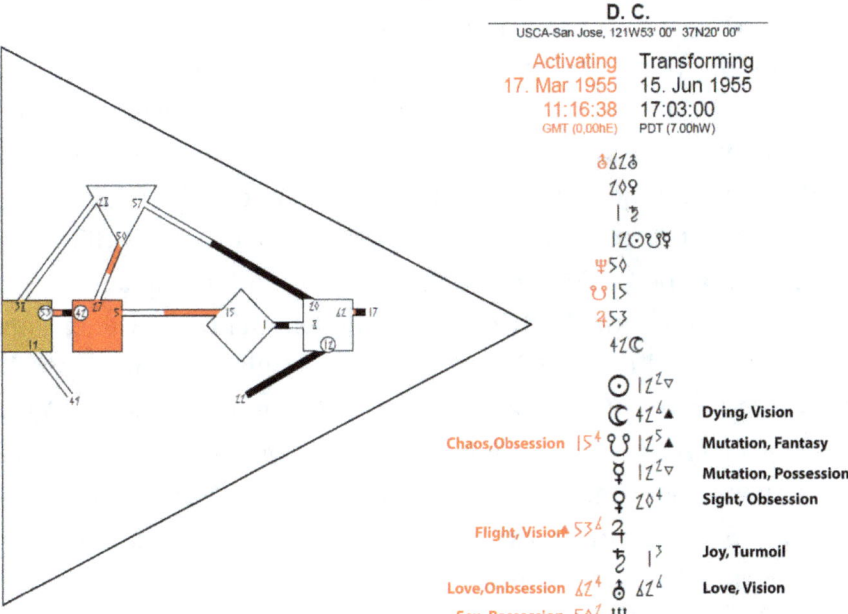

Lunar Sleep Design

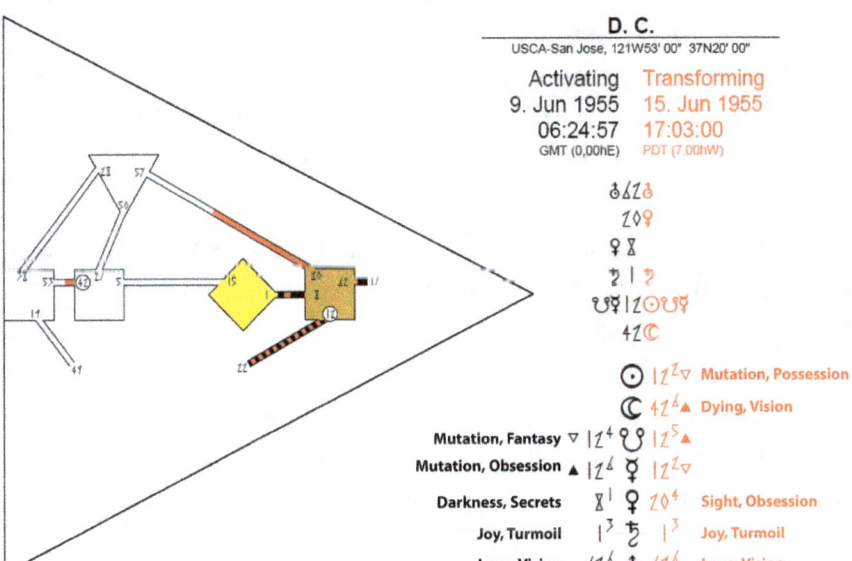

Figure 2.10: D.C.'s Solar and Lunar Dream Design Chart

What makes D.C. an interesting case example is that he is a different Type in each Matrix. In the Waking Rave Design (WRD), D.C. is a Split Definition Generator; in the Solar DreamRave (SDR), he is a Generator; in the Lunar DreamRave (LDR), he is a Projector. As noted in other materials published by RLS, most people are Reflectors in the SDR and the LDR (cf. Bibliography). Not only is it unusual to have a definition in the DreamRave (DR) but to have three different types within the Designs gives the TDM a profound impact.

The WDR shows an individual who is a Split Definition Generator. He has Channel 10-20 and Channel 56-11 defining the Identity/Self (G) Center to the Throat Center and the Throat Center to the Ajna Center. From the Throat Center, two additional Gates are active, Gate 12 and Gate 62. From the Identity/Self (G) Center, additional activations occur in Gates 15, 1, and 13. From the Ajna Center is an additional activation in Gates 43 and 24. The additional definition in D.C.'s WRD is Channel 53-42 defining the Root Center to the Sacral Center, with the additional activations out of these two Centers being Gate 29 out of the Sacral Center and Gates 58 and 39 out of the Root Center.

It is always very important to look at the activations coming out of Defined Centers along with the Channels defined because of the flavor these Gates add to the interpretation, and additionally, these activations may have strength as Portal Gates and as active Gates in the TDM. In this case, in particular, it is very important because both the 62nd Gate and the 12th Gate are Portal Gates and because the 1st Gate, the 15th Gate, and Channel 53-42 are all present in the TDM.

Again, at a superficial, mechanical level, look at the number of activations in the WDR that are part of the SDR and LDR Matrix. Note that in D.C.'s case, he has 11 activations in his WRD in Gates that are in the SDR and LDR Matrix. On the Personality side, D.C. has 7 activations, and on the Design side, he has 4 activations. Note also that both the 62nd and the 12th Gate are activations that connect with his Self-Center to Throat Center Definitions.

And importantly, both of these Gates are Portal Gates in the DreamRave Matrix.

Just from this structural standpoint so far, we know a great deal about the importance of the archetypal collective in D.C.'s life, and we also know that he came in as a translator of symbolic language even more than of verbal content itself. It is also clear, because the two Defined Channels that D.C. has in his WRD disappear in the DreamRave Matrix, that his idea about himself and his true purpose of being here may at times be confused consciously for him. I am also noting that the Planet Neptune activates the 50th Gate. The effect of Neptune is often experienced as cloudiness as well as an ability to tune in to the unconscious dynamics. Gate 50, we know, has to do with values and sex/Herding in the DR Matrix. Thus, the importance of what D.C. does in his life is a driving force related to the Survival of the species, yet it is not always clear to him what is behind it consciously in the WRD.

We can guess that when understood and recognized for his archetypal wisdom, D.C. feels finally understood and as though his communication suddenly has gotten heard. It is also most important to note that the Design (Unconscious) Gate activations in D.C.'s WRD and SDR are each in a different Realm of the Matrix, i.e., Gate 53 is in the Demon Realm, Gate 62 is in the Light Field, and Gate 50 is in the Earth Plane. We know from this information that D.C. is here to bring in information and that his vehicle is designed to be integrative and to be part of a collective synthesis as mirrored in the TDM itself.

I would guess from the WRD itself that D.C. is here with the purpose of communicating incoming collective patterns to the collective through some kind of process. This purpose is amplified by the fact that Pluto is activating the 5th Gate by Transit from 2000 to 2002 and that Gate then activates the whole Channel 53-42, 5-15, and 1-8, which is present in the SDR. So, in all three Matrices, with this Transit of Pluto, D.C. always has increased Definition in all phases of consciousness.

From the Line activations in the WRD, D.C. is profiled as a 2/4. However, we see from the Line side of the WRD Matrix, which constitutes Gates in the SDR, that in D.C., 7 out of the 11 SDR activations are in upper trigram Lines, i.e., 4, 5, 6. In the entire WRD 64 Gate Matrix, D.C. has 16 out of 28 Lines in the upper trigram and 12 out of the 28 in the lower trigram. It is, thus, clear that although D.C. is classified as a 2/4 in his WRD, his TDM shows most clearly where the emphasis really is for him, as a being who sleeps 1/3 of the time, as well as the contextual nature of how he can be transpersonal.

In the SDR, D.C. is a Generator. In the LDR, he becomes a Projector. This fact is very significant. It's very significant because the Sacral Center response is part of his waking life and exists in the early phases of sleep, then disappears during the deeper layers of sleep. And he is then really moving between the different realms in the SDR and the LDR. In just dealing with regular reading, I would be saying to D, "You might have a good sense of what is right for you when you go to sleep, but when you wake up, you may have a completely different sense of things; you may get very different information between the waking state and the sleeping state, the dream state."

The next thing to look at is which Gates are added or subtracted between the two states. So, we see that the reason the Sacral Center definition is gone is that the 42nd Gate remains, but the 53rd Gate is absent.

D.C. may have trouble getting to sleep. One of the basic things about the Matrix itself when looking at the SDR, is that when a person lies down, that Sacral Center still generates. The Fuel/Motor Center, in this case, two Motor Centers, keeps the Format Fuel/Motor Energy running. It can be much more difficult to quiet the body. In the deeper state, in the LDR state, where the generative capacity (Sacral Center Definition) disappears, something else happens.

In the LDR, you have a Channel 8-1 Definition. D.C. needs to make a Contribution throughout his Forms. He studies Design or other things to access that. But, of course, in the LDR, there is no Fuel/Motor Center, so D.C. is without the power to move this Channel to Manifestation. He may wake up in the morning with a sense of what his Contribution should be, but that, again, becomes different than the raw archetype for D.C. because his SDR is something different from his LDR; the SDR is very powerful. In your WRD he deals with the fact that he is a Generator; he cannot just rush out on that energy, on that need to make his Contribution. That need works on him, but he cannot just rush out in the morning and do it. He may wake up in the morning with frustration; he may have a hard time going to sleep at night and waking up in the morning because of the frustration; yet, if D.C. does jump out of bed and start moving, he can end up having a lot of difficulties. He has to wait for responses from within his Sacral Center Authority to make his integrated self feel and be healthy.

D.C. also has the 20th Gate and remember that the 20th Gate is part of the Acoustic Channel. We have noted that many people who have the 20th Gate wake up suddenly. They just wake up with a start. It's also rather interesting to note some of the Line differences. The presence of the 8th Gate is very significant, especially because D.C. has many activations in it. Most of the activations are in the Light Field. (Ed. Note: It is clear from the research on brain scans that language is not present in the centers of the brain that are active in sleep. It is, thus, in the TDM that the translation occurs between the images and the language the potential of these images and any content related to the Centers in the 64-Gate Matrix that is not present in the 15-Gate Matrix are given their meaning to bring them through into the WRD. All acoustic sounds in the sleeping state are symbolic sounds without content except as they are later interpreted through the "higher" cortical areas of the brain).

When you look at a DreamRave, it is not like looking at a Human Design database, i.e., a Body Graph. In the Human Design database, we all have the same number of activations. We all have two columns with activations in everything. But, when you look at the

DreamRave Matrix, that is not necessarily so. Some people may only have four or five activations in that Matrix and other people may have many. There is a difference in the way those people integrate and operate in their Waking Consciousness. There is much complexity, for example, in D.C., because the dream state is conditioned by imprinting and because of the many activations in the DreamRave itself.

We have seen with people with the kind of configuration that D.C. has in his DreamRave that many activations in the Light Field give a lot of information. With that much information coming into D.C., he then feels a need to pass it through in his consciousness to others; D.C. needs to speak about it, needs to express it. The 12th Gate, which is the Earth Plane Field of Mutation, results in a sense of responsibility to communicate the awareness; D.C. feels himself a part of this synthesis between the realms. That is both a blessing and a curse in the way D.C. operates. The awareness between Gate 1 and Gate 8, as an activated awareness that is part of the darkness, results in a real need to explain what it is he has gotten in touch with within the Dream Realm.

It is also significant that D.C. has two Portal Gates, the Gate 62 and the Gate 12. Look at how many activations are present in Gate 12; there are five activations in Gate 12 in the LDR and three activations in Gate 12 in the WRD and the SDR. D.C. ends up with five activations in the LDR in the 12th Gate. So, he is very impacted by the collective and by the astral and as a translator, especially in the transpersonal sense.

That's a lot of information just in terms of activation differences between the Raves and also coming into D.C. The DreamRave is always extremely significant because its definition is not as common, obviously, as in the WRD itself. The Channel 8-1 becomes very powerful for D.C. In the LDR, the activation is the 1st Line of the 8th Gate, so it shows something about the sequence. In other words, in the end, D.C. is driven to explore the Form to get the information he needs to finally get to the point where he can find a secure foundation. He is actually driven at the unconscious collective level to get to the bottom of it, if you will, to really find out how things work. He gets information along the way, coming through. Also, note when you look at the complexity in this, and you see all the different Lines, that you can see how we are all basically in the activation, in the prana ourselves. Part of us is active, and part of us is passive in the way information moves through.

The main definition that changes D.C. in the LDR is the 8th Gate. The 8th Gate is in the 1st Line. D.C. is an Alpha so his sense of himself and his Secure Foundation are dependent on him getting to a basis of this channel in himself. When he can explore the Foundation, he accesses his drive. Then, out of the dream state, he brings Light into the Darkness so he can see the foundation and he can see how things work. It's like going underneath your house; you take a light with you, and you check it out. That's what D.C. is being told to do in his programming. Look at how the TDM is configured, look at the contrast between the three designs, and integrate all three designs.

Focusing again on the content in the designs, we see that D.C. has Channel 20-10, but in his LDR, Gate 8 activates. How D.C. is given the information and explores the Darkness through Channel 1-8 in the LDR. But D.C. can only live it out in his WRD through his Gate 20 and only when it is recognized by others. Furthermore, when he has a dream experience, what happens is that his contribution formulates ideas at the moment. Ideas can start bubbling out of D.C. the moment he awakens. Automatically, all of the need to express himself is in the 1st Gate, so all that comes out through the Throat Center and impacts the Ajna Center. D.C.'s whole idea system is impacted.

Ideas get programmed in during the REM state and then the pressure is on D.C. in the waking state to bring out the ideas and the values and the understanding that was imprinted into the association areas of his brain and the cellular chemistry during this sleep stage. Remember, it is not personal. It is through a design like D.C.'s design that we especially understand the importance of not personalizing the collective archetypal information that comes through when we sleep and dream. Remember also that the translation from symbolic formulation into language occurs through the 12th Gate, which has its own Mutative agenda.

When you look at somebody's WRD and the person is a Generator, in this case, a Split Definition Generator, you know that even when the body is tired, the mind can still be busy and buzzing. In the Split Definition Generator, as in this case, the Centers of the Split do not connect to each other. The two different aspects function differently.

When D.C. lies down, the only thing left is his Generative capacity; it is work to let go.

An important piece of advice for Generators, particularly Generator children, is to let them go to sleep when they are dead tired because it is the only time that a Generator can sleep. If you order a Generator to go to bed early or force them to keep to their routine by telling them, "You have to go to bed at 10:00 o'clock, you've got to get your beauty sleep," then they have problems sleeping. A Generator needs to function according to the response system. A Generator has to respond to their fatigue. When they are tired, then they can go to sleep. But if they are not tired and they push themselves to go to bed, "I'm going to go to bed now, it's good for me," then they are going to lay there and thrash around and thrash around. That goes back to what it means to live out your Type. If you live out your Type, you are going to have a healthy life; you are going to have a healthy sleep, and you are going to have a healthy process. It always comes back to the same thing. Remember also that lying down does change the Design Matrix, but it is not just changed in that horizontal position. It seems from the kind of data we receive about sleep problems that shifts in consciousness are also important in activating the alternative Matrices through which we function. It is like a switch within us that allows the Triple Design Matrix to turn on.

So, to integrate all of that, these three different aspects of D.C.

show something very clearly: lying down is important because it gets D.C. out of the Mind (Ajna Center) but also puts him deep into his energy. Once past that threshold, he finally enters a peaceful place. Deep sleep is incredibly healthy for D.C., even if it doesn't last for a long time. All aspects are connected to it. In other words, as long as D.C. can get down to that LDR stage, he enters a stage where he really relaxes because he loses the whole Generative Field. He can simply float in that stage and feel quite refreshed when he comes back.

The Triple Design Matrix in Meditation

Certain kinds of meditation, like Transcendental Meditation (TM), which is done sitting up, activate the 15-Gate matrix in a 64 Matrix state. In this state, we can observe those Centers that are turned off when we are horizontal, but we can witness them because they are still active when we are vertical. The deep rest that we get in something like TM is that transition zone where we have access to that Matrix in awareness, in consciousness, in the human state, and not in a mammalian state.

Someone like D.C., where the Ajna Center is defined in his WRD, something like TM, where he has all four kinds of states of consciousness accessed, would be very important. So, some kind of sitting meditation, as well as that lying down state, could be very beneficial. For D.C., as he comes out of the dream state, there is this need to explain what he has obtained out of that collective unconscious.

The other thing that I want to make sure to mention again is one of the primary reasons I picked D.C.'s chart as a chart to look at. It has numerous activations. What I have seen in designs where you have Gates in all three of the spheres, and then you have activation that is somewhat different in the LDR is that people with this kind of configuration generally have a sense of an overriding purpose in life with which they connect.

They struggle deeply to integrate what it's all about because there are so many activations in all the different states of consciousness. There is not an easy way, especially with D.C.'s split, to understand what that is about. So, the mind comes in and wants to understand it, and yet, there is all of this drive that has nothing to do with the personal life. The Lines are very transpersonal in D.C.'s charts. This is a good integrative case in terms of that aspect of the analysis of the DreamRaves.

When you look at your DreamRaves, look at them in conjunction with looking at your Human Design. In other words, see them all together. Look for the obvious. Remember the very simple and obvious things that you can see because, as a formula, they are going to bring you the closest to the truth. When we were looking at the configuration of the SDR and the LDR of D.C.'s chart, we just saw the obvious: the obvious is that there is one state in which very powerful Fuel/Motor Centers are working and another state where suddenly the Fuel/Motor Centers are gone. By looking at your own TDM and just by looking at the very surface level, to begin with, you can begin to get a feeling of what the difference is in you in those three different states. After all, the beauty of the graphic of Human Design is that once you understand the components and how they operate, you can get a sense of what that is.

Also, look at the Lines. You need to see what aspects of your dreaming activation passive and what aspects of it are active and to see where they fit in terms of these different fields at which we have been looking. It is very important that you live out your Type while you are awake. If you live out your Type while you are awake, you feel healthy in your life; living your Type is the most important thing of all. It seems to be our karma; we will go deeper and deeper into our exploration to find all of these things. However, the real point is about you.

Conclusions

> I verified with statistics that Type holds up as a valid and reliable construct across populations, and Type is valid not just in the WRD but also in the SDR and the LDR. This verification means that Type is one of the great essential truths now available to us. It means that every one of you can participate in going through the experiment with what it is like to follow the strategy of your Type across the TDM; you will probably find that the other aspects of your life naturally come together.

Most human beings come to this knowledge because they are looking for exactly what the strategy of Type offers. That is what people have been looking for forever. It is not a belief, it is not a dream, it is not a hope; it is a very boring, mundane statistic. Living one's Type is something that anybody can accomplish in this life. That is really what is significant.

Right now, we have incredible themes at work. We have Pluto, for example, in the 5th Gate until 2002 (cf. "Pluto in Gate 5: A thought for Consideration," Eleanor Haspel-Portner, Ph.D., Rave Life Sciences, Web, 2000). It means that all of us are having our patterns impacted by the presence of Pluto. It impacts on our SDR and our LDR, as well as on our WRD. This may be a time when many people have difficulty. If you have the 15th Gate, for example, in your LDR, you may have a lot of trouble getting down to that deep state of sleep while Pluto is in the 5th Gate. We have the program, the program that impacts us. You have the basis, and you have a Matrix that you can work with. But, the most fascinating thing in Design, the way we learn in Design is by following the way the program works because it is a neutral teacher. You get to experience it all.

Ra's Experience

My first experience 13 years ago with my own long road of verification of this knowledge was simply to watch my movie, to watch the interaction, and to watch the program as it impacted me. And, of course, we all have deep places of vulnerability in our Design. I am open emotionally. So, in the course of a month, the Moon gives me six or seven different times with 10 to 12 hours of being emotional. I would just sit and watch the movie. I'd watch it. I'd feel. I'd go through the process. I got to a point where I was very sensitive. I lived a bizarre life then. I was very isolated. You get to a point where you can actually feel the Gates opening and closing. There is this clicking that goes on, and it moves through you. We are in the program.

Don't isolate this fixed matrix that gives you a way to see how you filter and how you receive it out of that matrix; the general programming throughout- the universe makes it all work. We all have specific themes at work for us while we are asleep. Those themes are controlled by the programming itself, slower moving objects programming us can keep certain themes active in us for years and keep active in us as a collective. So, by watching the program in association with the matrix, you see how that process works while you are asleep, i.e., during shifts in your states of consciousness.

What I would strongly recommend is that when you wake up in the morning, you take notes about what happened during the night without looking at your dream design with its Transits so that you have something of a real experiment to see if what you remember from the night is confirmed when you go back and look at the Transits. RLS has a program module in the NTW program that prints out Transit DreamRave composites with your design. It is designed for you to take notes on the sheets. Work with the information that belongs to you. It is your right

Book Two References

Dement, W. C., and Vaughn, C. 1999. The Promise of Sleep. Random House: New York.

"Preliminary Research on the Human Design System and Health." Eleanor Haspel-Portner, PhD, et al., Rave Live Sciences, 2000)

"Revised Research Verifies 5 Types in the Human Design System." Eleanor Haspel-Portner, PhD. Rave Life Sciences. August 2001.

"The Triple Design Matrix: Type Statistically Verified Across the Matrix." Eleanor Haspel-Portner, Ph.D. Rave Life Sciences. August 2001.

Newberg, Andrew, M.D., et al. 2001. Why God Won't Go Away.

Ballantine Books, New York.

Ra Uru Hu, et al. 1999 Living Your Purpose. Rave Life Sciences, Pacific Palisades, California. Science, Vol. 279, pp.91-95.

BOOK THREE

DreamRave Basics & Keynotes

Seminar Transcript & Updates
Recorded January 8, 2001
Vienna, Austria

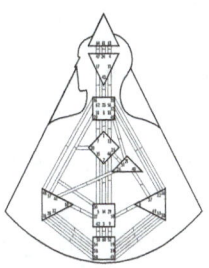

Introduction

In my process of bringing the knowledge that I was given into the world, there are many things that I have been hesitant to do. There are still things that I have not released because they tend to excite people, get them all cranked up, and get them lost in things that really are not important now. Many of you who have been students of mine for many, many years know how many games I've played with you when you would ask me about dreams. I would tell you, "Well, yeah, look at the 63rd Gate or the 64th Gate." I would have said anything to you to get you awake. It worked to a point. The fact is that the real difficulty of being honest in the work that I do and teaching you things as they truly are is that the whole business of understanding and dealing with dreams has been delusional from the start. It has been delusional from the start because, from the start, dreams were seen as personal.

You see my hat. For those of you who cannot read English, it says, "I am helpless and incompetent." I don't mind wearing this hat in public. I can handle it. "I am helpless and incompetent." You are all helpless and incompetent. We are all helpless and incompetent. Life is not personal. The great struggle of the Personality Crystal is to transcend the personalizing of life, of what it is to be in form, of what it is to live in these vehicles, of what it is to deal with consciousness in form. That we personalize everything is the great vanity of the world; it is the great vanity. We take it personally. You take your lives personally. You think you are personally responsible.

When Freud started to personalize people's dreams, we collectively started on a long road to confusion. I have nothing against Freud, by the way. Freud and Jung, for me, simply explored aspects of a foundation they did not grasp. They explored those things brilliantly for what they did. The reality is that dealing with the DreamRave is beginning to be it, you cannot truly take this knowledge in if you're taking this knowledge in to personalize it.

In your illusion of meeting your mother or your dead brother or a duck, whatever the case may be, in the illusion of the way in which you personalize, all of that has nothing to do with what the dream life is about. Nothing. It is a cruel joke, and it is the cruel joke of the Gods. They don't have much respect for humanity or humanity's intelligence or the capacity of humanity to wake up and be aware.

Basically, what it means is that the time that you are asleep. The time in which your stubborn personality, the vain personality, the personalizing, suffering personality finally shuts up, in that state of sleep, the real work gets done. The real work gets done because we take in the program without personality resistance. The program is for all of us. We all share the dream field together. We are all integrated into the same dream field. But as long as you are looking for the personalization, "Ah-ha, I have this Gate." As long as you try to personalize it, you will not understand it.

The DreamRave is a deeply, deeply mystical journey. It is a spiritual journey. It is a journey beyond the vanity of what it is to be awake. It is a journey into the totality. It's a journey into the consciousness of the One in which all of us participate in the consciousness of the One without the vanity of self-reflected consciousness, without knowing that we're really doing it.

There is an old tradition of the builders of the world. There are supposed to be beings on this earth who must be alive for the world to work. But you could never identify them because the moment you could identify them, they would hold the world to ransom. We are all builders of the world, but when we sleep, not when we are awake.

When I was given the knowledge, the basis of being given that knowledge was the fact that I was being given something that not only was mechanical and logical but because it was mechanical and logical, there was something that could be substantiated. The core of the scientific knowledge that I was given was the nature of the neutrino. At the time that I received the information from the voice in 1987, the neutrino was something that was not understood, not known. It was considered to be something that didn't have mass. When the actual proof came out about the nature of the neutrino, what was most fascinating for me was the way in which scientists discovered that neutrinos had mass. The way scientists discovered that neutrinos had mass was by measuring the oscillation of neutrinos as they moved through the Earth. In other words, neutrinos spin, and as they spin, they change. Now, of course, the whole nature of oscillation is that oscillation at any other level – if you want, we can call it music, or we can call it sound or whatever – and the old story in the Bible about "In the beginning was the word," well, "yes," in the beginning neutrinos oscillated, and neutrinos oscillating bring us information. We live in a Neutrino Ocean. We live in a Neutrino Ocean in which the Neutrino information comes from every conceivable direction.

Remember, in this little space here, three trillion neutrinos a second will go through that space, and they're not all going through in the same direction. It's an ocean of information; within the confines of our limitations, we are not designed to take in the whole ocean. We can't. It's not possible. So, each and every form, each species of life, all different things that we have, they all have different ways in which they take in the Neutrino Ocean and the Neutrino programming.

Human beings are very complex in the way they are designed. Illustration 3 shows the Design of Forms. Note that in the illustration of a plant, the plant's design is opposite our own. It is an upside-down triangle, in that sense. Plants receive their primary programming through the Earth first. The Neutrino Ocean goes through the Earth into the planet. The plant vertically receives its programming. It's actually 88 degrees, but I don't want to play games with Pythagoras. In other words, plants get a stream of information, and they're designed to take in the information this way.

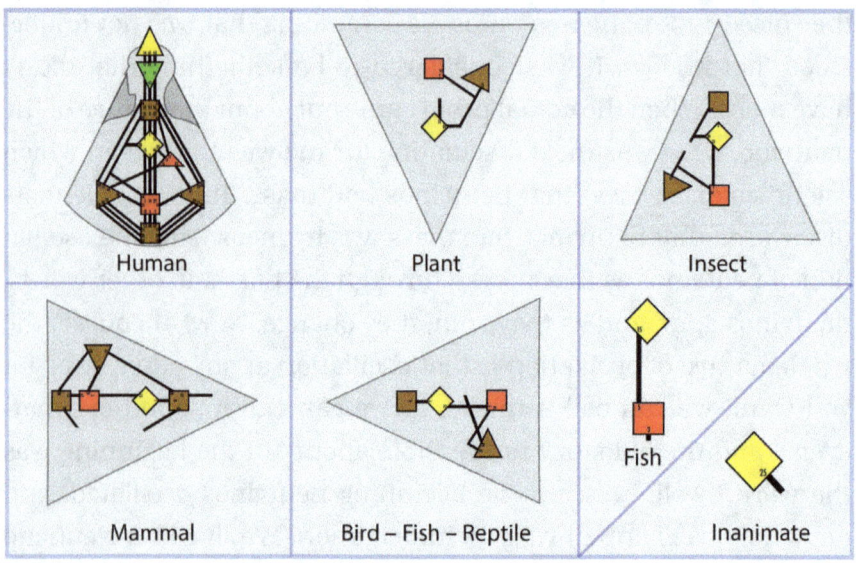

Figure 3.1: The Design of Forms

We know in looking at the Human Design Rave Chart that we are programmed the other way around. We operate in a field in which we take in the information vertically. As we walk along, we have a streaming of Neutrino information that goes into us, programs our crystals, and comes into us. Again, it's at an angle. It comes in at 88 degrees, and We have this continuing stream moving in. We don't get the other stuff. We don't get the same programming as a plant. The closest we get to plants is to eat them or to smell them, or whatever, but we do not get their programming. They have their own unique programming.

When it comes to the Mammal, which is the key to DreamRave, you can see that the Mammal receives its programming in a horizontal mode. If you love dogs, and I love dogs, the greeting between a dog and its master/mistress is always amusing to watch from this context. Either the human gets down on all fours, or the dog leaps up on its front paws and stands up against its master or mistress, trying to come to a common ground of programming. But it's natural in us. So, the Mammalian life form receives its information differently than the human. The Mammal is designed to receive this information in a horizontal mode. Of course, we know our evolution; we are, after all, Mammals. We have never, ever left our Mammalian design behind us. Once in a while we make love standing up, but it's not common. We are Mammals. We may be special Mammals. We have a uniqueness that, in Design, we can see comes from the Head Center, the Ajna Center, the Solar Plexus Center, and the Heart (Ego) Center. These Centers truly make us different as a species and as a form, yet at the same time, we've never left the Mammalian aspects of ourselves behind. So, when you lie down to go to sleep at night, you cut off, you disconnect from being this special higher species; you lose the connection to the active Head Center and to the Ajna Center. You disconnect the chaos of the Solar Plexus Center; you become a Mammal. You go back to your Mammalian source and roots, and in doing so, you change your program. You stop receiving the vertical program, and you enter into the world of the horizontal program. The horizontal program operates differently than the vertical program because there is no Personality Consciousness resistance at the horizontal level; it's not there. There is no Ajna Center, no Head Center, no Solar Plexus Center, and no Heart Center. Because there is no resistance, everything gets done.

If you look at the Illustration of Forms (Figure 3.1), you'll see that the most important absent Center is the Heart Center. There is no Heart Center (Ego) in the Mammalian world. It doesn't exist. We have all kinds of human beings who have forever tried to condition vanity into animals. If you've ever been to a dog show or a horse show, you know that. We work really hard at trying to condition animals. But the reality is that within the context of the form, there is no potential for vanity or free will. There is no assumption of being in control. Dogs don't walk around saying, "This is my life, and I'm going to live it the way I want to." That is not the way it works. You must understand that the only time that we're truly released from our vanity is when we're lying down. Isn't that funny? How many religions get you to get down on your knees and get Mammalian. "Get rid of your vanity, get rid of your vanity," then you can really get the program.

Look at the ceremonies where you have millions of people on their knees with their heads to the ground in this huge Mammalian field, with no vanity, no sense of being in control, no sense of knowing what to do. Helpless and incompetent is what we are, folks. That's why I teach you how to surrender, so you can see that everything functions properly. But if you take charge, and your life is going to be a mess. When we're horizontal, that doesn't matter. When you go to sleep, you join the rest of the workers who take in the program purely every moment of every day all the time. Every plant and bug and bird and beast and fish are all in the program without vanity.

That is my struggle. I came into the world with the biggest, bloody Ego you'll ever meet. I know the nature of vanity. I know it deeply within me, and I know it's the greatest curse of all. It's the curse that curses everyone. It's that assumption inside of you that makes you think that you can do something about anything. You can't. It happens. It's always happening. When we sleep, we are in the flow. When you make love, and you're about to have an orgasm, you don't know anything about vanity. You're just lost in the program; you're just lost in the flow. That's what it's all about. We do not do a good job with our waking consciousness. We always interfere with the program. We are the rebellious children.

Someone says, "Look, go to sleep, darling. Everything will be fine," When we sleep, the vanity is gone. Dreams are not meant to be personal. There is no reflective consciousness in dreams. There is no Ajna Center. There is no Head Center. And there is no neural soup that's there in the Solar Plexus Center. It's not there. All the things that make us human are not there. We can get back into the business of contributing to what it is for us to be informed and of what information we bring out of that to the whole without it being confused by our waking consciousness; that's when we're doing a good job. Most human beings only do a good job after they're dead, which isn't very rewarding.

I mentioned at the beginning that I've always had a hesitancy about bringing out certain information. The fact that DreamRave is even here is a byproduct of my relationship with Dr. Eleanor Haspel-Portner and Dr. Marvin Portner in California, where we began Rave Life Sciences. We began the process of scientifically substantiating the validity of Human Design. We established that Type is a legitimate construct; as a result of that verification, my attitude changed toward bringing out materials that I had considered what I call gray. I call it "gray" because the basic components of the material are mystical and have to be accepted or believed in order for the constructs that would follow to be accepted.

Over the years, I've given gray courses in which I've talked about cosmology. For example, I was given, by the voice, things that cannot be substantiated in fact. Please recognize this about the nature of the DreamRave, my resistance to bringing out the DreamRave is that the very basis of the DreamRave is the acceptance of what I have been told about the nature of crystals of consciousness. It is something that has yet to be proven, and it is important for you to recognize that. (Ed. Note: Since Ra presented this information, The DreamRave and the Triple Design Matrix have indeed been scientifically documented. cf. "The Triple Design Matrix: Type Statistically Verified Across the Matrix." By Eleanor Haspel-Portner, Ph.D. Rave Life Sciences. August 2001). That's why, with things like this, I am hesitant. However, given the substantiation of the basic construct of Human Design, I don't feel uncomfortable anymore releasing such material (cf. "Preliminary Research on the Human Design System and Health." Eleanor Haspel-Portner, Ph.D., et al., Rave Live Sciences, 2000) and "Revised Research Verifies 5 Types in the Human Design System." Eleanor Haspel-Portner, PhD. Rave Life Sciences. August 2001). The DreamRave Design System is published, and it is available (The DreamRave Design, Rave Life Sciences, 2000). The work itself is fascinating. I want you to recognize that it comes from a deeply mystical understanding of the way in which consciousness operates on this planet.

According to the voice in the way in which cosmology was described to me, we had in the beginning the personality and the design crystals, and when they met, they shattered, and they spread out into the expanding universe. Everything is endowed with crystals of consciousness, everything. The crystals of consciousness that are the embodiment of the consciousness field of our Solar system, i.e., what the Solar cell represents, is that the Personality Crystals and the Design Crystals have a different way of life if we can call it that. They have a different way of existence than what or how we experience them or can see them in form. For the crystals of consciousness as a totality, the form is transcendent, i.e., the form is the earth, and the form is the Solar system; in other words, the form takes on a much larger dimension. We are all inside of the womb, so we're all inside of the form structure itself, but we see it relatively differently.

There are more personality crystals than one could possibly imagine. If you could imagine all of the human beings incarnated now, if you could imagine all of the forms of life incarnated now, and I'm talking about every blade of grass, every ameba, every cell, I'm talking about all of them, if you imagine all of that, it is a fraction of the number of personality crystals that are here and that are part of the dynamic of our planet. The vast majority of personality crystals never, ever get to incarnate into any kind of form. Not only are we specialized as creatures, but those of us who are here have specialized personality crystals because we have always been in form. You do not get this job as a new job. This is an old job that all of us who are on this planet have participated in forever, i.e., we are specialized in entering into form, but we are a minority in the personality crystal structure.

If you could imagine what the earth really looks like, not the way our eyes see it, you know, it's pretty enough, this nice little marble there with all these blue waters and clouds going by, it's pretty, but that's the illusion. If you could really see the earth, first of all, you wouldn't see the earth. That's the first thing, you wouldn't see the earth at all because the earth is encased like a crystal ball. The earth is inside of, if you will, a crystal shell. It's a very old image. If you go back to some of the earliest concepts of the structure of heaven and all of these things, you'll see it's an old, old concept. Yes, we're in this shell; okay, we are. This is a personality crystal shell. But it's not a real shell, not in the sense that it's locked into a shell. It is all dynamic and moving. The so-called shell is made up of Crystal Bundles, personality Crystal Bundles. Personality crystals can operate in the environment of the earth from the ground, from the floor, from the earth's base up to the end of the atmosphere. There are no personality crystals outside of the atmosphere of the earth and there are no personality crystals that are below the earth. In other words, the personality crystal has a range. Personality crystals never travel alone. They are always part of a bundle.

Think about those beings who are sensitive and who have a feeling that there's a ghost in the house. Now, of course, all of that is mechanically real. It's delusional the way we see it, but it's mechanically real. If there is a personality bundle that's moving through this room, somebody's going to notice it. And that personality bundle is going to have millions of personality crystals.

The larger bundles we've already given names. We call them Christ Consciousness or The Buddha Field or Gabriel or whatever it is. Channellers give names to them all the time. That's all channellers do, by the way. They give names to the personality bundles to which they belong. See, that's why we're in form. Remember, we're only aspects of a huge, organized consciousness process. When you come into life, when you incarnate, you come out of your bundle. Now remember that the vast majority of crystals in that bundle are never, ever going to incarnate. They are dependent on you in that sense. You come into the Form, and by coming into the Form, what you experience can be brought back to the bundle when you're dead. Then your personality goes back up into your bundle and that information gets disseminated into the bundle through the Neutrino ocean. It is not, by the way, that that is conscious of itself being a consciousness field. It's not. It's just a mechanism at work. Self-reflected consciousness is something we play with only in our vanity; it does not operate at that level.

Recognize your nature. I've had people come to me over the years who hate themselves, and they are severely confused; they don't know anything, and they don't think there's any purpose, and they don't think they're of value. It's such a drag to not recognize your enormous privilege in being here. You're all doing a highly specialized job. You really are. It's an incredible work that you're doing. Fortunately, you don't know that. I mean, I've avoided telling people about their work because then, "they get off on it." They say, "Well, you know, I'm doing special work for the program," and they're right back into their vanity trip instead of finding their grace in all of that.

We are surrounded by a Crystal Bundle Field that's in the Neutrino Ocean, and it means that nothing gets to us, nothing, without being in the Neutrino stream that's gone through Mars before it comes through us. The Neutrino stream comes from the zillions of stars that feed our program. It is all conditioned by the Personality Crystal Field before it ever gets to us. That is one side of the dynamic: the personality bundles and the bundles literally covering the earth. Also, understand that all of the phenomena that turn people on, what I call science fiction phenomena, the UFOs, the Virgin Mary who stands in front of you, whatever the case happens to be, all of this is personality Crystal Bundles at work. As you will discover, you cannot trust them. They lie.

In The DreamRave Matrix, Figure 3.2, the personality crystal bundle is called the Light Field. The Personality Crystal bundle directly programs the Five Gates associated with the Light Field. These five Gates are always programmed directly by the Personality Crystal bundle. You cannot contribute to your bundle until you're dead. Think about that. Think about how this information is slanted.

The DreamRave Keys

The Mechanics of the Sleeping Life

Secrets	Possession	Turmoil	Obesssion	Fantasy	Vision
1	2	3	4	5	6

The Light Field

62 Love
20 Sight
57 Attunement
8 Darkness
1 Joy

The Earth Plane

12 Mutation
27 Yearning
50 Sex
8 Time
15 Chaos

The Demon Realm

19 Environments
53 Flight
42 Dying
38 Aggression
28 Fear

Figure 3.2: DreamRave Keys

Think about the way in which you are programmed. You're programmed by the light to be rewarded after death. This is one of the things that the light always tries to do. It always tries to say, "But we'll get you into heaven. We'll really reward you. Die now, okay? It's okay, you can die. It's all right." You go off and fight a holy war when you're seven years old. It's okay. "We'll give you the keys to the kingdom. You're going to go straight to God, baby." This is part of the Light Field conditioning.

The Light Field says, "Look, you're actually here to die. So, we'll give you many, many nice things to think about that makes death tastier: You're going to go to the Kingdom of God, you're going to be embraced by Jesus. Buddha and you are going to dance," you know, the whole story. And more important than that, when you die you get rid of the form. In those personality Crystal Bundles, you are here in form. There's no brain there. It's not like they're thinking about all of this. I mean that's one of the great jokes for me. You see, when you die, when your personality crystal leaves your vehicle, say "goodbye" because you're going into the emptiness.

These bundles, they hum. They are oscillating crystals. They carry within them incredible potential. Because as the Neutrino Ocean goes through this huge crystal consciousness that is Earth, it programs the whole universe, so it's really something. But it's not like they're aware of that. I can have contact with my father's personality crystal; it's up there somewhere in one of the bundles. And it so happens that there is a configuration and so forth and so on, and all of a sudden, I have this connection through a Neutrino stream directly to that crystal, and I think, "Jesus, that's my father," and I'm thinking about my father and have a sense of him being there. Now, I can experience that as reflected consciousness, but that crystal that is in the bundle that was once inside of what I called my father isn't aware that it's having a conversation with me, connected to me, or whatever the case may be.

I want you to be very careful. Though we tend to anthropomorphize these bundles, give them names, give them personalities, and give them everything we can, you don't want to be fooled. You are not being called to the Gates of Heaven by an attendant, present, self-conscious god; you're not. It is all an illusion. You're being called back into your source, which, by the way, as long as you're in there, as far as you are concerned from the consciousness that you have relative here, nothing will go on. You're not going to remember, to see, or to know. It's not like you're going to have access to anything that you are participating in because that's the whole point. The whole point is that while we are in form, we learn and slowly get to the point where we will ultimately control the form that is our body, but that is the greater body. It is something far beyond our potential to grasp. But we are at the forefront of reflective consciousness in form because, ultimately, that's what the totality is going to be. It's going to be some kind of extraordinary self-reflected consciousness. Now, we can't grasp that now.

So, understand that the personality field is a propaganda field as much as anything else. It is a propaganda field to imbue you with light so that you are ready ultimately to leave the form and come back and deliver the goods. Of course, the deepest dream of the Light Field is immortality. It is such a joke. You see, the personality crystals that are in all of you, that are in me, they've been here for the same amount of time. They've been here eternally. For over 15 billion years the personality crystals that sit inside of you have been in existence. They're really ancient, ancient, immortal things. For the vast majority of beings, it isn't that personality crystals don't get annihilated; they do on occasion, and great changes occur, one of which is coming up. But the fact is that immortality is the sucker pitch. It's the great pitch of the Light Field. The Light Field says, "Look, you are immortal. Just die." Isn't that a wonderful joke? I have a black sense of humor: "You are immortal. All you have to do is die. You'll see. You will exist forever. You'll see." It's true. The personality crystals tell you basically what's true. The personality crystal is sort of eternal. It'll probably last another 30, 40 billion years, something like that. It's relatively eternal. Of course, it's eternal without self-reflected consciousness. You know, that's a nice game.

There is a real difference, as in all the binaries of Human Design. There is a real difference between how the personality field operates and how the Design information operates. Design crystals do not form bundles. There's only one Design Bundle. It's had many, many mystical names. The very first time I came to teach in Vienna, I taught it as "Shambala." It's one of the many names of the Design Crystal. There is only one bundle. All of the potential of form is gathered together in that bundle which bundle operates within the earth, and it moves. You see, the teachers who came before me were personality bundle teachers, and they taught the perspectives of different personality bundles. They taught the perspective of the light. There have been many interesting and diverse teachers of the light. My experience 14 years ago was the experience of meeting the Design Bundle. It is where my information comes from. It is my archetypal joke that I am not the son of God, that is, the son of the yang personality, that I am a son of a bitch or, more nicely placed, the son of the mother; in other words, I am the messenger of form and the messenger of form knowledge.

There was a fascinating scientific discovery that took place about seven years ago. Scientists discovered through sonar experiments in the ocean that at the very core of the earth is a 2,000-kilometer-wide iron crystal. There is, figuratively speaking, in a real concrete sense, this huge, massive crystal that's at the center of what we call our earth. Now, of course, personality crystals have their own agenda. Well, so do design crystals. It is not like the form doesn't lie to you, and the light does. They both lie. They both have their stories to tell. They are caught up in what we have traditionalized in our mythologies as the eternal struggle between light and darkness. These are the great themes of the development of our self-reflective consciousness. These are the deep moral dilemmas that we have to deal with in the reality of what it is to be in form; there is constantly this dynamic between the forces of light and the forces of darkness and in the moralities that we've established because darkness eludes us, it remains the mystery. The darkness becomes associated with evil or with the negative, and the light is associated with the holy and the good.

It's such a funny joke for me. There have been people who have been telling me for years that I'm the devil. I'm not the devil. I'm older than all of that. These are relative concepts that have come out of the development of our civilizations. You see, in the Judaic-Christian mythology, in the Garden of Eden, when the snake arrives, the snake says, "Hey, form is really exciting. It's an incredible thing. Here's this apple. Here's the form. Go ahead and take a bite. Get out of this light trip. See how everything works."

Remember, we are here to be in form, to master what it is to be in form, not to be in the garden. You see, the evil of that is that when the snake came into the garden, the snake didn't give you anything except the bite, and everything else remained a mystery: "Well, how do things really work?" We become afraid of those who know about things and how they work and that we don't understand how they work. Knowledge becomes power, and the power of knowledge becomes the tool of oppression, of pain. We've lived all of that history. But, you see, I am still in this role of the snake in the garden. But there's a difference. The difference is that you can have the whole damn tree. You can have all the branches. You can have all the roots. Ignorance is what is evil. Once you grasp the essence of what form is, the question of good or bad or black or white is no longer a question because it is about ignorance.

I have met so many people who have lived out the tradition of personality light. I meet them wherever I go. It's one of my jokes. I meet all of these Holy Rollers. I meet all of these people who are filled with all that stuff. I look at them, and I think, "Polish your crystal because nobody can see your light, nobody." That's the whole business of the form. The whole business of the form is to say, "Look, the moment you surrender to your form, the moment you surrender to life, the moment you surrender to being in a body, that is when everything is correct." So, the Demon Realm hustles you in the opposite way of the personality. The personality says, "Look, get through life and die. It's terrible. Get through it. And while you're going through it, get down on your knees every once in a while, and try to get out of the pain of what it is to be in a vain body, and you can bring your glory afterward." The form side says, "Hey, excuse me, but there's nothing after life. You have to be in the life, and you have to be in the form." Both sides are after us.

You'll notice from the Division of the DreamRave/Mammalian Matrix that we're dealing with a trinity. We're dealing with a different kind of processing. The light on one side and the dark on the other side are in a constant battle. Now, there's a joke in that. They're both right. It's what it's all about. Only when you can live them both as one are you complete.

Many people on spiritual paths are not spiritual. They have a spiritual language. They have spiritual friends. They read spiritual books, but they're not spiritual. There is no such thing as a spiritual being until you are surrendered. You do not surrender to the light; you have to surrender to the darkness. You have to surrender to the form. The personality is a passenger in this vehicle. The passenger doesn't own this vehicle. This vehicle is a deep, deep privilege. We are here to be in the form, to experience the beauty, to experience the incredibleness of form. Only when you can accept your form, accept your Type, accept your Strategy, be a Passenger.

If you don't interfere, you can then have a polished crystal out of which the light can shine. But you have to accept the form first.

We are programmed deeply by both of these sides, each pulling us in its various directions. The Five Gates of the Demon Realm, the design, the dark forces, whatever you want to call them, program us to enter into the form, to embrace life for life's sake, to fear death, to hate death, to love only what it is to be, to live, to make love, to make more, to eat, to kill, to be in the form. We're all part of a form. It's a great thing. It's not a Light Field. It's a totality made up of all things. We have this struggle that goes on and which we each live out.

Ignorance and our binary nature have led to this conflict of light and darkness, as well as to the way we have anthropomorphized the conflict into our language, traditional stories, and concepts. Yet, this is a trinity, and we are programmed in three different ways in sleep. Obviously, by seeing that this relates to Gates, understand that all of us are mixes of all of these various ways in which we can be programmed. There is no true light, and there is no true darkness. What I like to call my mystical courses is a gray field. There is a place of synthesis. It has other names; you could call it the Tao. Whatever it is that you're looking for as a synthetic expression, that synthetic expression is found in the Earth Plane. When all of this was explained to me 14 years ago, this was the part that I found the most bizarre and the most fascinating. The obvious was clear to me. There is a programming from here and a programming from there, and these were the mythologies that I grew up with. Yet, the evolution of our process can be seen through the Earth Plane because this is the way the Earth Plane works.

[Editor's Note: With validation and substantiation of the Triple Design Matrix as a synthetic, integrative field during REM sleep, it is important to understand that during sleep, there is more than one synthesizing, integrative field: The Earth Plane, which is the Tao between the Demon Realm and the Light Field, and the Triple Design Matrix, which is the synthesizing, integrative field between the Waking Rave, the Solar DreamRave, and the Lunar DreamRave. At this point, this is the documented foundation of our mechanical understanding of the integration between the physiological psychological programming of the collective layers of the archetypal consciousness and our Waking awareness.]

When you all go to sleep tonight, any of these Gates that are there in the Earth Plane are Gates that are being programmed by human beings who are awake while you are asleep. I want you to think about that. You go to sleep in America. When you go to sleep in America, there is somebody in China who programs you. When that person in China goes to sleep in the evening, there is an American on the other side of the Earth programming them. I don't mean to personalize it. I just want you to have a sense of it. You see, The Earth Plane Gates form the synthetic field. By the way, there are some people on earth in certain locations on earth who don't have anybody on the other side programming them and that can be quite different. But we are all in a very special field in the Earth Plane because that's how we get in touch with how consciousness in form evolves on a day-by-day process through our development. Think about it. You see the East and the West; well, put them to sleep and see what happens. They program each other. Think about all of the poor people on the other side of the Earth from the rich people. Think about how the program feels to them and how their dreams are programmed by DVDs and computers, and whatever. We're not separate from each other. We constantly impact each other. The sleeping human being is programmed by the waking human being; we always exchange information. This is where the synthesis exists. This is where it meets in us.

Grasp something: The Earth Plane is a generative field. If you look at these Earth Plane Gates, you'll see that they create a generator. So, do the Demon Realm Gates. However, the Light Field is a Projection Field. That statement tells you a lot. But, to understand the nature of this Earth Plane generative field realize that it generates consciousness.

We respond to the program and our response to the program generates consciousness. This is life, and we program each other. Think about all the Generators on this planet. Seventy percent of the earth is made up of Generators and Manifesting Generators (cf. "Revised Research Verifies 5 Types in the Human Design System, "Eleanor Haspel-Portner, Ph.D. Rave Life Sciences. August 2001). Generators know that they are ignorant. They are caught in the web of evil, and the result is that they are frustrated, in pain, and suffering. What do you think it feels like when you are programmed by them? What do you think that feels like? We are not alone. It's not about, "Well, it's on the other side of the world. It doesn't affect me. It's okay that there are 2 billion of us who are hungry." Well, when you're sleeping, you get their program, and you have to deal with that, and it lives inside of you.

Without vanity, as all Mammals do within their kind, you find a way so that everyone, each and every member of the species, has an opportunity to live out its truth. We have a whole world of pain, and we take it in. You take in your Earth Plane. When you wake up in the morning, you carry the pain of the world inside of you. That's why I spend so much time in my life trying to wake up Generators so that we can evolve, so that we can move on. If everyone is being programmed by pain and suffering while they're asleep, they bring it into their daily lives. You are not separate from the pain, and you will never escape it.

One thing in the end that form teaches is that we are one form. Our vanity, our illusion of separateness, means nothing. It's just our movie. We are one thing. The most important knowledge that I can bring with the DreamRave is for everyone to recognize deeply within themselves that their advantage, their privilege is that you take the Oneness in all the time. You cannot escape the horror of the world. This is where we have a chance to see our development and growth. The Earth Plane is where the Tao is, and it is only when that Earth Plane is free of pain that we are going to have a world that wakes up in the morning and embraces life until death.

When we do a Mammalian calculation, the calculation is 88 degrees of the Moon before birth to establish what the Design information is. To get the Design data, unlike in a human being where you calculate 88 degrees of the Sun before birth, here you deal with 88 degrees of the Moon before birth, so you're dealing with a much shorter span. In a human being, you can see that the personality crystal actually comes in and spends one-third of the gestation process inside of us, that is, given a normal pregnancy. It takes a lot of time to get comfortable with sitting in the vehicle and all of those things. When you deal with Mammals, you are dealing with a less-than-a-week timeframe.

The personality crystal is yanked into the vehicle very, very quickly, so it has very little time in that vehicle before the actual birth takes place. However, it doesn't mean that in order to be able to understand the complete reality of what it is to be human, there are simply these two different Charts – there is the Solar Rave Chart, the Waking Rave Chart that we're all comfortable with, and then there is this Mammalian variation on the other side – but there is a third thing: The DreamRave, through the Mammalian design, operates through different calculations. When you go from being erect to being horizontal and you are waking, e.g., if I were to lie down here on this table, the calculation for my Mammalian Design would simply transfer what is in my normal Waking Rave chart and just put that in the 15-Gate Matrix. In other words, the Design Personality calculated for my individual Waking Rave is the same as what is called the Solar DreamRave. Basically, you can understand the Solar DreamRave by recognizing that it refers to you in a horizontal state being awake or being in the first stages of sleep. Consciousness can go from being awake and horizontal to being asleep and horizontal, but deep sleep is a different state of consciousness.

What that gives us is our regular Waking Rave. When we're awake, it gives us the Solar DreamRave; when we're awake horizontally or when we have just entered into sleep, or when we are just coming out of sleep; and then you have the Lunar DreamRave that is different because the Design is different.

In other words, the Design you've had in your Waking Rave chart could still be there if it was in these Gates in the Matrix, and that could still be there in the Solar DreamRave. In the Lunar DreamRave, suddenly, those Design aspects disappear, and new ones emerge because you have a new calculation. In this Design calculation, your Personality stays the same; it is consistent throughout. But when you do this calculation for the Lunar DreamRave, you go back to 88 degrees of the Moon from your birth. You calculate the Chart as if you were a Mammal, and that gives you a totally different configuration. One of the most important things in Lunar

DreamRave analysis is the difference between your horizontal Solar DreamRave and your deep sleep Lunar DreamRave. There is a transition between the two. We're seeing in our research (cf. Rave Life Sciences) that it really makes a difference. If something is present as you enter into sleep but disappears when you're in a deep sleep, and you have to come back and meet it again when you're coming out of sleep, it can be disturbing. We actually have three different Matrixes that we can look at to see the totality of our being: The individual Waking Rave chart, the Solar DreamRave, and the Lunar DreamRave. The three charts form what Eleanor has designated as the Triple Design Matrix.

> After this presentation, I used astrological calculations to delineate the Sleep Design of a Mammal. We know, factually, that Mammals have stages of sleep similar to those of a human. The Lunar DreamRave that Ra talked about is calculated at 88 Lunar Degrees before the Birth Time. I used the Lunar Minute calculation to look at a more sensitive Body Map, one that would differentiate twin kittens. Eight Charts form what I call Noble Energy Maps® and include the Mental/Waking, Spiritual/Archetypal, Emotional/Angelic, and Physical/Biological Worlds. The Four Worlds operate in different Matrices: The Mental/Waking World has 64 Gates, The Spiritual/Archetypal World has 15 Gates, The Emotional/Angelic World has 33 Gates, and the Physical/Biological World has 25 Gates. The validity of these calculations has been documented in Noble Energy Maps® on over 45,000 cases proving that 99% of the general population are Manifesting Generators.

When it comes to understanding or beginning to understand the nature of how we're programmed, the way I've described to you in the beginning, the programming of the crystal fields, and the ultimate synthetic programming of us programming each other, all of that takes place in the configuration of the Lunar DreamRave.

The Solar DreamRave is important, but it is important only from a different point of view. It is very important to understand that the transition between the deep Lunar Sleep and the deep Lunar Chart is unique in its nature because the calculation is different. It is here where the programming takes place at the deepest level and where you make your legitimate contribution to the totality. It is important to see that in terms of the way you use this information in analysis.

The description of the DreamRave and the way it operates describes the Lunar DreamRave. It involves stepping into that deeper state, and it is in that deeper state that the real programming takes place. (Ed. Note: Eleanor has documented that the actual programming with its integration takes place in the REM state, during which the information programmed into the neural circuitry is actually downloaded into the Hard Drive of the brain physiology). However, it is in moving back and forth between the Solar and the Lunar DreamRaves that we have a tremendous amount of information for physical and psychological well-being.

This information has a great deal of significance in potentially helping people who have medical, psychological, and/or sleep problems. The statistics (cf. Rave Life Science publications) indicate that the Triple Design Matrix can diagnose and help with sleep and other problems that are epidemic and enormous. Many, many medical and other insights are possible through understanding and providing service to people by understanding the relationship between the Lunar and the Solar DreamRaves.

This material is the mystical side of all of the information. Keep it in that context. See that there is deep, deep programming that goes on when we are absolutely uninvolved, and it's there to really see the magic of what it is to be human and, what it is to be in these forms, how profound our contribution actually is.

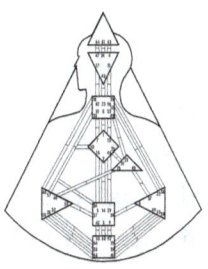

The Light Field

We're going to begin with the programming of the Light Field. Remember that the programming of the Light Field is the personality of Crystal Bundles and the impact that they have as mediums through which the Neutrino Ocean or the Neutrino Stream operates. We are deeply, deeply conditioned in terms of how we perceive the outside world by this Light Field. It's one of my jokes, one of the great jokes of my design is that, given the kind of man I am and given the kind of knowledge that I teach and given the kind of forces that I've dealt with. My Lunar DreamRave has Channel 8-1, Channel 20-57, and Gate 62. I don't have any of the other stuff. I don't have Demon Gates. I go into this deep, deep sleep, and all the light forces say, "Okay, let's get him. We got him." It's one of the ironies of my life.

Begin with the Light Field. But first, notice that the DreamRave Keys breaks the Body Graph into three areas of Five Gates each, i.e., there are 15 Gates altogether (see Figure 3.2 on page 273). At the top of each of these blocks of Five Gates, there is one Gate that is given a different color.

Look at the Mammalian Design. All forms of life, other than the Waking Individual Rave, the Human Rave, which is a closed system, all other forms of life, animate or inanimate, are designed to integrate with other forms of life. In terms of life forms, these are called Cross-Species Gates. If you have a dog and you happen to have Gate 49 and the dog has Gate 19, this is a cross-species bonding. It is a way in which two species can meet each other. It is the way we have met in the past. As a matter of fact, this connection to Mammals is where we captured them, bred them, and killed them for dinner, and while we were doing that, we blessed them, gave them godhead status, and honored them for feeding us.

The next Cross-Species Gate from the Mammal is Gate 12. It is there that the Mammal has the potential to have the 12th Gate but not the 22nd Gate. This potential for having the 12th Gate gives Mammals their connection, ultimately, to what is our Solar Plexus or our emotional system. This Center is where humans and Mammals meet as friends. It is a social connection. It is how, ultimately, humanity was able to survive by making friends with dogs. They were about the same weight, ate the same food, traveled in the same territories, and if we didn't make friends, it would have been a fight to the bitter end. This is the place where you make friends. This is a place where you can meet the stranger. Of course, there is a third Cross-Species Gate. Gate 62 is a potential in Mammals but Gate 17 is not. Mammals other than Humans do not have a neocortex. It is here that you train bears to ride bicycles. It's here where Pavlov trained his dogs to drool. It is here that you can train, that you can bring order, organization, and understanding as a Cross-Species field.

In Mammals, these are Cross-Species Gates. In the Lunar DreamRave, these are Portal Gates. It is both through Portal Gates and out of Portal Gates that information exchange actually takes place within the dream structure and how it gets to the Waking Rave and into the Waking consciousness. These Portals can bring the importance or the value of the programming that takes place. Through those Portals, the information/archetypes can be brought out into the larger world, into the larger Mental/Waking World.

Also, through those Portals, at the Lunar DreamRave level, information can come in from the outside.

When we're looking at each of these divisions, the Light Field, the Earth Plane, and the Demon Realm recognize some things: The Light Field is a projective field. We know what the projection field is, that is. The Light Field tends to bring us a great deal of bitterness because bitterness is a theme of projection; it is about recognizing and being recognized. The Light Field itself cannot do anything, so what it is there to do is to guide, just as the whole projector theme happens to be. If you look at the Earth Plane and the Demon Realm, you'll see that they are more similar to each other. They are both rooted in the Sacral Center. They are both rooted in Generative energy. Notice something else, also. When you look at the Body Graph and you look at the Throat Center, you see that there are only four Gates in the Throat Center in the Mammalian Matrix. The Demon Realm has no voice. It is part of what makes the Demon Realm dark to us. It cannot explain itself to us. It does not have that capacity to articulate. The Earth Plane has one Throat Gate; the Light Field has three voices. The capacity of light to fill us up, to stimulate us at the intellectual plane, to catch us in conceptualizations, that light "advertises" itself. Think about it. The Light Field and the Demon Realm have all the publicity. They have the whole thing. The power of the Light Field is that it can speak; it has a voice. Anybody who has a Lunar Gate in the Throat Center finds great importance when they speak in their sleep or when they hear dialogues in their head. Those things are very important collectively.

There have been many dream societies where the tribe gets up in the morning, and everybody shares the night's dreams. The experience is not personal. The people get in touch with the program. If you get up in the morning with your dream and you think your dream is about you, that's your illusion. It isn't. Many of us have the same dreams all the time. Those of us who are here are programmed by the same forces that are over there on the other side of the world. One of the things to recognize about the Light

Field is that the Light Field tends to dominate the information that we get from the dream state. That's neither good nor bad; it's just something clearly to be seen. It is all talk and no action. There's a lot of promising going on, but it doesn't mean it can be delivered.

Remember, you cannot trust either the Demon Realm or the Light Field. You can't. If there is anything we can trust, it is the Earth Plane programming because it represents us. It is humans as the Synthesis Field of the light and the dark as one together. I want you to understand why the dark side has always had a hard time. It has a hard time in terms of the way civilizations and philosophers attach names and concepts to these things. It's a frightening place. The Demon Realm has no voice, so we are dominated by this Realm. When this Piscean Age comes to an end, and it will come to an end, it will be seen how important it is to get the facts out. We're dominated by the belief systems; we are dominated by the dreams and illusions of the Light Field because that is what gets expressed at the verbal level through our Dream Field. Don't be fooled. Remember that the message of the Light Field is "die." Think about that. "Die and go to heaven." It's nice.

Channel 8-1

In Mammalian design, the 8-1 is the Channel of the Alpha. As the Channel of the Alpha, it gives the Direction. It is the place in which the direction of the program, the direction of our whole dream purpose, is given to us. In that sense, it is very, very powerful in its impact on us. One of the interesting things statistically about the nature of the Lunar DreamRave is that the majority of Lunar DreamRave beings have an undefined Self (G Center), which is different statistically from what occurs statistically in the Waking Rave (cf."The Triple Design Matrix: Type Statistically Verified Across the Matrix." By Eleanor Haspel-Portner, Ph.D. Rave Life Sciences. August 2001). Lack of identity is very, very important in the dream life. There are many people. There are examples here in this room of people whose Lunar DreamRave has no activation whatsoever. I know Mammals like that, no activation whatsoever. In many ways, that is the perfect state. People have asked about ideal charts; I say, "Yeah, sure, no activation." Then you have an ideal Chart because then you can take in everything and you can be one with the totality.

Gate 1

The 1st Gate is the Gate of Direction. It is the Gate of Direction coming out of the G-Center. You can see, of course, that that is the only direction that is possible coming out of the G-Center. So, the direction that comes out of the G-Center is keynoted: Joy. Look, I play a lot with light and dark as a game because, after all, it's been unfair: Light is able to get all of the publicity. Of course, it's essential for us to be pointed towards the light, obviously. It's essential for us to be pointed toward the whole. It is essential for us to recognize our relative immortality. It's essential for us to recognize not that we were created in God's image, but rather that we are God creating God. That is something we're here to discover.

The first thing to recognize about the basic direction that we have in this life, a direction that we're given in the program, is the direction of the joy of the light. We can see that in the terminologies that we have, e.g., "a light at the end of the tunnel." It is an illusion people have when they're dying that they see the light at the end of the tunnel; there are people waving at them and calling them; there is this whole family in the crystal bundle that is saying, "Come on back, come on back." That's what is there in that 1st Line theme. I have that in my design. I have the 1st Gate. I don't have the 8th Gate. I have the 1st Gate and I don't have the 8th Gate in my Waking Rave Chart or in my Solar DreamRave Chart. But in my Lunar DreamRave Chart, there is the 8th Gate.

That theme of darkness is actually the light describing the dark. That's like Hitler describing the Jews. Please understand that. Don't believe all that. In other words, the voice, that realm, has no voice.

The Light Field controls the way the program describes darkness to us. That's what I get when I go down into the deepest zone. It says, "Ah, you poor soul. You have to go live in the body, poor thing, the treacherous, ugly body, the weight of being in the world; the hunger, the anger, the pain, the savagery, all of those things, the barbarity to stay alive, that you must destroy and kill, all of that."

You see, you are entering into the darkness, knowing that at the other end of the darkness is the light. If it weren't for the 8th Gate in my Lunar DreamRave, I never would have had any capacity to be able to bring to you what darkness is, what form is. At the deepest level part of the program, the Light Field knows. It recognizes that we must be in form. It recognizes all of that because the form is everything. It just says, "Look, it's really ugly, but it's okay. You give unto Caesar what is Caesar's. There is a glory waiting for you, and that glory is something you can only know when you die." Basically, the Light Field teaches us that our motivation keeps us going in the hardship of the world because we know there is light on the other side. I could do a great Baptist imitation now about the cost of dealing with the devil in this life, that Satan is on your back, and you have to carry Satan across in order to get to the light. We all get it. It is part of the program. What to do?

Gate 57

The 57th Gate is a very important Gate at all levels in Human Design. Notice that the Light Field is the most deeply acoustic field. It is acoustic in terms of the individuality that is present as definitions but also in the fact that the individuality has outlets in the Throat Center. It is one of the things to understand about all experiences at the dream level: no matter what you think you see in a dream, you have actually heard it. Nobody sees anything in a dream. It is actually heard at many levels, but it's an acoustic experience that can be translated or transformed through the metamorphosis that takes place in the Throat Center. The 57th Gate is a Fear of

Tomorrow. We know that in terms of its context in design analysis. Something important to understand is that the Light Field and the Demon Realm are not to be trusted. They are both involved in the tension between each other, and both of them try to get us to accept death in different ways. It's not like they're really against each other; it's just their approach that differs.

The 57th Gate carries within it the deepest yearning for immortality. It doesn't want to be worried about tomorrow, the integration aspect of that, whether it can survive or not, the fears of not being able to have enough to eat, all of those things that drive integration. It is driven by a fear of mortality and by the dream of immortality. It is not the immortality of the flesh. It's the joke of the personality that says, "Yes, you are immortal." Your Personality Crystals have been here forever. You can maintain that immortality. Don't worry. Dying is okay. The moment you die, guess what? You have no fear of the now, and you have no fear of tomorrow. You see, the dreamer in the 57th Gate goes to a place of fearlessness, absolute fearlessness, as if they are eternal everything, always. That's the magic we're being offered. It's true, it's true, I know. I know that we are ancient. But that's the way it's presented.

These dreams of immortality are a way of getting us past the fact that we have a lousy job. We get constantly thrown into form. You've all incarnated over and over and over again. That's why you don't remember it. You would hate it. This is not for you. The totality doesn't give a damn about you and your relative life. It is about all of us: everything, every plant, and every fish. This is a vast consciousness program at work. Here is that immortality, the dream of reward, the beauty of light, the Buddhist dream: "Let's get rid of the body. Let's just be humming light," that's the dream reward. It helps us survive. It helps us survive the fact that life is hard; our jobs are terminal, and our bodies are rented. We survive being experimental, cyclical incarnators. We survive all of it. When it gets to be too much, and you get to the 20th Gate, you wake up in horror. That is the 20th Gate. The 20th gate brings you out of the deepest sleep instantaneously. You heard something you did not want to hear. It is vibrational. It shakes you right awake.

Love is the theme of the Light Field, and Love is in the details. In the end, the Light Field knows that it is only an aspect of the whole. The Fields point at each other, and true love comes with the Details.

Ultimately, in order for us to be of value to the totality, we cannot be ignorant. We are not here as Mammals; we are here to know at the deepest possible level of Knowing. Can't you see it? We are already in the business of creating Light. We genetically alter food; that process never existed before. We clone extinct animals and bring them into life out of the wombs of cows. We are going to create human beings according to what we need. We will. We are here to be the greatest, the ultimate creative force; that is our purpose. So, in the end, the Detail is our fulfillment. Through this Portal Gate, 62, some of the most important information we receive comes through. Through Gate 62 comes the Voice of Angels. It is the voice of God in your ear; true information, and messages from the Light Field point toward fulfillment of the Detail. Remember, their role is to give us the right drug to get us through the hardship of what it is to be in Form. That drug is Love, and the personification of that drug is a God that loves us, one who rewards us for our arduous task. It is nice.

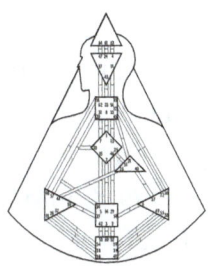

The Demon Realm

Channel 53/42

Whereas the Light Field brings us our direction, the Demon Realm brings us our format in terms of looking at the configuration of the Matrix. As we know, the format energy here in Channel 53-42 is the Format Energy in Design Analysis that we refer to as Maturation. It is one of the things to recognize. If the entire biverse, what I call the biverse, is to be awakened truly, if it's genuinely a totality of consciousness, then the mastery of form and the mastery of endowing form with light – if I were just black, you wouldn't have anything to do with it, it would be terrifying.

The whole thing to recognize is that the two aspects are part of the same thing. They are just polarities, after all. This is how we're programmed from the start, from the Demon Realm, in terms of our Format. The Format begins with the 53rd Gate, the Gate of Flight. It carries the classic dream of the Gate of Flight. I have had this dream in which I am flying, and while flying, I suddenly realize it's harder and harder to fly. In my case, my legs had bracelets on them that led to chains, and the chains went down toward the Earth. There were all kinds of what appeared to be ants in the dream, pulling the chains and yanking me back down. The Demon Realm starts off by saying, "Let's get out of the body."

It has a different purpose in that, by the way. It allows us to be able to kill. People in the 21st Century, at least some of us, get uncomfortable with that. But, after all, if we hadn't gotten to the top of the food chain, we would have been a terrible failure because we would have been eaten off by something else, and the whole prospect of consciousness in form never would have survived. But it's also essential to understand that out of the 53rd Gate, the very first thing that we get from the form is the recognition from the form itself that the form is a trip, and it would really be nice to get rid of it. But it's also telling us something else. On the other side of Gate 53 is Gate 42, the Gate of Dying. It's not really the Gate of Dying; you can call it the Gate of Decaying. Everything about the Demon Realm can be seen from its Portal Gate 19. It's about the Environment.

That Environment is your Body. That's the primary environment. It is all about the Form. What the Format says to us is that our literal escape from Form is to experience the Form decaying and dying. I had a conversation yesterday. I was talking about something, and I said, "Well, we're going to die, and that will be it." It's true. There is this deep recognition through this Format in all of us that these bodies are naturally decaying. When you're young, you may fear being old, but when you're old, isn't it funny to experience how the body says, "Hey, I feel good"? We learn to experience and accept decay; we accept our time as a limitation.

If you know that this miracle is dying, it's decaying; we must honor it. That's the whole point. The whole point of the Demon Realm is to learn to love not God but your Form, the privilege of the Form, the privilege of having a neocortex. I may love dogs but don't want a dog's life. There is a privilege in having a neocortex. It is the intent or the purpose of evolution that we are self-conscious at the highest possible level. We cannot do that unless we embrace the Form. That's our Format to start us off on that process.

In continuing with the Demon Realm, we've looked at a Format and a Format Energy that says to us that we are helpless in Form. I have heard so many so-called mystical, spiritual people talk about how you choose your parents. Yeah. The first thing you recognize about being in form is that they don't want you to understand how that works because you would rebel. In other words, this is a lousy job. You're not paid well. You suffer a lot. You have a billion people on this planet who have religious affiliation with somebody who was nailed to a cross and died. This is the Earth. One of the things to recognize about Earth is that Form says, "Okay, we realize that this is a tough ride. Don't be terribly concerned about it because the body is going to decay. You cannot stop the decay. You don't have to worry about being in form because the Form comes to an end. You will end up seeing that you live through the whole process whether you like it or not." You go from child to adult; you go from the vitality of youth to death.

Channel 28/38

Everything about the Demon Realm is about the Environment. That Environment, particularly in Channel 28-38 within the context of Human Design, is the Channel of Struggle. The 28th Gate in Design

Analysis is a Gate of the Fear of Death, i.e., the Fear of Purposelessness. But, the most mystical and magical thing about the 28th Gate is that that 28th Gate is there to bring us to the point of awareness because it represents a very profound fear; it carries the fear that the Form cannot handle the consciousness. It is the fear of whether or not the form can handle the consciousness. In other words, the fear is about whether consciousness at all can really work through the Form. Can we transcend being the beast? Can we transcend these things? Can we attain our Godhood? Can this Form really be endowed with consciousness? Some of our deepest graces come from that fear.

On the other side of Gate 28 is the 38th Gate, a Gate of Aggression. Human beings, being binaries, tend to moralize words, particularly words like "aggression." Aggression can be given a negative connotation. One of the things about this inherent Struggle is where Gate 28 Struggles for the growth of consciousness, the growth of awareness within the Form; the 38th Gate recognizes that to do that, you have to Survive. You have to eat. You have to kill. You have to be protected. You have to be alert. You have to be aggressive. You have to deal with the world. People who experience what is often called the "astral plane" will describe the astral plane as a frightening and often deeply violent field of energy. This very much describes the 38th Gate. It is very much about fierceness. Gate 38 means in a Mammal fierceness that is necessary to get to where we are.

I am not an apologist for being a killer ape. I'm not. What is the point of that? The fact of the matter is that the crudity and primitiveness of this Form is the fundamental limitation; the deepest Fear of Gate 28 is that "Ah, geez, it's such a limited Form, how are we ever going to wake up? How are we ever going to be enlightened? How are we ever going to be God?" Because of the Form's limitation and the struggle for the form, we have that Fear.

Those of you who have taken mystical courses with me before know that there will be a change in the Form. The Form will change. It will be a lot more sophisticated than this one. So, there is turmoil within us because we have to deal with the limitations of the Form. I get my angriest as a Manifestor when dealing with students for so long now. There's a part of me that says, "Their form is their limitation. They're never going to get past it. I might as well kill them." That's the deepest fear that comes from the Form itself: the Form itself is a limitation that will not allow us to transcend the Form itself. We are aspects of the whole coming to grips with our own inherent holiness. This programming is taking place at a very, very deep level inside of us. Everything about both the Light Field and the Demon Realm is coming to grips with the ordeal of the body. It is coming to grips with what it means to accept that living in Form is a difficult task.

What's interesting about the Demon Realm is that it is so deeply connected to food. That's what makes these machines so primitive. I had a fast of over 40 days, and it was one of the most delightful things not to have to eat at all, not to care about food, not to waste energy thinking about it, doing it, all of those things. Of course, if I had gone on any longer, I would have died. There is a compromise we make in being in Form. The Form must be satisfied. If you are someone who has Demon Realm activations in your Lunar DreamRave, and, particularly, if you have the 19th Gate, there is something very important to understand: You will wake up in the morning, and you will not remember your dream. But the moment you have your breakfast, you will. It's a very important thing to recognize and to be open in those moments and not be distracted. Suddenly, that dream will come back to you. It's deeply connected to food.

One of the most frightening things that exist for us is that because we are part of Mammalian biology, we are terrified of extinction. We have to accept that as part of the bargain for us. I teach you to let go of trying to control your form and watch your form with your light. When the two live together the way they were intended to live, the byproduct is that within you as a human being, there is an internal quietness.

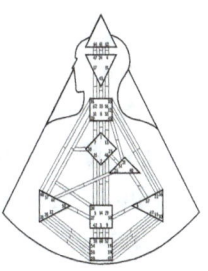

The Earth Plane

The Earth Plane is the only thing we can trust, and it's us. In other words, it's the synthetic result of what it is to be alive in the world. It is what it is to be in your Waking Human Design Rave, your waking life. It is to be through that whole process. All of that is synthesized here at the Earth Plane. You can see that the 12th Gate is its Portal, and the 12th Gate is named "Mutation," where it all takes place. There is programming on either side: the love on one side, the light on one side, the environment, the form, the body on the other side. But here in the middle, this is the Tao. This is the synthetic field. This is the place where true mutation takes place.

The essential ingredient in looking at the Earth Plane is to look at the Tantra. The Earth Plane has the only Tantric Channel in the Mammalian structure. Channel 15-5, Being in the Flow, is an enormously important channel because it is universal among all life forms, right down to the single cell. Channel 15-5 is one of the very basic channels of existence. We know it in the analysis as the Channel of Rhythm of Being in the Flow. Being in the Flow of the waking consciousness translates into what we call time.

Our relative waking universe is our relationship in the waking world to gravity. Gravity, by that very result, leads to our illusion of time, our measurement of movement. The personality is deeply concerned about time: "How much time do I have left today, tomorrow?" "How much time is left on this plane?" These are all questions of time in terms of when things have to be done, of all the timings that we have. This is the waking consciousness and its way of being in the flow. We say, "We all have to gather here at 10:00." We all come into the flow. In other words, time is essential to understand about the waking consciousness, but the sleeping life is very different.

Gate 5

The 5th Gate Keynote is Time. The way to understand it is as Timelessness. When you enter into the Dream Realm and fall deep into that Lunar DreamRave world, there is no time, no gravity, no movement in space. It is all relative to the Waking Consciousness. One of the glories of the 5th Gate is that you can be in the timelessness of everything. It is a magnificent place. By the way, that can become quite uncomfortable at the mundane level. For example, if in your Lunar DreamRave, you have the 5th Gate, and you go into deep timelessness in your deepest sleep, and when you come to the surface, if that isn't there, oh, how disturbingly you get thrown into it. These are people who hate alarm clocks. They come out of timelessness into, "Gees, I only have ten minutes to go…" How uncomfortable that is.

Gate 15

On the other side of this Tantric Gate 5, you have Gate 15. Gate 15 is keynoted Chaos. Here, time completely breaks down as a continuum. I had a wonderful dream in which my dead father and my dead dog were with me in the future. This is a classic Gate15 dream. The yesterday, the tomorrow, and the now get all jumbled up together, resulting in incredible Chaos. At the same time, there is magic in that. The past can speak to you through Gate 15, i.e., through Gate 15, you can meet the past. People with the 15th Gate are convinced they have had a past life. Something is banging into other time frames that says, "Well, wait a minute. I must have been there." We were all there over and over and over again. If you knew that, you'd be very angry because it doesn't seem like there's any reward for it. We're too dumb. It's really, really difficult.

Gate 28

We do have the fear of Gate 28; we do have a limitation. I cannot see microwaves. I cannot watch the Neutrino stream move through me. I cannot consciously access all of that. I have deep, deep limitations as a form. Of course, in the flow of evolution, that's obvious. We are allowed the awareness that the limitation will tolerate. My job is to get us to the point where, at least, we fulfill the limitation; if you fulfill it, you can ultimately transcend it.

The whole basis of the absolute truth of the program is that we are part of the timelessness and timeliness of all things. We are everything. We are the alpha and the omega. We are all things. We are all time and part of an all process. That's the magic that's there that we call the Tantra that leads to the love of humanity. That is our uniqueness. We are beyond time. We are so far beyond time that we are so ancient. It is all there. It is all a part of us. That's its real beauty.

By the way, those beings who carry a great deal of the Earth Plane, and in particular those who carry the Gate 5 or the Gate 15, can have contact with information that's been in existence, that's been in the world, they can be in contact with information that hasn't come yet. There is no time in that concept; there is no time, so all times are possible, no matter how difficult that is for the waking consciousness to deal with. It is the waking consciousness that's described in what is called physics. The waking consciousness says we're moving in space, that it's time, and it's this, and it's that, etc. At the deepest dream level, at the deepest level of receiving programming, we are immortal. We are outside of time, and none of that matters. All things are possible as information that can come through. It is ultimately expressed through the Portal. It is eventually expressed mutatively to transform us. Prophecy comes through the Dream Realm. The voice of prophecy can speak and articulate mutation. We are constantly mutating. We are continually moving in the waking context toward the future that we are always in contact with at the sleeping level, always.

Channel 50/27

You can see that in the Earth Plane, you have the Channel 50-27. The Channel 50-27 is the only sexual channel in a Mammal. It is the equivalent of Channel 59-6 in a human being. It's where the genetic structure of their sexuality is determined. The way Mammals live together through sexual bonding is determined in Channel 50-27. There is not any sex in the dream life in the context of how that word is normally understood. It doesn't operate that way. However, something goes on in terms of the way bonding takes place. We have a lot of trouble getting along with each other. That is part of being human.

One of the things you lose when you're in the Lunar DreamRave stage is that you stop being human in terms of a functioning neocortex. One of the things possible then is that you can bond in a way you've never bonded before. This is the herding instinct in a Mammal built into a hierarchical structure. The 50th Gate is the Gate of the Law, and the law constantly mutates. One of the most important things about Gate 50, the Gate of the Law, is control of how we bond. In human beings, all the sexual rules come from Channel 50-27: whether somebody is circumcised or not, when they bond and mate or not, what they do in terms of mating, and so forth, and so on. All of those structures are established in Gate 50. Grasp that it is in the Earth Plane where the most mundane, cliched spiritual expressions occur in Gate 50, e.g., "We are all brothers and sisters," "Love thy neighbor as thy self," All of that is possible in the bonding that takes place at the deep Lunar DreamRave level. That bonding that takes place according to Type does not occur according to the Type you have in your Waking Rave but according to the Type that you have in your deep Lunar DreamRave.

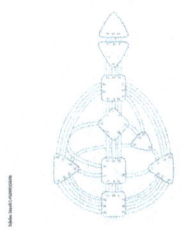

Conclusion

You can never escape the hierarchy or hierarchies. You can never escape these distinctions. In partnership classes now, I tell people, "If you are a Manifestor, be with a Manifestor. If you're a Generator, be with a Generator. If you're a Projector, be with a Projector. If you're a Reflector, be with a Reflector. If you must be with a different Type than your own, be an energy Type with an energy Type, or be a non-energy Type with a non-energy Type." Ultimately, that's the way that it's going to work. Ultimately, the organization of the totality has to do with the way we intrinsically operate. The real mutation takes place while there is all this pain on the surface of the waking life. We have people here who hate people there. We have all of these distinctions creating the dilemma of being able to come together. In the deepest dream state, however, we make deep bonds with the other.

Now, remember, through your Triple Design Matrix, you're bonding with something other than just yourself. You are programmed people who are awake while you're asleep in the Earth Plane. This is where we truly make contact with each other. If you have a sexual dream, you wake up, and you transform the acoustic phenomena. It's all acoustic. You transform it into a visual. Please understand that you didn't have a sexual dream, but you bonded deeper than you've ever bonded in your waking life. That's how you know it actually happened; it was there, but it's the only way we translate it through the waking consciousness (Ed. Note: this process occurs in the REM state of sleep, i.e., the Integrated Field of Consciousness). It is so important to see that we work together at a level much deeper than we're able to recognize, even among those of us who work deeply and cooperatively together. It is nothing in comparison to what's going on in this field.

I have some advice for you: Don't sleep with anybody. I've been telling people this forever: don't sleep with anybody. Don't sleep with people. Don't do that (Ed. Note: Research clinically has demonstrated that it is beneficial for some people to sleep in the same space, while it is detrimental to others). You don't want someone messing up your enlightenment, do you? Understand that. It's really what it's all about. It's essential that you grasp the importance of being in your own aura. I've been giving that advice to people for a very long time with this knowledge underneath. I've been telling them over and over again. I try to provide the mundane values of that, i.e., you don't want to be filled up by somebody's center, which they have, and you don't. You would have to deal with that energy afterward; you would not wake up like yourself and the rest of these obvious things.

The most important thing of all is that you have to do your job when you're unconscious. When you're asleep in your deepest state, it's the most beautiful thing you do. That's one of the things that gives humanity grace. We're not totally useless. We have enormous problems with awakening to the beauty and the grace of life. We have big problems with it, yet there is an aspect of our nature: one-third of our lives that we spend in this state where we do enormously valuable work, in which we truly are a community of love and growth. It's very special. It may be frustrating that you don't actively participate, but that's our limitation.

This is the first time ever that this knowledge, that this Gateway, has opened up so we can even understand what is really going on here. It isn't about what you do with this knowledge. This knowledge is at a very deep level. We are helpless; we are incompetent. Stop interfering. Greater things are going on in this life than ever imagined. Your absolute value to the totality is far beyond anything you've ever been able to grasp. We are truly magical creatures. On one side, we make our contribution to the whole, yet we make it unknowingly, selflessly, with no vanity, with no guilt, with no shame, with no blame, with no need for reward, with no need for the conflict of light or dark or this or that; we are magnificent in that state. Despite whatever the conscious, awake suffering happens to be, it's so important that at least you know that we are participating at that level and that we are true of value. Recognize that what we are doing in our waking consciousness is desperately seeking to mirror what we learn at the deepest levels while in our deepest sleep. We want to be able to bond in perfection.

We are all capable of the deepest love. We are here to shine with light. We are here to totally accept the grace of being in form. We are here to be God. That is us, and that is our journey. Feel adequate in your waking life and in the pursuit of coming to grips with what is true for you. Recognize that you are always making a contribution, an extraordinary contribution at a state of awareness of consciousness, and if you could see that at your waking level, you would really stun yourself because none of this stuff burdens us.

It is important that each and every one of you live out your waking strategy. After all, that's what waking consciousness is all about. The Triple Design Matrix and beyond is about the fact that we are already in the "correct state" of deep sleep. Hopefully, none of you will mess with that. Human Design brings awareness to you while in all states of consciousness. That's an essential journey. You get to that journey by living out your nature, and you get to that journey by living out your nature and not sleeping with other people so that you can continue to be pure in what you truly do at your deepest level in this life. Remember, not sleeping with somebody is not about sex or love. It is not about acceptance or rejection. It is simply wise. It is better to be wise than not to have the chance to be awake and be clear. [Ra's adamant view about sleeping separately can be healthy for some couples and unhealthy for others. Please note that Ra spoke about this subject in 2001 when my research was in its infancy. Type, as Ra presented it in Human Design, has been proven statistically and through multiple forms of validation to be an incomplete system. The Human Design Body Graph is a partial picture of how a person's energy develops and how cosmic energy influences them. Noble Energy Maps® has documented that 99% of the population function as Manifesting Generators in their Integrated Energy Map, and it shows how they are influenced by cosmic energy that activates all Four Worlds at specific times over the first three months of life. I recommend you read the material in this book as source material and do further exploration and research.]

Book Three References

"Preliminary Research on the Human Design System and Health." Eleanor Haspel-Portner, PhD, et al., Rave Live Sciences, 2000)

"Revised Research Verifies 5 Types in the Human Design System." Eleanor Haspel-Portner, PhD. Rave Life Sciences. August 2001

"The Triple Design Matrix: Type Statistically Verified Across the Matrix." By Eleanor Haspel-Portner, Ph.D. Rave Life Sciences. August 2001.

About the Author

It is my great honor and privilege to share my knowledge with you and to use it to help you live a life of fulfillment and recognition of your divinity.

My interest in astrology began in 1971 when I was told that astrology is the most scientific of the esoteric disciplines. At the time, I had just completed my doctorate at the University of Chicago, was well versed in psychology, sociology, anthropology, and biology, and had done extensive research on world religions; however, hearing that astrology was scientific intrigued me.

I found an astrology bookstore near my home and proceeded to learn how to calculate an astrology chart. It proved to be the hardest thing I had ever attempted to learn. The language was symbolic and the mathematical calculations complex. But I persisted and began to understand basic astrological work.

Two years later, I was deeply honored and blessed to book an astrological reading with Katherine de Jersey. The reading with her showed me the power and depth of astrology in the hands of a Master. I studied astrology privately with several astrologers and was also in training as a Jungian Analyst. I also focused on Kundalini energy and meditation because I was having Kundalini energy experiences, and I wanted to understand them and my psychic abilities.

In 1996, I encountered the Human Design Mandala, a complex, yet intriguing system that intertwines psychology, astrology, and developmental science. My fascination with the Human Design System deepened with each passing year.

Through my research, I had a staggering revelation: 99% of humanity possesses the inherent potential to manifest their true selves. Tragically, the majority of people remain oblivious to the existence of the Four Worlds — the Mental, Spiritual, Emotional, and Physical dimensions that govern our daily reality.

While their lack of awareness is not inherently "bad," it is a missed opportunity for growth and fulfillment. When individuals are unaware of the Four Worlds, they navigate life without understanding the diverse dimensions of their consciousness. They may feel disconnected, struggling to align actions with their true selves, and miss out on the profound impact that recognizing and harmonizing with these dimensions can have on their overall wellbeing.

It was then that my mission crystallized in my mind: to illuminate these dimensions, to guide individuals towards a conscious existence that embraces the essence of their soul.

Noble Energy Wellness®

Noble Energy Wellness® focuses on Energy Medicine and Holistic options for healing and health. Dr. Marvin and Dr. Eleanor® teach energy wellness in their weekly Manifest Your Dreams Webinar. Through the webinar, you can learn how to live authentically while manifesting your actual potential by understanding and integrating the Four Worlds into your daily life. Register to learn how you can manifest your dreams by attending these weekly webinars.
https://www.nobleenergywellness.com

Noble Energy Maps®

Noble Energy Maps focus on Dr. Eleanor's proprietary and innovative system for mapping how cosmic energy impacted you during your childhood development and how you can use this knowledge to optimally time your decisions, identify your life purpose, and live a self-realized life. Dr. Eleanor statistically validated her system through over 45,000 cases and uses Noble Energy Maps to guide clients toward wholeness and empowerment.
https://www.nobleenergywellness.com/energy-map/

The Noble Logo has a special place in Dr. Eleanor's heart. Her first cat, Noble, lived to age 22 and was an inspiration and guide during important times in Dr. Eleanor's growth and studies. He worked with her and Dr. Marvin when they hosted weekend groups for over ten years. Noble always helped guide them toward whom to work with next, as well as to the area that clients needed to work on. Dr. Eleanor uses calculations based on research done on her two homegrown twin kittens. The critical human developmental times used in Dr. Eleanor's proprietary maps, have proven accurate clinically and statistically, which map the Four Worlds in your energy field and how you can best function.

The Mandala of Synthesis® describes the elements coded into Dr. Eleanor's proprietary Noble Energy Maps. The Mandala of Synthesis includes the Kabalistic Tree of Life, Chakras, Astrology, the Hexagrams of the I-Ching, and critical times in early Human Development. Dr. Eleanor calculates her maps and integrates the information coded into a graphic illustrating the way you use your energy, where the flow of energy becomes clear. Dr. Eleanor's extensive education as a social scientist, researcher, and clinician has empowered her to formulate a complete system that recognizes the complexity of your consciousness and shows how you can best use it for growth and expansion of consciousness.

https://www.nobleenergywellness.com/mandala-of-synthesis

www.ingramcontent.com/pod-product-compliance
Lightning Source LLC
Chambersburg PA
CBHW070048080526
44586CB00013B/954